CLASSICS
AND
TRASH

THEORY/CULTURE 1

General editors: Linda Hutcheon and Paul Perron

Traditions and Taboos in High Literature and Popular Modern Genres

HARRIETT HAWKINS

University of Toronto Press
Toronto   Buffalo

First published in Canada and the United States by
University of Toronto Press 1990
Toronto and Buffalo

ISBN 0 8020 2767 9 (cloth)
     0 8020 6813 8 (paper)

Canadian Cataloguing in Publication Data

Hawkins, Harriett
Classics and trash

(Theory/culture)
Includes bibliographical references.
ISBN 0 8020 2767 9 (bound) ISBN 0-8020-6813-8
(pbk.)

1. Criticism.   2. Canon (literature).   3. Popular
literature - Great Britain - History and criticism.
4. Popular literature - United States - History and
criticism.   5. Literature and society.   I. Title.
II. Series.

PN81.H39 1990   801 .95   C90-093588-X

Printed and bound in Great Britain
by BPCC Wheatons Ltd, Exeter.

For Anna, Allen, Mike, Christine and, as always, Eric

On traditions and taboos:

> Mankind never lives completely in the present: the ideologies of the superego perpetuate the past, the traditions of the race and the people, which yield but slowly to the influence of the present and to new developments, and, so long as they work through the superego, play an important part in man's life, quite independently of economic conditions.
>
> Sigmund Freud

*   *   *   *

On 'high literature' and popular genres:

> All normal people need both classics and trash.
>
> George Bernard Shaw

> According to his powers each may give;
> Only on varied diet can we live.
> The pious fable and the dirty story
> Share in the total literary glory.
>
> W. H. Auden

Contents

List of illustrations

Preface

The drama's laws the drama's patrons give,
And we that live to please, must please to live.

Samuel Johnson

*   *   *   *

In American popular genres, a man portrayed as an intellectual is traditionally bound to be either ineffectual, homosexual or villainous. And so he *never* gets the girl in the end. By contrast, in English popular genres, especially in novels by female authors, intellectual men may finally win the heroine's heart and hand. Lord Peter Wimsey in Dorothy L. Sayers's detective novels, is a female fantasy, an ideal 'Ladies' Man'. Thus art not only tends to give its patrons what they want: from generation to generation it also shapes the romantic, sexual and ideological fantasies by which it was shaped and can therefore be described as a creator of the culture by which it was created (see Montrose (1983) for further discussion of this historical process). The introductory section of this book, which is primarily devoted to 'Men's Men' and 'Ladies' Men', surveys the differing fantasies, traditions and taboos governing the portrayal of typical heroes, anti-heroes and villains in Anglo-American 'high literature' and 'popular genres' alike. The second section, 'Some parables of a woman's talent', deals with dramatically comparable portrayals of talented heroines and their 'Svengalis' in works ranging from *The Phantom of the Opera*, *Trilby* and *The Red Shoes*, to Henry James's *The Bostonians* and George Eliot's *Daniel Deronda*. Informal interviews with women professionally engaged in the arts today suggest that the conflicts between dedication to an artistic vocation and devotion to a husband and children are still as active in real life as they are in some of these melodramas. The third part, 'From *King Lear* to *King Kong* and back', treats the influence of Shakespearian drama on popular modern stage-shows and films. Questions of literary 'identities and identifications' – especially those of gender – which are raised by

xiii

different works considered throughout the book, are discussed in the final section.

Professionally speaking, this book grew out of a paper that I originally wrote for a symposium on 'High Literature and Popular Genres' which was held at Oberlin College in 1984. But my personal conviction that a recognition of the continuing cross-fertilisation between 'high' literature and popular genres inevitably enhances our understanding and appreciation of both, had its origins in the years spent, many decades ago, as a child and then an adolescent watching practically every movie shown in the small town where I grew up.

Speaking in terms of the critical tradition, it should be noted from the outset that until very recently it would most certainly have been, even as in certain circles it may still be, academic suicide to admit to any interest in, much less an enjoyment of, certain works popular with 'bourgeois' (middle-class, middle-brow) audiences. For instance: not so very long ago, to mention George du Maurier's bestselling novel about Trilby and her Svengali, to say nothing of Gaston Leroux's penny-dreadful, *The Phantom of the Opera*, in the same chapter or even in the same breath as a novel in the 'Great Tradition' by George Eliot or by Henry James would have been deemed blasphemy deserving a death-threat by a critic such as F. R. Leavis. By much the same critical token, reporting on the centenary of T. S. Eliot's birthday (*Time* magazine (1988), 26 September, p. 55), Paul Grey respectfully cited various scholarly celebrations, such as a lecture at the Library of Congress, a conference at Washington University in St Louis and a symposium in Japan, before adding:

> And then there is *Cats*, Andrew Lloyd Webber's extravagant adaptation of Eliot's book of light verse, *Old Possum's Book of Practical Cats* (1939). The smash show has been seen by some 25 million people in 15 countries and contributed more than $2 million in royalties to the Eliot estate. Purists shudder at such commercial success and its spin-offs. Says critic Hugh Kenner, 'Eliot wanted to connect with a popular audience, but *Cats* wasn't what he had in mind.'

Queries: How does he know? And why on earth wouldn't any author, whether 'high' or 'low', be delighted by a popular success of this magnitude? The odds are that, like his widow, who gave the adaptors a previously unpublished poem about 'Grizabella the Glamour Cat' and also wrote a note 'Apropos of Practical Cats' for the show's souvenir brochure, Eliot himself might have hugely enjoyed the stupendous success of *Cats*.

But be that as it may. As the critical dismissal of *Cats* reported in *Time* clearly illustrates, although it has long been considered respec-

table in academic circles to take seriously as well as to enjoy popular
'Folk' art, proletariat art and non-bourgeois art-forms such as jazz,
folk songs and soul music, comparably 'popular', commercially
successful, bourgeois, middle-class, middle-brow art of the kind
attracting audiences of twenty-five million people in fifteen different
countries has traditionally been ignored if not deplored in certain
intellectual circles or dismissively put down, in terms of 'distant' and
distancing distinctions, as the kind of thing that '*other* people like'.
Thus *Gone With the Wind* is often patronised as 'a woman's novel' or
as 'a film popular with adolescent females' and so on (for further
discussion of 'distant' distinctions, see John Caughie's major essay on
'Popular culture: notes and revisions' in MacCabe (1986), p. 170).
The interest in cultural studies over the past decade seems to me to be
one of the most important educational trends to emerge in the late
twentieth century. But, of course, the technological means of study-
ing films at our disposal today were not available to previous
generations, and a book such as this one could not have been written
before it was possible to play so many of the films discussed here
again and again.

Yet long before the advent of video, or even of television, popular
films did as much to shape the imagination of young people as they
do now. And the truth is that as children and adolescents, most of us,
whatever our sex or class, have immensely enjoyed popular works
(films, stage-shows, TV programmes) of the kind that we
ourselves may later sneer at as 'bourgeois'. For that matter, as
Caughie has also observed (p. 168), whenever we 'identify ourselves
with a collective past' or as members of a given generation, those
books and films and television shows and popular music that we
especially enjoyed as children and adolescents (from *King Kong,
Casablanca* and *Gone With the Wind* to *Star Wars* and *E.T.*) 'are what
constitute our collectively shared experience'. Virtually everyone
who grew up in western Europe in one generation remembers the
advent of the Beatles just as everyone in the previous generation
remembers the impact of Marilyn Monroe in *Niagara*, of Elvis
Presley singing 'You ain't nothing but a hound dog', and of Marlon
Brando's electrifying performances on stage or on screen in *A
Streetcar Named Desire* and/or in *The Wild One*. People growing up
now will, likewise, forever remember Michael Jackson and Madonna,
and so on.

Since this book focuses on popular conceptions about 'high'
literature and 'bourgeois' genres alike, the various books, reviews,
journals and commentaries cited, like the novels and films that are
discussed in detail, were necessarily selected from works available in

the 'public domain'. Virtually all of them are available in paperback, in non-specialised bookshops or in public libraries. More specialised critical and feminist theorists from whom arguments here have been derived are cited by the contributors to Colin MacCabe's valuable anthology of essays on *High Theory/Low Culture* and other works cited in the bibliography, but the major arguments concerning gender that I've posited in the final section of this book are, put simply, that certain 'popular' classics such as *Gone With the Wind*, as well as certain 'canonised' classics such as *Daniel Deronda*, are positively liberating in so far as they dramatically stress the likenesses, as opposed to the difference, between individual members of the opposite sex, even as a masterpiece such as *Wuthering Heights* stresses the sameness between the child Cathy and the child Heathcliff while simultaneously stressing (with equal relevance to both sexes) the values of compassion, mercy and empathy traditionally associated with 'the feminine principle'. Thus two seemingly self-contradictory arguments that feminist theorists have posited over the past several decades come closer to reconciliation in literary practice than might appear conceivable in theory. Time after time, works of art dramatically refute fallacious, patriarchal conclusions concerning the differences between men and women that have traditionally been – and still are being – used to deny women equal rights. Yet they also take positive stands in affirmation of principles traditionally deemed 'feminine' – and thus often denigrated as effeminate, weak, sentimental, sissified – such as pity, kindness, peace and love. The political as well as the critical arguments about *Othello* and *The Tempest* (in Chapters 3 and 4) were posited in dialectical opposition to Allan Bloom's reactionary assertions about Shakespearian drama, and 'high literature' generally, in his bestselling book on *The Closing of the American Mind* (1987) as well as in his previous book on *Shakespeare's Politics*.

By now, so much has been made of this fact (both *pro* and *con* by Bloom and others) that it might seem too obvious to need saying that, like each generation's superstars, certain books (such as *The Lord of the Rings* or the 'Oz' books by L. Frank Baum), films (such as *The Wizard of Oz*) and television shows (such as *Star Trek*) that were first encountered in childhood or adolescence by successive generations, may 'do more to shape the imagination and its style' than all of our 'later calculated readings of acknowledged masters' – see Vidal (1983), pp. 75–6. As Gore Vidal goes on to observe, like creative writers generally, scientists tend to be remarkably candid in their acknowledgement of this fact: thus the effort by the American space programme to find life elsewhere in the universe, called 'Operation Ozma', was most appropriately named after Baum's 'Lost Princess of

Oz'. Like classical Gods and Goddesses, stars like Bogart and Monroe exemplify traits and types (Monroe is clearly 'of the genus Venus') to their countless votaries in successive generations, even as lines like 'Round up the usual suspects', 'The stuff that dreams are made of' and 'Toto, I have a feeling we're not in Kansas any more' are as recognisable to 19-year-old film fans today as they are to their parents and grandparents.

As suggested by the epigraphs from Shaw and Auden, the literature and criticism I have read while working on this book have consistently reinforced my long-standing personal conviction that 'high' artists have, historically, derived far more enjoyment and inspiration from popular and 'bourgeois' artists – and vice versa – than certain academic theories and canons would suggest (for further discussion, see Butler (1987), pp. 3–22). In so far as this is in fact the case, the artistic tradition which thrives on generic out-breeding (certain in-bred Hollywood stereotypes are a different matter – see Chapter 1) has in practice if not in theory been a great deal more democratic and far less élitist, even as it has often been demonstrably less sexist than the academically closeted critical tradition. Or so it will be argued later on.

To illustrate central points about traditions and taboos both of genre and of gender that are involved in the portrayal of various character-types and stereotypes that occur in 'high' and 'low' works alike, I have cited multiple examples of sympathetic monsters (Caliban, King Kong, the Phantom of the Opera), talented heroines (George du Maurier's Trilby, Henry James's Verena Tarrant, the dancer played by Moira Shearer in the ballet film, *The Red Shoes*), and attractively wicked women in differing popular and classical works, so that readers unfamiliar with one character will probably recognise another example of the type. For instance, if you are not already acquainted with the deliciously wicked Marquise de Merteuil, who deceives others into believing that she is a perfectly virtuous woman in the notorious eighteenth-century French epistolary novel, *Les Liaisons Dangereuses*, and in the twentieth-century film and stage-play based on it, you may vividly remember the comparably wicked first wife of Maximilian de Winter whom everyone else, including the readers of Daphne du Maurier's novel and the audiences viewing Alfred Hitchcock's classic film or the subsequent TV series based on it, had believed to be the perfect woman until the surprise ending of *Rebecca*. Everyone will, of course, think of other examples of various character-types and stereotypes, such as the ineffectual (usually American) or villainous (usually 'foreign') male intellectual; or the sexually attractive single woman who is treated rather like a loose cannon on the gun-deck, in so far as she must be either destroyed (killed off, as in *Fatal Attraction*) or ultimately controlled (in holy wedlock, as in *Baby Boom*). And so on. Given the unending interest and limitless complexity of the subject, this book can only serve as a starting point for further discussion.

ACKNOWLEDGEMENTS

The ballad, 'Ballerina', by Carl Sigman and Bob Russell, is quoted from the 'Best of Vaughn Monroe', MCA Records, Inc., Universal City, California, 1983. 'Brush up your Shakespeare' and 'Don't fence me in' are quoted from *The Complete Lyrics of Cole Porter*, edited by Robert Kimball, Vintage Books, New York, 1984. The lines from the lyrics, 'Angel of Music' and 'The Phantom of the Opera' are from the libretto of the musical play by Andrew Lloyd Webber, Charles Hart and Richard Stilgoe, as published in *The Complete Phantom of the Opera* by George Perry (1987), Pavilion Books, p. 145. Copyright © The Really Useful Group P.L.C. 1987.

Page references to books and articles cited in the bibliography are inserted in parentheses at the end of quotations. Longer, illustrative or explanatory footnotes appear at the end.

A preliminary version of Chapter 3, 'From *King Lear* to *King Kong* and back', was originally presented as a lecture at Oberlin College in 1984 and subsequently published in *'Bad' Shakespeare: Revaluations of the Shakespeare Canon*, ed. Maurice Charney (1988), Associated University Presses, pp. 37–55. An early version of Chapter 2, 'Angels of music, demon lovers and red shoes', was first presented as a lecture sponsored by the Woman's Studies Program at Vassar College in 1987.

For information, offprints, references, answers to queries and invaluable criticisms of my own arguments, I am most grateful to Rosalind Miles, Catherine Belsey and Linda Woodbridge, as well as Helen Coker Akins, Ann Bartlett, Tina Brownley, Alistair Buckley, David Carter, Oriel Cooper, Emmie Farrow, Emogene Grill, Genevieve Hawkins, Christopher Hill, Sara McCune, Juliana Michie, William H. Rothwell, Jr, Evert Sprinchorn and Norman Talbot. Numerous examples of connections between 'high' art and popular works that are cited here were suggested by students from St Hilda's College, Southern Methodist University and Emory University, as well as by my former students at Vassar College. I owe particular thanks to Paula Volsky for permission to use her original ideas on pp. 71–4, and continuing gratitude to Marguerite McDonald for taking me to see so many movies, so many times.

Illustrations

The publisher is grateful to the following for permission to reprint material in copyright:
Scene stills of Michael Crawford costumed as the Red Death and as the Phantom, from the Andrew Lloyd Webber musical, *The Phantom of the Opera*, 1986. Copyright Clive Barda/London. Reproduced by permission. Scene stills of Lon Chaney in *The Phantom of the Opera* (1925) and of Herbert Lom in *The Phantom of the Opera* (1962). Copyright Universal Pictures. Courtesy of The Kobal Collection. Reproduced by permission. Scene still of Claude Rains in *The Phantom of the Opera* (1943). Courtesy of The Kobal Collection. Reproduced by permission. Scene still of Maximilian Schell, in *The Phantom of the Opera* (1982). Copyright © 1982 CBS Inc. All rights reserved. Courtesy of The Kobal Collection. Reproduced by permission. Original illustrations which accompany George du Maurier's novel, *Trilby* are by the author. This edition, J.M. Dent and Sons Ltd., Everyman's Library, 1931. Last reprinted 1978. The cartoon of King Kong is used by permission of the cartoonist, Rick Mayrowitz and previously appeared as an illustration to Harriett Hawkins's essay, 'From *King Lear* to *King Kong* and Back' published in *'Bad Shakespeare: Revaluations of the Shakespeare Canon,* ed. Maurice Charney, Associated University Presses, 1988, pp. 37–55. Scene stills from *Rebecca* (1940). Copyright Selznick International. Courtesy of The Kobal Collection. Reproduced by permission.

CHAPTER ONE

'Such stuff as dreams are made of'

INTRODUCTION: 'HIGH' LITERATURE AND 'POPULAR' GENRES

We are such stuff
As dreams are made on . . .
　　　　　　　Prospero, in Shakespeare's *The Tempest* (1611)

POLICE INSPECTOR. What is it?
SAM SPADE. The stuff that dreams are made of.
　　　　Screenplay, by John Huston, of *The Maltese Falcon* (1941)

*　　　*　　　*　　　*

In Steven Scheuer's film guide for 1988 (p. 493), John Huston's version of Dashiell Hammett's *The Maltese Falcon* is most succinctly described as:

> The stuff that dreams are made of. Two previous screen adaptations of Dashiell Hammett's classic hard-boiled novel exist . . . but they have been swept under the rug in the light of this, the definitive version. A new sort of hero, a rough draft for the sixties/seventies antihero, was introduced to the screen in Bogart's Sam Spade. 'Falcon' also began a new career for screenwriter John Huston as a director. Huston's talent lay not only in his taut, concise scripting and his dark, drama-laden images (which paved the way for the film-noir style); he also assembled a cast made in Heaven. The film's plot, involving Spade and a cast of shady characters in a search for an elusive, priceless statuette, has been endlessly imitated but never, never duplicated.

Huston also added a final line to his screenplay that does not appear in Hammett's novel and gives the film's ending an unforgettable, elusively poetic quality of its own: 'It's heavy', says Ward Bond, as the police inspector picking up the fake falcon: 'What is it?' 'The stuff that dreams are made of ', answers Humphrey Bogart, thus summing up, in a cynically elegaic line, the disillusioned yet ultimately romantic nature of the film's antihero, Sam Spade – and of John Huston's movie masterpiece itself.

For admirers of Shakespeare, the climax to this film seems wonderfully enhanced by the cynical detective's inspired echo of perhaps the most haunting of all lines from *The Tempest*: 'We are such stuff/As dreams are made on' (IV, i, 156–7). Conversely, to admirers of the film who subsequently encounter the original line in Shakespeare's

3

play, Prospero's famous speech seems, not at all inappropriately, to echo and complement Bogart's. Indeed, common memories of the movie version of *The Maltese Falcon* may explain why so many people, including myself, unconsciously tend to substitute 'of' for 'on' when quoting Shakespeare's line: Huston's version well-nigh indelibly amalgamates in the memory with Shakespeare's to become 'such stuff as dreams are made of'.

Even as a subsequent chapter surveys, in more detail, the relationships between Shakespeare's works and popular modern films, plays and novels, it should be stressed from the outset that comparable interactions, deliberate echoes, conscious fusions and unconscious confusions between 'high' art and 'popular' genres such as detective stories occur all the time. To give a more recent example, in Tom Wolfe's bestseller *The Bonfire of the Vanities* (1988), Maria, the gorgeous young mistress of the protagonist, Sherman McCoy, thus complains to her lover about having been smugly put down by an insufferably snobbish Englishman because she had unwittingly confused Raymond Chandler's detective, 'Philip Marlowe', as played by Robert Mitchum, with Christopher Marlowe, the great Elizabethan playwright.

> 'Sherman, who's Christopher Marlowe?' . . .
> *Christopher Marlowe?* 'I don't know. Do I know him?'
> 'The one I'm talking about was a writer.'
> 'You don't mean the playwright?'
> 'I guess so. Who was he?' Maria continued to look straight ahead. She sounded as if her last friend had died.
> 'Christopher Marlowe. . . . He was a British playwright, about the time of Shakespeare, I think. Maybe a little before Shakespeare. Why?'
> 'Which was when?' She couldn't have sounded more miserable.
> 'Let's see. I don't know. . . . The sixteenth century – 15-something. Why?'
> 'What did he write?'
> 'God . . . beats me. Listen, I thought I was doing well just to remember who he was. Why?'
> 'Yes, but you do know who he was.'
> 'Barely. Why?'
> 'What about Dr. Faustus?'
> 'Dr. Faustus?'
> 'Did he write something about Dr. Faustus?'
> 'Mmmmmmmmmmmmmmmm.' A tiny flash of memory; but it slipped away. 'Could be. Dr. Faustus . . . *The Jew of Malta!* He wrote a play called *The Jew of Malta*. I'm pretty sure of that. *The Jew of Malta*. I don't even know how I remember *The Jew of Malta*. I'm sure I never read it.'
> 'But you do know who he was. That's one of the things you're supposed to know, isn't it?'

And there she had put her finger on it. The only thing that had truly stuck in Sherman's mind about Christopher Marlowe, after nine years at Buckley, four years at St Paul's and four years at Yale, was that you were, in fact, supposed to know who Christopher Marlowe was. But he wasn't about to say that.

Maria then proceeds to describe the indignity she had suffered at the hands of the Englishman:

'He couldn't wait to tell me he was a movie producer. He was making a movie based on this play, *Dr. Faustus*, by Christopher Marlowe, or just Marlowe. I think that was all he said, just Marlowe, and I don't know why I said anything, but I thought somebody named Marlowe wrote for the movies. Actually, what I think I was thinking about was, there was this movie with a *character* named Marlowe. Robert Mitchum was in it.'
'That's right. It was a Raymond Chandler story.'
Maria looked at him with utter blankness. He dropped Raymond Chandler. 'So what did you say to him?'
'I said, "Oh, Christopher Marlowe. Didn't he write a movie?" And you know what this . . . bastard . . . says to me? He says, "I shouldn't think so. He died in 1593." *I shouldn't think so . . .* I couldn't *believe* the . . . snottiness. . . . Sherman, tell me the honest truth. If you don't know who Christopher Marlowe is, does that make you stupid?'
'Don't be ridiculous. I could barely think of who he was, and I probably had him in a course or something.'
'Well, that's just the point. At least you had him in a course. I didn't have him in any course. That's what makes me feel so – you don't even understand what I'm talking about, do you?'
'I sure don't.' (pp. 74–7)

As Tom Wolfe himself no doubt knew, the fact is that Maria's association of Raymond Chandler's 'Philip Marlowe' with 'Christopher Marlowe' is historically valid. As a boy in England, Raymond Chandler attended an exclusive boarding school at Dulwich that was founded by Edward Alleyn, the Elizabethan actor who created the roles of Dr Faustus and the Jew of Malta in Marlowe's plays. The hall of residence that Chandler lived in there was named after the playwright and so, years later, was the cool, attractive, wise-cracking, lonely detective hero of his novels, who was played by Dick Powell in 1944, then by Bogart in 1946 and subsequently by Robert Mitchum in the 1976 and 1978 film versions of *Farewell, my Lovely* and *The Big Sleep*. Chandler's portrayal of Philip Marlowe also owes something to his admiration for the author of *The Maltese Falcon* and to Hammett's hero, Sam Spade – see Drabble (1985), p. 183; and see also the 1980 film, *The Man With Bogart's Face*, whose private-eye hero was as it were inevitably named 'Sam Marlowe'.

As his allusions to Chandler's 'Marlowe' and to Marlowe's 'Dr

Faustus' likewise serve to illustrate, Tom Wolfe's novel itself clearly exemplifies the continuing process of cross-fertilisation between the highest of 'high art' and popular genres.[1] For that matter, there is no knowing how many works, from Christopher Marlowe's tragedy to Goethe's drama and Gounod's opera, have in turn been based on the German legend of John Faust, the necromancer who sold his soul to the devil for ultimate knowledge, power, wealth, beauty, fame. In English and German dramas and in several operas based on the legend of the man who sold his soul to the devil for more-than-mortal power the gifted hero must ultimately choose to serve one of two masters. He must decide whether to obey his 'good angel' and abandon his 'art', or to obey his evil angel and persist in it. And it could be – see below, p. 76 – that all these works reflect a tendency on the part of the human brain to narrow major choices and options down to two ('He who is not for us is against us'; 'You cannot serve both God and Mammon'; and compare also W. B. Yeats's conclusion: 'The intellect of man is forced to choose/Perfection of the life or of the work . . .').

For instance, in the beginning of Christopher Marlowe's *Tragical History of Dr. Faustus*, the gifted scholar has any number of intellectual pursuits available to him: he initially considers law, medicine and logic. But his choice soon gets narrowed down to the ultimate decision whether to devote himself to 'divinity' (theology) or to 'necromancy' (black magic) – that is, whether to serve God or to serve Lucifer. To the bitter end of the tragedy his soul is torn between these mighty opposites:

> O soul, be chang'd to little water drops
> And fall into the ocean, ne'er be found.
>   *Thunder, and enter the Devils.*
> My God, my God! Look not so fierce on me.
> Adders and serpents, let me breathe awhile.
> Ugly hell, gape not! Come not, Lucifer!
> I'll burn my books.

And in the end his body, likewise, is 'torn asunder' by the very forces he himself initially chose to summon and serve. As we shall see, with more detailed reference to specific works in Chapter 2, a gifted woman's choice between the claims of her art (her profession as a singer or a dancer) and her heart (the man she loves) has, tradition-ally, been treated as comparable in magnitude to the Faustian choice between serving God and the Devil. Thus, in works of differing genres, a woman's refusal to serve man, whether as a daughter or wife or mother, is most dramatically portrayed as comparable to Faustus's damnable ambition to rise beyond his subservient relationship to God.

For that matter, the Faust legend underlies innumerable popular as well as classic portrayals of characters who make bargains they cannot get out of and are ultimately enslaved by the forces they sought to master or finally destroyed by the demons – the Lucifer and Mephostophilis – that they once summoned to command. For instance, the endings of countless science fiction films echo the moral message in the concluding lines of Marlowe's tragedy:

SCHOLAR. Well, gentlemen, though Faustus' end be such
    As every Christian heart laments to think on,
    Yet, for he was a scholar once admir'd
    For wondrous knowledge in our German schools
    We'll give his mangl'd limbs due burial,
    And all the students cloth'd in mourning black
    Shall wait upon his heavy [sad] funeral.
                                      Exeunt.
               [Epilogue]

CHORUS.
    Cut is the branch that might have grown full straight,
    And burned is Apollo's laurel bough,
    That sometime grew within this learned man.
    Faustus is gone: regard his hellish fall,
    Whose fiendful fortune may exhort the wise
    Only to wonder at unlawful things,
    Whose deepness doth entice such forward wits
    To practise more than heavenly power permits.

'He was a great man', someone almost invariably says of the brilliant researcher likewise doomed by his search for ultimate knowledge in all those science fiction films: 'but there are things mankind had better leave alone'.[2] The host of twentieth-century variations on the Faustian legend also obviously includes Thomas Mann's *Doctor Faustus*, Klaus Mann's *Mephisto* (filmed in 1981), and other films of virtually every genre, such as *Cabin in the Sky* (1943), *Dr Faustus* (starring Richard Burton and Elizabeth Taylor in 1967), *Bedazzled* (1967) and *Angel Heart* (1987), as well as the American baseball musical wherein the hero sells his soul to the Devil to assure that the Washington Senators will beat the New York Yankees in the World Series. As Steven Scheuer's film guide notes (p. 181), both the stage and screen productions of *Damn Yankees* featured the incomparable Gwen Verdon as the delectably demonic temptress, Lola ('Whatever Lola wants, Lola gets,/And little man, little Lola wants you'), and musical-comedy buffs will forever remember her magnificent dancing in the 'Two Lost Souls' number.

Speaking of lost souls, 'What availeth a man. . .' wonders Sherman McCoy, the doomed protagonist of *The Bonfire of the Vanities* (p. 263), and thus Tom Wolfe likewise raises the identical Biblical questions posed throughout Christopher Marlowe's *Dr Faustus*. 'For what shall it profit a man, if he shall gain the whole world and lose his own soul? And what shall a man give in return for his soul?' (Mark 8:36). Moreover, even as Wolfe combines features of his own 'New Journalism' with social satire (in the manner of Ben Jonson or of Thackeray in *Vanity Fair*) and other techniques derived from major realistic novels by Balzac and Zola, his bestseller is likewise enriched by explicit as well as implicit allusions to Charles Dickens's *A Tale of Two Cities* (both novels begin with a rich man's vehicle running down a child of the poor and subsequently chart the nemesis that follows) and to Edgar Allan Poe's 'The Masque of the Red Death'. For instance, the novel's innocent young black victim, Henry Lamb, lived in 'Edgar Allan Poe Towers' a housing project in the festering South Bronx district of New York where Poe himself once lived, while a tabloid newspaper features an article about Lamb's case that is explicitly entitled '*A Tale of Two Cities*':

> A long caption began: '*Two vastly different New Yorks collided when Wall Street investment banker Sherman McCoy's $50,000 Mercedes Benz sports roadster struck honor student Henry Lamb. McCoy lives in a $3 million, 14 room, two-storey apartment on Park Avenue. Lamb, in a $247-a-month three-room apartment in a housing project in the South Bronx.* (p. 485)

Earlier, in a central episode stressing the modern relevance of 'The Masque of the Red Death' to the chic guests at a flamboyantly extravagant Park Avenue dinner party, a character dying of AIDS describes Edgar Allan Poe as an artist with 'prophetic vision', who wrote 'a story that tells all we need to know about the moment we live in now'. He then outlines Poe's fable of the fabulously rich Prince Prospero, who was determined to insulate himself and his friends from the mysterious plague ravaging the countryside around his castle. Having laid in provisions of food and drink that would last for two years, the Prince summoned all the best people to his castle and then closed its gates 'against the outside world, against the virulence of all lesser souls, and commenced a masked ball that was to last until the plague had burnt itself out beyond the walls'. Prince Prospero's party is 'endless and seamless', it takes place in seven great salons,

> and in each the revel becomes more intense than in the one before, and the revelers are drawn on, on, on toward the seventh room, which is appointed entirely in black. One night, in this last room, appears a guest shrouded in the most clever and most hideously beautiful costume this company of luminous masqueraders has ever seen. This guest is dressed as Death, but so convincingly that Prospero is offended and orders him ejected. But none dares touch

Michael Crawford costumed as the Red Death in the Andrew Lloyd Webber musical,
The Phantom of the Opera, *1986*

> him, so that the task is left to the Prince himself, and the moment he
> touches the ghastly shroud, he falls down dead, for the Red Death
> has entered the house of Prospero. (p. 355)

'And now' – to conclude the fable in the words of Poe himself – 'was
acknowledged the presence of the Red Death'.

> And one by one dropped the revelers in the blood-bedewed halls of
> their revel, and died each in the despairing posture of his fall. And
> the life of the ebony clock went out with that of the last of the gay.
> And the flames of the tripods expired. And Darkness and Decay and
> the Red Death held illimitable dominion over all.
> *Tales of Mystery and the Imagination*, p. 308

Like Shakespeare and Dickens, Poe is one of the writers whose work
and influence has erased the boundaries between 'High Art' and
popular genres. His work simultaneously points upwards, towards
highbrow post-structuralist theory, and downwards to a popular
series of horror films starring Vincent Price; it looks backwards to
Shakespeare and the English Romantic poets, and forwards and
outwards across national and linguistic boundaries (Poe has always
found special favour in France). For instance: the name of 'Prince
Prospero' obviously recalls the name of Shakespeare's Duke of Milan
in *The Tempest*, just as the 'precursor' of Vladimir Nabokov's Lolita,
the 'initial girl-child' who Humbert Humbert likewise loved with a
love that was more than love, back when he was a child and she was
a child in a 'princedom by the sea', has the name of Poe's 'Annabel
Lee' (*Lolita*, pp. 11–14). And Poe's tales are not only the ultimate
plot sources for the horror-film director, Roger Corman, whose 1965
version of *The Masque of the Red Death* is generally agreed to be the
best of the American International Poe Series. They have also served
as an inspiration to the French theorist, Jacques Lacan, in his
influential and controversial 'Seminar on *The Purloined Letter*' (see
also Muller and Richardson (1988)).

So far as popular modern genres are concerned, Gaston Leroux,
the author of *Le Mystère de la Chambre Jaune* (*The Mystery of the
Yellow Room*, 1907) and *Le Fantôme de l'Opéra* (1911) was most
explicitly indebted to Poe as the originator of the horror/detective
story (see Peter Haining's foreword to *The Phantom of the Opera*
(1986) p. 14). Indeed, the entrance of the Phantom himself, in the
hideously beautiful costume of Poe's 'Red Death' at the opera's
masquerade ball, is a climactic scene in Leroux's original novel and
also in the 1925 film version starring Lon Chaney, as well as the high
point of the most spectacular production number in the musical
version by Andrew Lloyd Webber. Very like the final reckoning in
the fable of Dr Faustus (will he or won't he? can he or can't he avert

his own damnation?), the inescapable nature of the Red Death haunts
the imagination of highbrow and lowbrow authors and audiences
alike. In Wolfe's novel, the terrified protagonist, Sherman McCoy,
hears Poe's tale as if 'the dying voice' that told it to the unheeding
guests at that Park Avenue dinner party had been 'the voice of an
oracle' dispatched by God Himself and speaking straight to him:

> Edgar Allan Poe! – *Poe!* – the ruin of the dissolute! – in the Bronx –
> *the Bronx!* The meaningless whirl, the unbridled flesh . . . and,
> waiting in the last room, the Red Death. . . . He felt dizzy. In
> addition to being consumed by fear, he was drunk. His eyes darted
> about the lobby. . . . He half expected to see the shroud. (pp. 357–8)

Indeed, comparable warnings to the super-rich, the smug, the selfish,
who, like Prince Prospero, believe they can insulate themselves from
'the virulence of all lesser souls', pervade Wolfe's novel from the
beginning:

> You, you Wasp charity-ballers sitting on your mounds of inherited
> money up in your co-ops with the twelve-foot ceilings and the two
> wings, one for you and one for the help, do you really think you are
> impregnable? And you German-Jewish financiers who have finally
> made it into the same buildings, the better to insulate yourselves
> from the *shtetl* hordes, do you really think you are insulated. . . ?
> And Staten Island! Do you Saturday do-it-yourselfers really think
> you're snug in your little rug? You don't think the future knows
> how to cross a *bridge?* (p. 7)

Thus, one of Poe's *Tales of Mystery and Imagination* serves, in this
parable of New York in the late 1980s, as a metaphor for specific
social and historical realities, telling us 'all we need to know' about
the way certain things actually are 'at the moment we live in now'.

   Given their comparable themes, origins and frames of reference
why are some of the works and not other works just mentioned, from
Dr Faustus and 'The Masque of the Red Death', to *The Phantom of
The Opera* and *The Bonfire of the Vanities*, treated as equally 'high'
literature and/or discussed together in terms of their equally popular
and sometimes identical genres? In the dialogue about 'Marlowe'
quoted earlier on, Tom Wolfe conveniently provides us with one
manifestly clear, albeit wickedly ironic account of what, to many
people, distinguishes certain authors such as Shakespeare, Marlowe,
Milton, Dickens and Poe from lesser beings. That is, in order to
establish one's own superior *social* status as the right kind of person
who has been educated in the right kind of schools (Buckley, St
Paul's, Yale), one is 'supposed to know who Christopher Marlowe
was'.

   By very much the same token, Gore Vidal provides us with an

equally ironic and comparably valid class distinction between 'good' literature and 'popular' writing. In certain academic circles, 'good' writing means 'that which is taught to involuntary readers' while 'bad' writing means popular writing that is widely read (Vidal (1987) p. 52). By both definitions, although and arguably *because* Chaucer and Shakespeare and Marlowe and Dickens and Poe all originally claimed their share of the total literary glory as a result of having written plays, poems and novels which people once voluntarily read, went to see performed, loved, hated, were moved by, were shocked by, came to know 'by heart', parodied, adapted, lifted titles from, used as starting points for other kinds of art (ballets, operas, musicals and so on) they are now academically if not artistically insulated against the outside world, against the virulence of all lesser souls. Thus Shakespeare is, on the one hand, critically canonised and on the other hand, anathematised in arguments that have less to do with his artistic influence than with his academic status at the top of the Anglo-American list of those institutionally sacrosanct Authors known by their last names only ('just Marlowe'), who (like Sherman) you have, or (like Maria) you have not, 'had in a course'.

As Wolfe's novel reminds us, the real reasons why in certain circles it is *de rigueur* for you to know 'who Marlowe was' have everything to do with the semiotics of status – that is, with your social and educational credentials – and nothing to do with genuine knowledge or intelligence, or indeed with Christopher Marlowe's literary achievements. Therefore the answer to Maria's question, 'Sherman, tell me the honest truth. If you don't know who Christopher Marlowe was, does that make you stupid?' is, obviously, 'No'. To know who he was is an obvious badge of cultural literacy (Hirsch, 1987) but not to have 'had' Marlowe in a course does not 'make you stupid'. Indeed, in many ways, Wolfe's street-wise Maria seems a lot brighter than his pampered preppy, Sherman McCoy. It should also be noted that for reasons not unrelated to the artistic traditions and taboos discussed below, in differing social and institutional circles – e.g. among certain students in certain high schools – there is a stigma attached to any writers or works that you might be, or might once have been, required to read in a course. All of them are presumed to be equally boring and irrelevant. Therefore not to know, and above all defiantly not to care, and certainly not to *want* to know who Christopher Marlowe was, would be a mark of status, a source of pride. Knowing who 'Philip Marlowe' was might be OK and indeed could be a sign of insider-status in yet other circles. Ditto for Roger Corman and Jacques Lacan: to know, or not to know – or not to want to know – who they are would immediately define one's status as an insider or as an outsider, as a friend or a foe, to all devotees of horror films and/or students of critical theory. And so on.

These points and other arguments concerning how, why, who and what gets into or is excluded from the established canons of Anglo-American literature deserve, and will get, further discussion later on. But of equal importance for our purposes here, Wolfe's dialogue also demonstrates the kind of first-hand knowledge of 'high' art that it is (on the one hand) taboo for a virile American hero, but (on the other hand) traditional for some insufferably snobbish, snotty, British or otherwise un-American villain to possess. Can you imagine John Wayne playing a character with a first-hand knowledge of the works of *Christopher Marlowe*?

THE UN-AMERICAN VILLAIN
AND THE ALL-AMERICAN MAN'S MAN

There are rare exceptions to this rule (e.g. *The Dead Poets Society*) but generally speaking, a man portrayed as a hero deserving of a red-blooded young man's admiration or emulation in any popular American film, TV series or novel produced during or after the Second World War *cannot* display any interest in poetry, to say nothing of any appreciation for or knowledge of classical music, art or ballet. For it is traditionally taboo for an All-American Male to display any artistic or intellectual knowledge, passions or interests of the kind invariably associated with a range of villains from the evil scientist (with a middle-European accent) who seeks to dominate the world, to the succession of cultivated murderers brought to justice by Peter Falk in *Columbo*. Indeed, in American popular genres, unless it is treated as a conspicuously incongruous, specialised interest on the part of some beauty-loving beast or an otherwise tough gumshoe-type, any knowledge of the 'fine arts' such as the opera or the ballet, and certainly any interest in matters intellectual, is virtually bound to mark a male character as either a sissy (by implication a homosexual), an ineffectual intellectual (a wishy-washy liberal), a doomed and damnable Faust-type scientist or a sinister, un-American villain. The historical origins of this Hollywood taboo may stem from the premium traditionally placed on the egalitarian virtues of frontier times, when a man was judged by what he was and not by what he knew and the lack of a classical education did not count against you. It may also have to do with the traditional, mythical opposition between the unfallen Adam and the serpent in the Garden of Eden, as well as the ancient, pastoral opposition between the decadent city and the unspoiled country and so on through to the conflict between the sophisticated, polished, silver-tongued, lecherous, treacherous city-slicker and the plain-spoken frontiersman exemplifying homespun American virtue, who was so perfectly embodied on screen by Gary Cooper in *The Plainsman* (1936) and Henry Fonda in *The Trail of the Lonesome Pine* (1936). And, of course, by the honest, populist Jimmy Stewart as opposed to urbane Claude Rains, who played the most corrupt and worldly wise of all the senators in *Mr Smith Goes to Washington* (1939).

Yet this historically based, albeit dangerously fallacious, American equation between the most admirable of all its democratic, populist, agrarian, egalitarian values and a manifestly and indeed virulently anti-educational, anti-intellectual tradition that later lent strength to McCarthyism was most indelibly reinforced in innumerable Second World War movies defining the hero, who personified natural and national virtue, in dialectical opposition to an autocratic, aristocratic, and always well-educated Enemy–Alien–Other, who personified un-American vice. Thus, the ultimate enemy of the American way of life was the sadistic, smiling, fiendishly treacherous Japanese officer who spoke impeccably polished English as a result of having been educated 'at Havahdt' and who, it could go without saying, had obviously been a straight-A student there. There were other ways of stereotyping Japanese characters. In contrast to the Harvard-educated commanding officer stereotype, Japanese soldiers were portrayed as subhuman monsters, as Grendels, as gooks (see Chapter 4).[3] But the traditional hostility to the aristocratic, élitist, European tradition that so many Americans had originally crossed the ocean, or gone West to get away from, was most dramatically – and arguably most perniciously – reinforced in the stereotype of the cultivated German villain who appeared in practically every Hollywood film dealing with Nazis and their atrocities during the Second World War.

> Smooth, suave and cultured, with a predeliction for classical music and paintings, knowing the best wines and the histories of their occupied chateaux, the movies' conception of the Nazi villain was one of the most stereotyped.
>
> (Bowen (1972), p. 212)

Ergo: virtually every male character who displayed comparable cultivation in a Hollywood movie made during the Second World War or subsequently was marked as villainous and/or as un-American, if not unmanly.

The Hollywood stereotype of the cultured Nazi villain was decidedly not based on real life, but in large measure derived from the

First World War stereotype of the sadistic Prussian officer-aristocrat portrayed by Erich von Stroheim ('the man you love to hate' in silent films – and see also his portrayal of Rommel in *Five Graves to Cairo*, 1943). It thus gave rise to some continuing historical confusions. It is certainly true that a premium on high culture and education has not resulted in the moral perfection of humankind. But then neither has ignorance of the creative arts and sciences. And if virtue knows no social, sexual, intellectual, racial or educational distinctions, neither does vice. There is no doubt that some European intellectuals, such as Martin Heidegger and the young Paul de Man, willingly or reluctantly collaborated with the Nazis, wrote anti-Semitic propaganda, etc. Conversely, however, many victims of and refugees from the Nazis (Einstein, Eric Auerbach, Ernst Gombrich, Bruno Bettelheim, Karl Popper, and so on and on) indisputably knew a lot more about science, literature and the fine arts than their oppressors. Indeed, it is hard to name any regime that has, historically, been more hostile to intellectuals in general and to the creative arts and sciences in particular than the Third Reich. The rise of the Nazis thus resulted in the immediate termination of the German film industry's historical claim to international distinction, as its most creative people fled to Britain and the United States. For that matter, the Nazi scum who participated in the beer-hall putsch and smashed windows on Kristallnacht no doubt had far more in common with today's nigger-hating, Jew-baiting, native-American-agrarian Ku Klux Klan or with the all-English proletariat Paki-bashers in the National Front than they had in common with, say, the devastatingly attractive (to women – he was a real ladies' man) romantic actor Conrad Veidt, who escaped from Hitler's Germany with his Jewish wife and subsequently made a career in Hollywood films playing suavely sinister Nazi villains, such as Major Strasser in *Casablanca*.

To compound the confusion, comparably cultured Nazi villains were played by British actors with upper-class accents such as Cedric Hardwicke, George Sanders, Herbert Marshall and Basil Rathbone (Bowen, pp. 212, 220). And in so far as they were likewise portrayed as profoundly hostile to the American way of life as well as to the American ideal of manhood, the smooth, well-educated German or Japanese officer-villain blended with and finally merged into the general stereotype of the cultivated villain as played in a host of Hollywood films by the self-same British actors, from George Sanders and James Mason on to Terence Stamp in *Superman II* (1981) and *Alien Nation* (1989), who could and did play romantic leads in English movies, but whose accents generally typed them in Hollywood films as educated, cultured, un-American, evil. Or as ineffectual or effete.

And so (to add to our list of un-historical incongruities) in the quintessential Hollywood swashbuckler, *The Adventures of Robin Hood* (1938), the decadent Norman (French) aristocrats, as played by Basil Rathbone and Claude Rains, spoke with posh *English* accents while the good, hardy, democratic Saxon (British) outlaws led by the dashing (Tasmanian born) Errol Flynn spoke with *American* accents. By very much the same token, the Americans Kirk Douglas and Tony Curtis led the heroic gladiators in their revolt against the decadent Romans, played by Laurence Olivier, Charles Laughton and Peter Ustinov, who spoke with cultivated British accents in *Spartacus* (1960). Placed in the enviable position of being ardently sought after by both Kirk Douglas and Laurence Olivier the beautiful slave girl, Jean Simmons, remained true to the American Spartacus and equated the embrace of the elegant, patrician Olivier with a fate worse than death. Of course, this practice of portraying manly, heroic embodiments of national virtues as irresistible to women of all nationalities, while simultaneously stereotyping the national enemy male as decadent (comparably effeminate) goes back a long way. In Shakespeare's *Henry V*, for instance, the French are portrayed as snobbish and effete in contrast to the hardy English 'band of brothers' led by manly King Harry, who eloquently inspires his troops with his impassioned patriotism and Churchillian rhetoric, but subsequently woos the French princess in the down-home language of an English yeoman, presenting himself to her as a 'plain soldier' with a true heart, who 'hath not the gift to woo in other places'. He thus sounds very much like an Elizabethan Gary Cooper, Jimmy Stewart, or the young John Wayne proposing to the pretty school-marm, 'Aw, shucks, ma'am, I'm not much good at sayin' things, but. . . .' 'Do you like me, Kate?' the tongue-tied King Harry of England asks the elegant Princess Katherine of France,

> I am glad thou canst speak no better English; for if thou couldst, thou wouldst find me such a plain king that thou wouldst think I had sold my farm to buy my crown. I know no ways to mince it in love, but directly to say, 'I love you.'
>
> (see *Henry V*, V, ii, 121–6)

The virile national heroes and decadent foes of the English (Robin Hood against the aristocratic Norman overlords; King Henry V against the French) have thus been dramatically stereotyped in ways comparable to the stereotype of the American hero opposed to the suave Nazi villain – and so, no doubt, have the traditional heroes and enemies of many other nations and cultures. But in Hollywood the equation between education, culture and vice became internally as well as externally axiomatic: the foreign intellectual was a villain; and if the native American intellectual was not himself the villain of the piece, he was almost invariably a traitor, a communist dupe, a homosexual. Thus, in post-war Hollywood, un-American (treacherous, ineffectual, unmanly) behaviour was equated with education and culture in general and not just with suave enemy aliens. In any event, by the middle of the twentieth century, a familiarity with the fine arts and a cultivated British accent were all it took to establish a given male character as an enemy of the American way of life. And well nigh invariably in American popular genres even the most attractive gentlemen of the British school were unfavourably contrasted to the all-American man of action. On the New York stage and then on screen, the English heart-throb, Leslie Howard, played the intellectual who was dramatically overpowered by Humphrey Bogart as the escaped killer – the man of action – in *The Petrified Forest* (1936). Prior to *The Dead Poets Society* (1989), this tradition was so strong that virtually every intellectual *American* male character portrayed in a Hollywood movie is either (a) shown up as an ineffectual wimp like Ashley Wilkes (also played by Leslie Howard) or (b) politically stereotyped as an indecisive, wishy washy liberal humanist such as the Stevensonian character played by Henry Fonda in *The Best Man* or (c) ultimately revealed to be the villain. And so the ultra-sophisticated Waldo Lydecker, who was played by Clifton Webb in *Laura*, as it were inevitably turned out to be the murderer in the end.

And no matter who plays them, or in what kind of Hollywood movie they appear, if there is a contest for the heart and hand of an attractive and virtuous heroine, the anti-intellectual or non-intellectual male will invariably win the girl in the end and thus, like the hero of an old-time melodrama, rescue her from the clutches of a sinister, sophisticated villain. In the one classic Hollywood movie I know of where the cultivated male does get the woman he wants, she is just as villainous as he is, and to be possessed by him is her ultimate damnation. 'You belong to me. . . . We deserve each other', says the devilishly suave drama critic, Addison de Witt (as played by George Sanders) to the treacherous upstart, Eve (played by Anne Baxter), when he claims the body and soul of the gifted actress whose ambition has doomed and damned her to belong to him – and so in effect wedded her forever to the theatre – in the Faustian denouement of *All About Eve*. By contrast, the hearts and hands and bodies of all really nice young heroines, such as the lovely Gene Tierney in *Laura*, invariably go to an all-American, anti-intellectual type such as the gum-chewing, baseball-loving gumshoe played by Dana Andrews, rather than to her cultured Svengali, Waldo Lydecker (for further discussion, see Chapter 2).

All this seems designed to reassure certain men in the audience that they don't need book-learning or good manners or anything else but their God-given all-American gun-toting masculinity to attract the best women imaginable. And all this is of course quite at odds with the fact that some of the most glamorous and desirable of all women in real life, and perhaps most notably in Hollywood itself, have so often preferred intellectual men to the hunks beloved of masculinist fiction. Both Mia Farrow and Diane Keaton (for instance) went for Woody Allen. The glorious Marilyn Monroe herself initially adored Arthur Miller even as her personal pin-ups were Albert Einstein and Abraham Lincoln. And the witty and urbane Adlai Stevenson was as devastatingly attractive to Lauren Bacall as he was to Marlene Dietrich (Bacall (1979), *By Myself*, pp. 203–5, 213–14). Thus, the only true answer to the question 'Do women prefer cave-men to gentler men?' obviously has to be 'Some do; some don't'. For that matter, so great is the appeal of intellectual men to some women that, as any faculty wife will testify, the male lecturer at a university who is so unattractive that none of his female students ever developed a crush on him has yet to be born.

One British 'gentleman star' whose film persona was simply too sexy for him ever to be cast as any character other than the man-who-gets-the-girl-at-the-end-of-the-movie was Cary Grant. But, perhaps significantly, even the wryly urbane, British-born Grant seemed positively American when Hitchcock cast him in opposition to such suavely sinister, sophisticated, cultivated – and far more British-sounding – villains as Claude Rains in *Notorious* (1946) and James Mason in *North by Northwest* (1959). In contrast to the Hollywood he-man stereotype, however, he was 'consummately romantic yet consummately genteel'. Indeed, as Tom Wolfe observes in his tribute to 'The Loverboy of the Bourgeoisie' (p. 137) the emergent era of macho Brandoism in movie heroes left Cary Grant as it were 'by default', in sole possession of what 'turned out to be a curiously potent device'. 'Which is to say' to women he was 'Hollywood's lone example of the Sexy Gentleman.' Wolfe also notes that it was none other than the 'tall, dark and handsome' young Grant who Mae West (playing the finest woman who ever walked the streets in *She Done Him Wrong*) originally invited to come up and see her sometime. And it was, by the way, the self-same Cary Grant to whom she likewise referred in the immortal one-liner: 'When they make better men, I'll make 'em'. Yet in spite of his phenomenal popularity – he was one of the top ten box-office draws for eight consecutive years beginning in 1959 (see Shipman (1970), p. 263) – Cary Grant had no successor. He was the last of Hollywood's Sexy Gentlemen.

Yet apart from such atavistic stuff as the most chauvinistic American fantasies are made of, there seems no reason why, in an ever-increasingly complex, specialised, technological culture, the succession of male role models produced by the Dream Factory since the Second World War (up to and including the American man's man's favourite cousin from Australia, Crocodile Dundee) has reinforced the same, ego-reassuring, albeit ultimately pathetic male fallacy, just as the more urbanised and middle class many Americans became in real life, the less urbane, and the more brutally macho and primitive became Hollywood's male icons. Contrast, for instance, the debonair image of the laughing cavalier, Errol Flynn, who set out to win the Second World War single-handedly in *Desperate Journey* (1942), with Sylvester Stallone retrospectively fighting the Vietnam War in *Rambo: First Blood Part II* (1985). Flynn, by the way, was also a native Australian, but in contrast to Paul Hogan's 'Crocodile Dundee' his film persona seems infinitely more urbane and closer in sophistication to that of his English successor, James Bond, albeit nothing like so ruthless towards women. The dashing heroes portrayed by Errol Flynn genuinely loved and ultimately married the fair heroines portrayed by Olivia de Havilland. By contrast, in Bond's case his ubiquitously irresistible sex-appeal triumphantly overcomes female frigidity and lesbianism, while he himself remains both sexually and emotionally 'aloof and finely controlled, alert and unencumbered for the tasks ahead' (Glover (1989), p. 70), and so fits the masculinist image of a virile man as one who devalues his relations with women, and at the same time sleeps with lots of them. By the same historical token, as compared to the macho personas of Clint Eastwood and Lee Van Cleef, the earlier Western heroes such as the late, great, Gary Cooper, Henry Fonda and James Stewart were positively chivalrous in their attitude towards women. And so, like all the greatest stars of both sexes, they bridged the gender gap in so far as they were exceptionally popular with men and women (and for that matter with homosexuals, heterosexuals, lesbians, bisexuals and trisexuals) alike. Or, as Julie Burchill puts it (*Girls on Film* (1986), p. 180), 'Damn damn damn damn damn damn damn': why can't a male hero nowadays 'be more like a – Gable, Tracy, Fonda, Bogart – man?'

For, of course, the more dominant, and indeed the more wildly romanticised and unrealistically idealised[4] the chauvinistic fantasy of the triumphant (over all enemies, over all females) all-American he-man became, the more hostile, contemptuous, and downright brutal became his treatment of women. Thus the persona of Bogart, the ultimately romantic tough-guy in *Casablanca*, gave way to the anti-romantic tough-guy personified by Marlon Brando as Stanley Kow-alski in *A Streetcar Named Desire* and so on through to Jack Nicholson in *One Flew Over The Cuckoo's Nest*, that 'primal male whine in which women are either jailers or whores' – see Burchill (1986), p. 179. And which was celebrated as a positive 'triumph of the human spirit' by the Hollywood establishment which awarded it more top Oscars than any film since *It Happened One Night* (Maltin (1988), p. 774).

One might argue that, looked at in political, allegorical and ideological terms, the ubiquitous triumph of the he-man over the gentle-man in Hollywood movies, represents the triumph of the virile American proletariat over the decadent (Old World) aristocracy. Or you could argue that it represents the dictatorship of an anti-intellectual American proletariat at the box-office, and/or the dictatorship of a kind of in-house un-American activities committee, if not a male chauvinist conspiracy, in the head office. For as everyone has noticed, the films made since the emergence of feminism in the 1960s have stereotyped women in every conceivably con-temptuous way: as bimbo, as career-bitch, as fair game. But in any case the fantasy triumph of the anti-feminist, anti-intellectual man's man obviously has to do with desires, with wish-fulfilment, with dreams, with sexually as well as nationally chauvinistic – and conspicuously atavistic – articles of faith. For that matter, as Leslie Fiedler observed in his ground-breaking study of *Love and Death in the American Novel*, there is a masculinist 'boy's own' strain in American literature which has always been profoundly hostile to the town-based ideology that tended to sanctify work, education, duty, home, cleanliness, marriage, chivalry, motherhood (p. 587). For instance, in Mark Twain's archetypal home-town there are 'no bad girls, only good ones, marriage with whom means an initiation into piety and conformity, the end of freedom' (p. 581). And so Huck and Jim flee to the raft to escape the twin tyrannies of law (slavery) and women (domesticity):

> The Widow Douglas, she took me for her son, and allowed she would civilize me; but it was rough living in the house all the time, considering how dismal regular and decent the widow was in all her ways; and so when I couldn't stand it no longer, I lit out.
>
> (*Huckleberry Finn*, p. 2)

Thus, from the Widow Douglas and her Old Maid sister, Miss Watson, to Ken Kesey's Big Nurse Ratched in *One Flew Over the Cuckoo's Nest*, the woman who embodies order, cleanliness, domesti-city, piety, civility, etc., is the foe of freedom, the ultimate tyrant to be feared and fled, the Holy Terror as well as the arch-enemy of man and boy who is by instinct and on principle out to stop his fun.

And so, in both 'classic' and popular American fiction, any male who conforms to the town-based ideology is anathematised as a collaborator with the enemy: as a sissy, a mama's boy, a ladies' man. By contrast, the man who retains his freedom, riding off alone into the sunset, is the ultimate American hero whose theme song (based on an original refrain by Bob Fletcher – see Kimball (1984), pp. 179–80) is, paradoxically, a send-up of this whole tradition by the most urbane and sophisticated of all American popular song-writers, Yale's own Cole Porter:

VERSE 1.
> Wild Cat Kelly, looking mighty pale,
> Was standing by the sheriff's side,
> And when the sheriff said, 'I'm sending you to jail,'
> Wild Cat raised his head and cried:

REFRAIN.
> Oh, give me land, lots of land under starry skies above,
> Don't fence me in.
> Let me ride through the wide-open country that I love,
> Don't fence me in.
> Let me be by myself in the evening breeze,
> Listen to the murmur of the cottonwood trees,
> Send me off forever, but I ask you, please,
> Don't fence me in.
> Just turn me loose,
> Let me straddle my old saddle underneath the Western skies,
> On my cayuse,
> Let me wander over yonder till I see the mountains rise.
> I want to ride to the ridge where the West commences,
> Gaze at the moon till I lose my senses,
> Can't look at hobbles and I can't stand fences.
> Don't fence me in.

VERSE 2.
> Wild Cat Kelly, back again in town,
> Was sitting by his sweetheart's side,
> And when his sweetheart said, 'Come on, let's settle down,'
> Wild Cat raised his head and cried:

REPEAT REFRAIN

The identical sentiments are, of course, expressed in the last lines of *Huckleberry Finn*: 'I reckon I got to light out for the Territory ahead of all the rest, because Aunt Sally she's going to adopt me and civilize me, and I can't stand it. I been there before.'

The jail=female refrain in American literature, would seem to reflect the self-same, primal terror of Woman as equated with domesticity, convention, law, that is so perfectly encapsulated in Karen Blixen's portrait of the imaginary 'Madam Knudsen', the archetypal domesticating woman who is out to ruin the pleasure of man and 'therein is always right' in *Out of Africa*. Old Knudsen, a Dane who lived on Blixen's farm and loved to tell her tall tales about his past life, had experienced many things: shipwrecks, plague, fishes of unknown colouring, drinking-spouts, three contemporaneous suns in the sky, false friends, black villainy, short successes and showers of gold that instantly dried up again. He often spoke of his abomination of the law, and all its works and all its doings: 'for the good citizen he had a deep contempt, and law-abidingness in any man was to him the sign of a slavish mind'. But he never in his narrations mentioned the name of a woman. It was, Blixen observes, 'as if time had swept his mind both of Elsinore's sweet girls, and of the merciless women of the harbour-towns of the world'.

> All the same, when I was talking with him I felt in his life the constant presence of an unknown woman. I cannot say who she may have been: wife, mother, school-dame or wife of his first employer, – in my thoughts I called her Madam Knudsen. . . . She was the wife of the curtain-lectures, and the housewife of the big cleaning-days, she stopped all enterprises, she washed the faces of boys, and snatched away the man's glass of gin from the table before him, she was law and order embodied. In her claim of absolute power she had some likeness to the female deity of the Somali women, but Madam Knudsen did not dream of enslaving by love, she ruled by reasoning and righteousness. Knudsen must have met her at a young age, when his mind was soft enough to receive an ineffaceable impression. He had fled from her to the Sea, for the Sea she loathes, and there she does not come, but ashore again in Africa he had not escaped her, she was still with him. In his wild heart, under his white-red hair, he feared her more than he feared any man, and suspected all women of being in reality Madam Knudsen in disguise. (pp. 204–5)

Likewise, various heroes of American literature (man and boy) light out for the Territory – the wild, the river, the sea, the mountains, the forest, the wars – wherever 'she' (who rules by reasoning and righteousness and must therefore be obeyed) does not come. Compare, for instance, Blixen's description of Madam Knudsen with Huck Finn's virtually identical description of the ways of the Widow Douglas:

> 'The widder wouldn't let me smoke, she wouldn't let me yell, she wouldn't let me gape, nor stretch, nor scratch before folks.' Then, with a spasm of special irritation and injury: 'And dad fetch it, she prayed all the time! I had to shove, Tom, I just had to. And besides, that school's going to open, and I'd a had to go to it; well, I couldn't stand that, Tom. . . . No, Tom . . . I like the woods, and the river, and hogsheads, and I'll stick to 'em too.
>
> (*Tom Sawyer*, p. 219)

Historically speaking, as Jane Tompkins notes (in Longhurst

(1989), pp. 28–9), for most of the nineteenth century the places that women could call their own in the social structure were the home and the church (and of course, the schoolroom). It therefore seems no accident that men 'gravitated in imagination towards a womanless milieu that, when it did not reject culture itself, featured, prominently, whisky, gambling and prostitution' – three main targets of women's reform in the later years of the nineteenth century. 'Can it', Tompkins asks, 'be an accident that the characteristic indoor setting for Westerns is the saloon?' The Western, she concludes, is not – or at least not primarily about the American desire to escape the problems of civilisation: 'It is about men's fear of losing their hegemony and hence their identity, both of which the Western tirelessly reinvents.' And so, even as Huck escapes to the river, the mainstream American literary tradition, 'popular' as well as 'canonical', has (as Leslie Fiedler also observed) historically tended to emulate its heroes, to take to the raft, to fear above all the stigma of being sissified and thus to exclude women from the central action. Or to marginalise them. And ditto, historically speaking, for the American critical tradition. Hundreds, if not thousands of students in innumerable American high schools and universities have studied Mark Twain's institutionally canonised books about boys for every one who knows that he also wrote about the young heroine, Joan of Arc. Twain's moving and sympathetic (*to young girls*) account of her great quest, her adventures, and the friends she made along the way has, in effect, been academically erased: long since dismissed as too sentimental for male critics to stomach.

Although there are some highly significant exceptions to this rule (see below), women are generally excluded from heroic quests. In John Huston's classic adventure films the quest for the Great White Whale and the treasure of the Sierra Madre, like the search for the Lost Kingdom of Kafiristan are undertaken by men only. And so is the heist in *The Asphalt Jungle*. Generally speaking, in adventure films as well as in popular thrillers (see Bromley, in Longhurst (1989), pp. 102–3) women are constructed passively (like Doll and Angela in *The Asphalt Jungle*) or they are not allowed to survive. Threatening (e.g. active) female figures such as Brigid O'Shaughnessy in *The Maltese Falcon* are finally eliminated. And, of course, Huston's 'quest' films, such as *Moby Dick* and *The Man Who Would Be King* are as often derived from 'high' literature as they are from popular modern genres such as the detective story, even as B. Traven's story of the quest for the Treasure of the Sierra Madre, on which Huston's film was based, in turn had a plot markedly similar in outline to *The Pardoner's Tale* by Geoffrey Chaucer. In any event, in works of 'high' and 'popular' art alike, and on screen as in the novel, women are marginalised as Ishmael joins with Queeg-Queeg to go on Ahab's quest for Moby Dick just as Huck and Jim team up on their raft, and so forth and so on, from classics of American literature by Melville and Mark Twain, through all those 'buddy' dramas of the fifties, sixties and seventies, where the occasional woman was only inserted to make sure (and to assure the audience) that Wyatt and Doc, and Butch and the Kid, and Starsky and Hutch sexually stayed on the straight and narrow.

Women are likewise marginalised in popular Western films as well as war movies where the hero's primary duty is to his regiment, his men, to his badge of office as sheriff (see *High Noon*), etc., so any woman who interferes with that duty is an impediment. To qualify as such, the hero *has* to have a higher goal than love, domesticity, private life. Therefore, although it seems paradoxical, he has generally been required to take up arms and leave the girl he loves, as it were to prove himself a hero worthy of a woman's love. Or so the seventeenth century cavalier poet, Richard Lovelace, observed in his poem 'To Lucasta, Going to the Wars':

> Tell me not (Sweet) I am unkind,
>   That from the nunnery
> Of thy chaste breast, and quiet mind,
>   To war and arms I fly.
>
> True: a new mistress now I chase,
>   The first foe in the field;
> And with a stronger faith embrace
>   A sword, a horse, a shield.
>
> Yet this inconstancy is such,
>   As you too shall adore;
> I could not love thee (Dear) so much,
>   Lov'd I not honour more.

Making exactly the same points in *Gone With the Wind*, Rhett Butler quotes this poem to Scarlett O'Hara, before he leaves her on the road to Tara and quixotically goes off to join the army (see Mitchell (1936), pp. 389–90):

> 'Oh, Rhett . . . how can you do this to me? Why are you leaving me?'
> 'Why?' he laughed jauntily. 'Because, perhaps, of the betraying sentimentality that lurks in all of us Southerners. Perhaps – perhaps because I am ashamed. Who knows? . . . No matter. I'm off to the wars.' He laughed suddenly, a ringing, free laugh that startled the echoes in the dark woods.
> ' "I could not love thee, Dear, so much, loved I not Honour more." That's a pat speech, isn't it? Certainly better than anything I can

think up myself at the present moment. For I do love you,
Scarlet. . . . Be patriotic, Scarlett. Think how you would be sending
a soldier to his death with beautiful memories. . . .'

When the furious Scarlett says she hopes a cannon ball lands right on
him and blows him to a million pieces, Rhett wryly replies, 'When
I'm dead on the altar of my country, I hope your conscience hurts
you.'

Thus, as Rhett so ironically reminded Scarlett, the right kind of
man's woman has traditionally and unselfishly and proudly waved
her hero off to glory, just as in all those Westerns the heroine
dutifully blinks back her tears as John Wayne or Errol Flynn rides
out of the fort at the head of the US Cavalry. For a woman's duty as a
woman is to see that her man does his duty as a man; to send her
soldier to his death with beautiful memories, etc. Alternatively, the
primary duty of a beautiful native woman (Sioux, Apache, Navajo or
Mexican) is to sacrifice her own life by throwing her body in the path
of the bullet aimed at her all-American hero and so make sure that his
love for her does not interfere with his primary duty to his own tribe.
He is supposed to die for his country, not for her; she is supposed to
die for him.

Yet from Venus imploring Mars to make love, not war, to Dido
pleading with Aeneas to stay with her, to Grace Kelly trying to
uphold pacifist Quaker principles in *High Noon*, women in love in art
through the ages have also, traditionally, sought to turn the hero
away from his vocation as a warrior, and given a pro-war ideology,
they therefore seem rather like anti-heroic versions of the demonic
spirit in the form of Helen of Troy who tempts Marlowe's Dr
Faustus away from his primary allegiance to God. Significantly,
however, as Jane Tompkins has observed (Longhurst (1989), pp.
25–6), in popular Westerns such as *High Noon* 'the discourse of love
and peace which women articulate' is always rejected, for it
obviously belongs to the 'discourse of Christian domesticity – of
Jesus, the Bible, salvation, the heart, the home – that the Western is at
pains to eradicate'. Indeed, the viewpoint women represent 'is
introduced *in order* to be swept aside, crushed, or dramatically
invalidated'. For instance,

> Near the beginning of *The Searchers* (1956), after a woman and her
> older daughter have been raped and murdered and a younger
> daughter carried off by the Indians, Ethan Edwards (John Wayne),
> who is heading up the search party, is addressed by an older woman,
> who says, 'Don't let the boys waste their lives in vengeance.' He
> doesn't even dignify her words with an answer, and the movie
> chronicles the seven years he and his adopted nephew spend looking
> for the lost girl. In this story, as in many Westerns, women are both

the motive for male activity (it's the women who are being avenged, it's a woman the men are trying to rescue) and at the same time what women stand for – love and forgiveness in place of vengeance – is precisely what that activity denies.

Ultimately, Tompkins concludes, 'the women and children cowering in the background of Indian wars, range wars, battles between outlaws and posses, good gunmen and bad, legitimize the violence men practise in order to protect them.'

Conversely, however, today as yesterday, individual artists may take the side of Venus against Mars just as Rubens did in a painting of 1637/8 for the Grand Duke of Tuscany (Gombrich (1972), pp. 126–7). The painter himself thus retrospectively describes the symbolism of a picture that came to be known as *The Horrors of War*:

> The principal figure is Mars [writes Rubens] who . . . advances with his shield and his bloodstained sword, threatening the nations with great devastation and paying little heed to Venus his lady, who strives with caresses and embraces to restrain him, she being accompanied by her Cupids and lovegods. On the other side Mars is drawn on by the Fury Alecto, holding a torch in her hand. Nearby are monsters, representing Pestilence and Famine, the inseparable companions of war; on the ground lies a woman with a broken lute, signifying harmony, which is incompatible with the discord of war; there is also a mother with her babe in her arms, denoting that fecundity, generation and charity are trampled underfoot by war, which corrupts and destroys all things. In addition there is an architect, lying with his instruments in his hand, to show that what is built for the commodity and ornament of a city is laid in ruins and overthrown by the violence of arms . . . you will also find on the ground, beneath the feet of Mars, a book and some drawings on paper, to show that he tramples on literature and the other arts. . . . [The] Matron clad in black and with her veil torn, despoiled of her jewels and every other ornament, is unhappy Europe, afflicted for so many years by rapine, outrage and misery, which, as they are so harmful to all, need not be specified.

As portrayed by Rubens, Gombrich observes (pp. 128–9), 'Mars is not a heroic warrior, he is a brutal butcher, rather stupid in bearing and physiognomy – and who would not be stupid to allow the Fury Alecto to drag him away from the embraces of Venus? The Fury is a demon'. The painting thus 'teaches and preaches the blessings of peace and the horrors of war by placing the contrast between the two before our eyes', and it is 'precisely the strength of the tradition on which Rubens drew that divinities who are imagined as human and even all-too-human, shade over into personifications [such as 'unhappy Europe'] who are far from "bloodless" '. Likewise looked at symbolically and psychologically, it is, *mutatis mutandis*, as if the flesh-and-blood women who stand for mercy, pity, peace and love in art are, simultaneously, externalised embodiments of the internal impulses *within* the hero (the psyche, the species, the nation) to lay down his arms, to abandon the feud, to make peace with the enemy, etc., and so their influence must finally be suppressed or exorcised or otherwise expelled from his soul and body when he dons the mantle of a tribal hero.[5] Thus, as eternally opposed to the full-metal jacket of he-manhood, any impulses towards charity, compassion, peace, domesticity, sensuality and love, whether from within or without – like works of art advocating them – have traditionally been character-ised as 'effeminate'. 'O sweet Juliet,/Thy beauty hath made me effeminate,/And in my temper soft'ned valour's steel!' exclaims Romeo, immediately before he takes up the sword again to kill Juliet's cousin (*Romeo and Juliet*, III, i, 110–12). On account of irrational passions that probably have to do with atavistic tribal priorities (the war must go on until the enemy is either totally crushed or killed; there will be an eye for an eye until all the world is blind; the feud must go on until 'by and by everybody's killed off, and there ain't no more feud' – *Huckleberry Finn*, p. 126), what is supposed to come first for a woman – domestic tranquillity, personal relationships, love, private life, and so on – must come second to a man. But there are, of course, obvious dramatic as well as ideological reasons for this dialectic.

It is, for instance, hard to imagine a literary or dramatic let-down comparable to the one that would occur if, at the eleventh hour, Melville's Captain Ahab had decided to heed the virtuous Starbuck's good advice, abandoned his vindictive quest for Moby Dick, reversed the course of the *Pequod* and headed home to live out his golden years with his dear wife and children back in Nantucket. By the same token, if Hamlet had heeded Gertrude's advice and made peace with Claudius, or if Romeo had spared Tybalt and so made his peace with the Capulets, the show could not go on. Likewise, in innumerable other instances, there are virtually identical dramatic reasons why the hero can turn his full attention to the woman only *after* his primary goal has been achieved; and so (as in the case of Shakespeare's King Henry V) his proposal of marriage signals 'The End' of the great adventure, of the quest, of the film or the novel. By contrast, in the romantic, chivalric tradition, of which certain stories and novels by Scott Fitzgerald – notably *The Great Gatsby* – are comparatively rare American examples, to win the woman herself may be the primary object of the hero's quest, even as the main goal traditionally sought by any woman in literature, high or low, is to find herself a man.

WHAT DO WOMEN REALLY WANT?
THE LADIES' MAN AND THE SINKING OF THE
'LOUISA'

Generally speaking, 'high' literature and popular genres alike would seem to confirm Lord Byron's conclusion that whereas 'Man's love is of man's life a thing apart,/Tis woman's whole existence' (see *Don Juan*, Canto 1, verse 94). For if this statement is not necessarily true in life you would never know it from traditional portrayals of women where the heroine's love-life *must* come first. 'With man', Simone de Beauvoir observed in 1949 (*The Second Sex*, p. 291), 'there is no break between public and private life: the more he confirms his grasp on the world in action and in work, the more virile he seems to be.' By contrast, 'woman's independent successes' have traditionally been deemed to be 'in contradiction with her femininity'. 'In men's eyes – and for the legion of women who see through men's eyes – it is not enough to have a woman's body nor to assume the female function as a mistress or mother in order to be a "true woman" ': the 'true' woman is required to accept herself as her man's ancillary, as his 'inessential Other'. And so, as if to illustrate de Beauvoir's points, in the classic Hollywood film about the theatre, *All About Eve* (1950), Margo Channing, the great star played by Bette Davis has, finally, to say that what she really, *truly* wants is to be a 'real' woman; that is, a 'married lady' busy 'doing things around the house', instead of starring in a major new play *'for want of anything better to do at night'* [my italics]. It is impossible to imagine any actor playing a male superstar of comparable magnitude making a comparable statement about his professional or domestic priorities.

Of course, portrayals of individual women today are less bound by the traditions and taboos of the feminine mystique than they were in 1950. Yet, generally speaking, it still seems mandatory for a 'real' woman's love-life to be treated as if it were, or ought to be her 'whole existence' and never, like man's love, 'a thing apart'. For instance, Karen Blixen's love for Denys Finch-Hatton was decidedly not the major subject of, and indeed was treated with determined reticence in, her memoir, *Out of Africa*, a book which is crowded with innumerable other, equally memorable relationships, incidents and characters. But Blixen's love-life was the central subject of the film, *Out of Africa* (1985) starring Meryl Streep and Robert Redford. Likewise, Beryl Markham's love affairs were of no significance whatsoever in her memoir, *West With the Night*, but they were treated as the most important aspect of her life in and out of Africa in the TV mini-series based on her biography. By very much the same token, a dramatically pointless love affair was gratuitously inserted, as if we might otherwise forget that the protagonist was a woman, in the film about Dian Fossey's desperate efforts to save her *Gorillas in the Mist* (1988).

By contrast, if his love for a woman is of overriding importance to a male protagonist, he is, traditionally, doomed. Scott Fitzgerald's Jay Gatsby and Shakespeare's Mark Antony, venture, and as it were inevitably lose, all for love. And so it is, primarily, as cautionary, admonitory examples of misplaced values and misguided passions that their love stories have been admitted into the established academic canons of 'high' literature. Had Antony renounced Cleopatra for the sake of Rome, or had Gatsby heroically renounced Daisy – or had Edward VIII renounced Mrs Simpson because England expected him to do his duty as king – their status as men's men might have been maintained along with their status as romantic martyrs. But not otherwise. Fitzgerald attempts to make his *nouveau riche* hero, Jimmy Gatz, acceptable as a man's man as well as a romantic dreamer by giving him a shady past as a racketeer. Yet the character who fell in love with Daisy, fought in the First World War, then went to Oxford, etc., would not seem significantly different if he had inherited his immense wealth from some bootlegger uncle or, for that matter, from a perfectly respectable father in trade. Thus Gatsby's career as a gangster and bootlegger never seems anything like as credible as his romantic quest for the golden grail-girl, Daisy, whose real worth turns out comparable to that of the Maltese Falcon. By contrast the persona of Bogart, who gives up the heroine for the sake of a higher cause in *Casablanca*, successfully fuses the tough-guy (the man's man) with the romantic hero (the ladies' man). Bogart's Rick is credible as the coolly cynical owner of a gin-joint as well as the idealist who did, in fact, fight in the Spanish Civil War, and his love for Ilse Lund is as enduring as Gatsby's love for Daisy. And so, as he tells her in the end, they will 'always have Paris', even though they both realise that the happiness of two little people doesn't amount to a hill of beans in a world at war. Thus to men and women alike, Humphrey Bogart seemed the perfect American hero, the quintessentially romantic tough-guy, when he and Ingrid Bergman heroically parted company at the airport – even as Trevor Howard seemed the quintessential gentleman-hero, the ultimate British 'loverboy of the bourgeoisie', when he and Celia Johnson parted forever in the train station at the end of their *Brief Encounter*.

Perhaps because, from Sir Philip Sidney to John Wilmot, Earl of Rochester, to Lord Byron, some of England's most glamorous

national heroes, legendary rakes, and most romantic heart-throbs
have themselves been poets, the British literary and cinematic tradition has historically allowed for brilliant, witty, urbane, cultivated
and sensitive as well as gentle heroes – as opposed to the all-American
tough guy. They are generally, however, also men of action who risk
all for some higher cause (such as rescuing French aristocrats from the
guillotine) *as well as* for the women they love. Obvious examples of
this type are Sir Percy Blakeney, as portrayed by Leslie Howard in
the 1934 film version of *The Scarlet Pimpernel*, or Sidney Carton, as
played by Ronald Colman, who died so romantically in *A Tale of
Two Cities*. There are no comparable matinée idols in British films
today. In the TV remake of *Brief Encounter*, the far more rugged
Richard Burton replaced the soft-spoken Trevor Howard. And in
remakes of the old costume dramas the male leads are generally
played by less mature, more boyish-looking actors, such as Anthony
Andrews (who played Sir Percy Blakeney in the TV version of *The
Scarlet Pimpernel*) or the American Richard Chamberlain, who
originally made his mark as the juvenile heart-throb Dr Kildare. Yet
the fact that many women on both sides of the Atlantic still like the
older, Trevor Howard/Leslie Howard/Ronald Colman type of
gentleman-hero is surely what accounts for the success of the TV
series that starred Edward Petherbridge as Dorothy L. Sayers's
aristocratic, intellectual detective-hero, Lord Peter Wimsey.

Like Baroness Orczy's Sir Percy Blakeney, Karen Blixen's Denys
Finch-Hatton[6] and Ngaio Marsh's superhumanly intelligent and
sensitive and divinely handsome detective inspector Roderick
Alleyn, Dorothy Sayers's quintessentially aristocratic Lord Peter is a
woman's fantasy-ideal if ever there was one. And although some of
his upper-class mannerisms and assumptions seem at best ludicrously
dated to me, it is easy to understand his appeal. In his relationship
with Harriet Vane, Lord Peter is portrayed as a kind of romantic
version of Sherlock Holmes whose own, absolutely phenomenal
popularity is attested to by the fact reported by Magnus Magnusson
on the television quiz programme *Mastermind*, that he has been
featured in more (no less than *200*) films, plays and television shows,
even as he has been played by more actors than any other character.
As a brilliant amateur detective, Wimsey's prototype is obviously
Holmes, while in his relationship with his beloved Harriet, Lord
Peter's prototype is the most romantic and chivalric of all ladies' men.

Like a twentieth century Sir Launcelot (who defended the life and
honour of his beloved Guinevere) Lord Peter Wimsey rescues
Dorothy Sayers's heroine from the hangman's noose. He is thus
Harriet Vane's chivalric champion, as well as her infinitely patient

and undemanding suitor, her adoring lover, devoted husband and esteemed comrade in detection. In short, he is an updated version of the lady's perfect 'courtly' (that is, simultaneously Platonic, romantic and sensual) lover and knightly champion. For that matter, the courtly ideal that flowered in the waning Middle Ages and which Dorothy Sayers herself knew a great deal about (she translated Dante) was originally nourished, just as it has been subsequently sustained by the female as well as by the male imagination, in literature high and low. For instance, Marie de France (fl. 1160–90) wrote Breton *Lais* that served as sources for successive English writers from Chaucer (see *The Franklin's Tale*) to John Fowles. In the preface of his own translation of Marie's 'Eliduc', Fowles perceptively stresses the crucial importance the feudal system placed on promises sworn between vassal and lord and the comparable emphasis on keeping faith that was applied to sexual relations by the code of courtly love.

> It was not only that the power structure depended on a man being as good as his word; all civilized life depended on it. Today we can go to law over a broken contract; in those days you could only take to arms. . . . [By the same token] *amour courtois* was a desperately needed attempt to bring more civilization (more female intelligence) into a brutal society, and all civilization is based on agreed codes and symbols of mutual trust.
>
> (See *The Ebony Tower* (1974), pp. 118–22)

So far as 'female intelligence' is concerned, the most celebrated of all medieval authors of courtly romances, Chrétien de Troyes – albeit perhaps not without irony – attributed the sentiments and subject (*sen* and *matière*) of his own *Lancelot* (*c.* 1177) to his patroness, Marie de Champagne, while the primary authority on the art of courtly love, Andreas Capellanus, also claimed to be a courtier of hers. In any event, looked at both culturally and historically, there obviously may have been – just as in many places on earth there still are – very practical reasons why women's dream-men so often tend to combine the sterling qualities of a stalwart champion and a *cavalier servant*; a tender lover and a rich and/or noble as well as intelligent protector; a loyal friend and trusted comrade: in a dangerous and potentially violent and brutal world where hostile men have, historically, been *women's* tyrants, exploiters, seducers, rapists, judges, jailers, juries and executioners, what woman might not dream of just such a devoted knight in shining armour?

The premium placed on reliability helps explain why the heroes of romantic novels written by and popular with women on both sides of the Atlantic so often suffer from unconsummated or unrequited love for the heroine: that is the ultimate test and proof of their devotion. For that matter, virtually all of them suffer from secret sorrows and/ or have gentle and sensitive souls as well as powerful physiques. As a result of embittered love, they may be cruel or heartless to others but they would never betray the one woman they truly love: 'I seek no revenge on you', Emily Brontë's Heathcliff tells his soul-mate, Cathy. 'The tyrant grinds down his slaves and they don't turn against him, they crush those beneath them' (p. 112). '*Why* did you betray your own heart, Cathy?', he asks his dying love. 'I have not broken your heart – *you* have broken it – and in breaking it, you have broken mine.' If the true romantic hero leaves the heroine, he never does so because he has fallen in love with some other woman. As Cathy observes it is, for instance, unthinkable that Heathcliff should ever forget her and find happiness in marriage to Isabella Linton (or anyone else on earth) and so say to someone, twenty years hence,

> That's the grave of Catherine Earnshaw. I loved her long ago, and was wretched to lose her; but it is past. I've loved many others since – my children are dearer to me than she was, and, at death, I shall not rejoice that I am going to her, I shall be sorry that I must leave them!
> (*Wuthering Heights*, pp. 158–9)

If Edgar Linton could not love Cathy as much in eighty years as Heathcliff could in a day, it is equally impossible that Heathcliff could love a comparably insipid, paltry, slavish, pitiful, abject creature such as Isabella (pp. 151–3). Heathcliff jeers at and despises Isabella because she had so foolishly pictured him as 'a hero of romance', which of course he is. But not hers: never Isabella's. He is *Cathy's* Heathcliff – '*my* Heathcliff', she calls him: 'I shall love mine yet; and take him with me – he's my soul.' And so she does, even as he pleads with her to haunt him from beyond the grave: 'Be with me always – take any form – drive me mad! only *do* not leave me in this abyss, where I cannot find you! Oh God! it is unutterable! I *cannot* live without my life! I *cannot* live without my soul!' (p. 167). And of course, had Cathy herself not so wilfully and cruelly left him, then nothing 'that God or Satan could inflict' – not misery nor degradation nor death – could ever have severed them (p. 161).

Differing romantic heroes may have differing vices, but a wimpish or fickle betrayal of the heroine is *never* one of them. 'Damn Ashley's honour!' Scarlett thought: 'Ashley's honour has always let me down. Yes, from the very beginning when he kept on coming to see me, even though he knew his family expected him to marry Melanie. Rhett has never let me down, even that dreadful night of Melly's reception when he ought to have wrung my neck. Even when he left me on the road the night Atlanta fell, he knew I'd be safe.'

For years she had had her back against the stone wall of Rhett's love and taken it as much for granted as she had taken Melanie's love, flattering herself that she drew her strength from herself alone. And even as she had realized earlier in the evening that Melanie had been beside her in her bitter campaigns against life, now she knew that silent in the background, Rhett had stood, loving her, understanding her, ready to help. Rhett at the bazaar, reading her impatience in her eyes and leading her out in the reel, Rhett helping her out of the bondage of mourning, Rhett convoying her through the fire and explosions the night Atlanta fell, Rhett lending her the money that gave her her start. . . . Suddenly she felt strong and happy. She was not afraid of the darkness or the fog and she knew with a singing in her heart that she would never fear them again. . . . She caught up her skirts to her knees and began to run lightly. But this time she was not running from fear. She was running because Rhett's arms were at the end of the street.

(Gone With the Wind, pp. 1021–2)

The implication here as elsewhere is that what counts most, in the long run, in our relationships with individuals of both sexes is their reliability as allies, as help-mates in our 'bitter campaigns against life'. For the same point traditionally holds true of the ideal man's man as portrayed by Gary Cooper, John Wayne and Randolph Scott: they are, likewise, absolutely trustworthy. Thus, what, in the long run, anyway, many women (and men?) most need and want are loyal comrades, allies and champions and what they most fear are the traitors, saboteurs and enemy agents that could be concealed behind even the most attractive or romantic persona of the Opposite Sex. The man you think adored you as romantically as Heathcliff loved Cathy may treat you as brutally as Heathcliff treated Isabella Linton. Similarly, many men still nurse a suspicion, in their heart of hearts, that all women are in reality Delilahs – or worse still, Madam Knudsen in disguise.

It is, therefore, heart-warming to learn that, after old Knudsen died, Karen Blixen was left to sort out a disagreement with the Nairobi Municipality about his funeral arrangements: it developed into a heated argument and she had to go into town about it more than once. 'It was a legacy left to me by Knudsen, a last tilt, by proxy, at the face of the law. Thus I was no longer Madam Knudsen, but a brother' (*Out of Africa*, p. 209). Elsewhere, one of Blixen's characters observes that it is so many years now since Adam and Eve were first together in the garden that it seems a great pity that the two sexes still seem unable to take a confident and friendly interest in each other. 'I wish that once, in all the time of men and women, two ambassadors could meet in a friendly mind and come to understand each other' (Blixen, 'The Roads Round Pisa' in *Seven Gothic Tales*

(1934), p. 24). Happily, this is exactly what happens in one of the most beloved of all movies – *The African Queen* starring Bogart as Charlie Alnutt and Katherine Hepburn as his Rose – wherein the heroine's chivalric champion (she calls him 'the bravest man in the world') takes the form of a gin-swilling, profane old river rat while the prim Old Maid, who turns out to be the genuine article very much worth fighting for and dying with, at first appears like the dreaded Madam Knudsen herself, who rules by reason and righteousness when she throws Charlie's gin-bottles overboard, cleans him up, straightens him out: 'Nature, Mr Alnutt, is what we are put in this world to rise above.' It's as if the most antithetical of all male and female stereotypes here join forces as comrades, embrace as lovers and are finally wedded as absolute equals. Portrayed both literally and symbolically in the same boat, each is the other's ultimate test, reward, judge and friend in exactly the kind of ideally reciprocal relationship described by Simone de Beauvoir (p. 277): 'Two who know each other in love make a happy couple, defying time and the universe; such a couple is sufficient unto itself, it realizes the absolute.' And so, as the warship *Louisa* that Charlie and Rosie set out to sink goes down, they literally as well as symbolically swim to shore together. There are good reasons why, fifteen years after this picture was released in 1951, the readers of the *Los Angeles Times* voted *The African Queen* their all-time favourite movie (Shipman (1970), p. 279). It is one of the few movies wherein the man and the woman join forces in a common cause and are allies and comrades, and not the One and the Other.

This form of mutual trust – of comradely, brotherly or sisterly support – that may exist independently of any sexual strings attached to it, as well as in conjunction with a romantic or erotic alliance, also explains why (see the discussion of the Svengali paradigm in the next Chapter) in a surprising number of ways the ideal ladies' man has more in common with certain ostensibly villainous characters (such as Waldo Lydecker and Addison de Witt) who lend support to and further the careers of the gifted heroines than with their macho rivals who see the girl solely as a love-object. For instance, although he could well afford to support his wife in grand style, Rhett Butler actively encourages Scarlett to keep on running her store and her mills: 'I don't care what fools say. In fact, I'm ill bred enough to be proud of having a smart wife' (p. 859). Rhett is also as well educated as Ashley Wilkes and ironically quotes Latin epigrams, the Bible and Shakespeare, along with those lines from Lovelace on going to the wars. And, of course, had she only let him, he could have loved Scarlett 'as gently and tenderly as ever a man loved a woman' (p.

1030). In *Casablanca* Bogart was, likewise, as appealing to women as he was to men because he played such a romantic and, ultimately, supportive tough-guy and so emerged as the heroine's chivalric champion, knowing what was, in the long run, the right thing for both of them to do. And as Woody Allen conclusively demonstrated in *Play It Again, Sam*, the Ghost of Bogart can provide any man, today as yesterday, with at least as desirable (to women) and certainly no less realistically achievable role model than, say, the boy's-own personas of Jack Nicholson in *One Flew Over the Cuckoo's Nest* or Sylvester Stallone as Rambo.

It is often observed that audiences especially tend to like characters whom they can 'identify with' – that is, they prefer those characters who most resemble themselves – and these and other arguments about fictional 'identities and identifications' are the main concern of the final chapter of this book. Yet it should be noted here that, at least as often as not, the most adored of all characters are not the ones most of us really *do* look or act like but the ones that we would most like to be like. Or love to be loved by. And the most beloved of all superstars combine both components: they are like ourselves, vulnerable or flawed in some ways, but better (more glamorous, etc.) in other ways. Thus the enduring appeal (to both sexes) of Humphrey Bogart in *Casablanca* may have to do with the way his persona combines an ideal integrity, cool strength, etc., with various other qualities that most men possess, but in the personas of such figures as, say, Clint Eastwood as 'The Man With No Name', etc., are treated as incompatible with macho manhood. Indeed the Bogart persona that has captured the imaginations of successive generations and both sexes is characterised by the fusion of opposites: e.g. idealism and cynicism; toughness and vulnerability; uncommon wit and common sense; and so on. Thus, that haunting allusion to Shakespeare's line about the 'stuff that dreams are made on' at the end of *The Maltese Falcon* could only enhance Bogart's enduring romantic appeal, along with the poetic appeal of Huston's film as a whole.

Of course, what is most romantic about *The Maltese Falcon*, what comes first to the mind when the film is mentioned, and lingers longest in everyone's memory of it, is obviously not the love-story: Bogart turns Mary Astor over to the cops out of loyalty to his dead partner. It is the image of that bird. And what captures the imagination is the unending quest for the film's holy grail – the stuff that dreams are made of here is indisputably that priceless, ultimately illusory statuette. For here as elsewhere the ultimate romance, the ultimate value, lies not so much in attaining the object sought for but in the search itself. The great director John Huston once observed that 'all human endeavor, virtuous or evil or simply plodding, receives the same honorarium, a check in the amount of zero' (Avedon and Capote (1959), pp. 10–11). And so the Maltese Falcon, over which all the characters fight to the death, is not the jewelled and genuine item but a leaden fake, a cheat. Likewise, at the end of *The Treasure of the Sierra Madre* the gold is blown away by the wind – and the same theme or denouement occurs in *The Asphalt Jungle* and, of course, *Moby Dick*. In fact, the only compensatory reward for all the effort undertaken in a Huston quest-film or indeed in life, as Michael Caine observes to Sean Connery when they are confronting certain death in *The Man Who Would Be King*, is having had experiences and established relationships along the way that one wouldn't have wanted to miss. And, of course, the grizzled old souse Bogart and the prim Old Maid, Katherine Hepburn, say exactly the same thing about their experiences together when they face death in *The African Queen* – a film that, to its eternal credit, took some of the most tenacious of all the gender stereotypes surveyed here and shattered them.

Likewise, in another all-time favourite film, *The Wizard of Oz*, the brave and resourceful Dorothy and her beloved comrades, the Scarecrow, the Tin Woodman and the Cowardly Lion, join forces (their hearts, their brains, their courage) on their quests to find the Wizard and destroy the Wicked Witch of the West. And, of course, equal measures of *True Grit* are displayed by the upright fourteen-year-old heroine Mattie Ross and the grizzled, hard-drinking, double-tough marshal Rooster Cogburn when they go into the Territory to avenge her father's blood. Thus, popular as well as high art need not necessarily reinforce gender stereotypes to achieve tremendous commercial success. But *True Grit, The African Queen* and *The Wizard of Oz* are rare exceptions to the rule whereby collaborative endeavour in the pursuit of a larger (non-or-extra sexual, non-or-extra romantic) goal is traditionally restricted to men. Indeed, one reason why the TV series, *Widows*, by Lynda la Plante, was such a joy to behold was the way it so brilliantly exploited, even as it reversed, all the conventions of the 'heist' genre by showing women successfully pulling off a robbery. Yet even so, the magnificent 'Dolly Rollins', who organised the heist, in the end proclaimed her undying love for the man who had betrayed her.

And so portrayals of women in popular films such as *Baby Boom* and in the mass media generally (Tuchman *et al.*, (1978), pp. 3–38) still tend to confirm rather than challenge Lord Byron's law, just as home life – domesticity – is commonly deemed to constitute woman's happiness. To give perhaps the most classic of all examples from one of the most popular of all films, having initially dreamed of flying somewhere over the rainbow and having found her way to the Emerald City and having destroyed the Wicked Witch of the West, Dorothy's ultimate discovery at the end of *The Wizard of Oz* (1939) is that 'There's no place like home!'. By contrast, at the end of the comparably glorious adventure film, *The Thief of Bagdad* (1940), Dorothy's male counterpart, the brave and resourceful young Sabu, having stolen the All Seeing Eye from the Temple of the Goddess of the Dawn and destroyed the evil magician, waves goodbye to the rightful king he restored to the throne of Bagdad and flies away over the rainbow on his magic carpet in his unending quest for 'some fun, an adventure'.[7]

For that matter, apart from the filmed tributes to Joan of Arc and other historical as well as fictional profiles in courage, such as *Carve Her Name with Pride, Secret Army* and various Second World War films, wherein women risk their lives alongside men in the Resistance, the only truly communal form of endeavour traditionally permitted between men and women in popular works is in show business and even then the heroine is virtually obliged to give her love-life top priority. Nevertheless, in certain works discussed in the next chapter the authors themselves seem to join forces with their fellow artists, regardless of sex. And in so doing they open up alternative possibilities and multiple choices for their own readers and audiences, if not to the heroines themselves.

CHAPTER TWO

Some parables of a woman's talent

ANGELS OF MUSIC, DEMON LOVERS AND RED SHOES

But the [movie] I liked best was *The Red Shoes*, with Moira Shearer as a ballet dancer torn between her career and her husband. I adored her: not only did she have red hair and an entrancing pair of red satin slippers to match, she also had beautiful costumes, and she suffered more than anyone. I munched faster and faster as she became more and more entangled in her dilemma – I wanted those things too, I wanted to dance and be married to a handsome orchestra conductor, both at once – and when she finally threw herself in front of a train I let out a bellowing snort that made people three rows ahead turn around indignantly. Aunt Lou took me to see it four times.

Margaret Atwood, *Lady Oracle*

Melodrama is the naturalism of the dream life.

Gail Godwin, *The Odd Woman*

*   *   *   *

What on earth do works so different as Gaston Leroux's *The Phantom of the Opera*, George du Maurier's *Trilby*, the ballet film *The Red Shoes* and Henry James's *The Bostonians* have in common with each other? With two major exceptions – and however much they differ in other respects – the various works discussed in detail in this chapter can all be interpreted as parables of a woman's talent, or as forms of a morality play in which a talented young woman must finally choose between her life as an artist and the young man she loves. The first exception is Christ's original 'Parable of the Talents' as recorded in the Gospel according to St Matthew. As we shall see, that parable's relevance to men has gone unquestioned for centuries, but whether or not it is equally relevant to women is a subject of continuing debate. The other exception is George Eliot's *Daniel Deronda* wherein the contrast between the two talented Jewish singers, the delicate Mirah Cohen and the formidable diva, the Alcharisi, to which I give special attention, is not the novel's central concern.

Perhaps significantly, in virtually all of the other works surveyed here – from popular novels, films and stage shows such as *The Phantom of the Opera*, *Trilby* and *The Red Shoes* to Henry James's portrayal of the 'gifted' Verena Tarrant in *The Bostonians* – the

41

*Claude Rains wears the mask of the Phantom in the 1943 film
version of the legend.*

contradictory claims of the heroine's art and her heart are shown to be
as fundamentally and profoundly opposed to each other as the forces
of good and evil that contend for the soul of the hero in a medieval
morality play. In their differing portrayals of essentially the same
conflicts, these films, novels and plays likewise serve to take us into
an imaginative twilight zone that lies somewhere between myth and
propaganda, fact and fiction, realism and symbolism, life and art.
Indeed, one can track some of their characters across the borderlines
from story to legend and on into myth as in ways markedly
comparable to the stories of Pygmalion and his Galatea, or of
Cinderella, Frankenstein, Dracula and Faust, the stories of Trilby
and her Svengali and the Phantom of the Opera and his Christine
have inspired successive reinterpretations, re-makes, adaptations, and
translations into differing media.

For instance, George du Maurier's original novel, *Trilby* (1894),
was turned into a hit stage-play that has inspired (at least) three

Michael Crawford's Phantom in Andrew Lloyd Webber's musical adaptation of 1986.

different films starring, in turn, John Barrymore (1931), Donald Wolfit (1955) and Peter O'Toole (1983). A hat still worn today is called a 'Trilby', while du Maurier's villain has become an archetype in his own right. People who have never heard of the novel *Trilby* will know what you mean if you mention 'a Svengali'. By now there have been at least four different film versions of *The Phantom of the Opera*, not to mention spin-offs such as *The Phantom of Hollywood*, *The Phantom of the Paradise* and *The Phantom of the [Grand Ole] Opry*. At the time the copyright on Gaston Leroux's 1911 novel was due to expire, plans were announced for no fewer than three competing musical *Phantoms*. And it has repeatedly been rumoured that Steven Spielberg hopes to make a film version of the smash hit musical adaptation by Andrew Lloyd Webber which opened in London in 1986 and New York in 1988.

But why should the legend of the Phantom of the Opera so persistently continue to haunt the imagination of theatrical entrepreneurs and audiences alike? Reviewing Lloyd Webber's musical in the London *Times* (11 October 1986), Irving Wardle, to my mind accurately, described Gaston Leroux's original plot as 'God's gift' to the musical theatre: 'It wraps up the legends of Faust, Svengali, and Beauty and the Beast into a grand death rattle of romantic agony.' By the same token, William Livingstone (*Opera News* (16 January 1988), pp. 22–5), stressed the potency of Leroux's fable with reference to its extremely effective fusion of melodramatic, operatic, and mythic themes and images:

> The musical relationship between Christine and the Phantom (whose music lessons do improve her singing) suggests the artistic domination of the soprano Trilby by her mentor Svengali . . . [while] an operatic parallel exists in the last act of *Les Contes d'Hoffmann*, in which Dr. Miracle and Hoffmann compete for power over Antonia and her voice. . . . The theme of searching for identity reaches a climax in *The Phantom of the Opera* when Christine insists on unmasking the Phantom. . . . This dramatic moment is similar to the scene in *Lohengrin* when Elsa demands to know her husband's name. Both recall the myth of Psyche, who defied all warnings to gaze upon the face of her lover, Cupid. . . . Near the end of Leroux's novel, the crucial kiss that Christine bestows [on the Phantom] also recalls the fairy tales of *Beauty and the Beast* and *The Frog Prince*. If the roots of *The Phantom of the Opera* draw strength from European folklore, they reach even deeper into myth. Reduced to essentials, the book echoes the story of Pluto, who kidnaps the beautiful Proserpina and takes her to live in his kingdom of the underworld. Given these potent themes and many melodramatic high points, it is not surprising that different writers and producers have sought to reinterpret the story of the young nobleman and the ugly monster competing for the love of the beautiful singer.

On the other hand, *Time* magazine's critic, William A. Henry III, felt that the plot of Leroux's penny-dreadful – 'part horror melodrama, part bodice-ripping gothic' – was 'too grim and kinky' for a musical. The central character is, after all, 'not only hideously ugly, but an extortionist, kidnapper . . . and megalomaniac – and the heroine must at least halfway fall in love with him.' What seemed to strike *Time*'s critic as *especially* kinky was the 'alternately thrilled and terrified' heroine's 'neurasthenic obsession with the Phantom'. For this, he observed, is 'unquestionably a love story, just as much for the heroine, a baffled girl from the chorus, as for the masked enigma who spirits her down to the labyrinthine bowels of the Paris opera house to teach her to become a star' (*Time* (26 October 1986), p. 36).

This critic is, certainly, right about the love story. But 'neurasthenic' – which is defined in the dictionary as 'a functional nervous weakness' – is not, I believe, the right way to describe the heroine's alternately thrilled and terrified responses to the Phantom of the

Opera. Her love for, and fear of losing him are here portrayed as an artist's love for, and fear of losing her own special genius, her inspiration, her daemon, her muse, combined with her terror at the unconditional allegiance and devotion demanded of her by her art, even as (in the new musical and the original novel alike) the Phantom communicates to Christine through her dressing-room mirror: 'Look at your face in the mirror – I am there inside!', sings Lloyd Webber's 'Angel of Music' (Perry (1987), p. 145). For that matter, the identical questions raised by *Time* magazine's reviewer were – as it were rhetorically – originally raised as well as answered by Leroux himself:

> To what extent . . . was she really a victim? Whose prisoner was she? What influence had she undergone? What monster had carried her off and by what means? . . . By what means indeed but that of music?
>
> (*The Phantom of the Opera*, p. 106)

If ever there were a parable of a woman's talent, *The Phantom of the Opera* is one, and since it encapsulates so many of the conflicts to be discussed later on, here, for the purposes of further reference, is an outline of the original fable.

'THE ANGEL OF MUSIC'

> What thou seekest is in thee! Look, and find
> Each Monster meets his likeness in thy mind.
> Alexander Pope (*The Dunciad*, III, 251–2)

> And though you turn from me, to glance behind,
> The Phantom of the Opera is there –
> Inside your mind.
> 'The Phantom of the Opera' (lyrics by C. Hart,
> R. Stilgoe and M. Batt)

The heroine of Gaston Leroux's novel, Christine Daaé, is a talented young singer whose father, a Scandinavian peasant who was himself a gifted violinist, had brought her up on stories about the Angel of Music:

> The Angel of Music played a part in all [of her father's] tales; and he maintained that every great musician . . . received a visit from the Angel at least once. . . . Sometimes the Angel leans over their cradle . . . and that is how there are little prodigies who play the fiddle at six better than men of fifty. . . . Sometimes the Angel comes later, because the children are naughty and won't learn their lessons or

practise their scales. And sometimes he does not come at all because
the children have a wicked heart or a bad conscience. No one ever
sees the Angel; but he is heard by those who are meant to hear him.
He often comes when they least expect him, when they feel sad and
discouraged. Then their ears suddenly perceive celestial harmonies, a
divine voice, which they remember all their lives long. Persons who
are visited by the Angel . . . cannot touch an instrument or open
their mouths to sing, without producing sounds that put all other
human sounds to shame. Then people who do not know that the
Angel has visited these persons say that they have 'genius'. (pp. 71–
2)

Christine's father told her that he himself had never heard the divine
voice, but promised that when he died he would send the Angel of
Music to her.

As a child, Christine's playmate was, for a time, the young
Vicomte, Raoul de Chagny, who loved her but knew that they must
finally be separated by the difference in their social stations. When he
kissed his childhood sweetheart goodbye, Raoul said 'Mademoiselle,
I shall never forget you', but he went away regretting his words, for
he knew that the daughter of a peasant could never be the wife of the
Vicomte de Chagny.

> As for Christine, she tried not to think of him and devoted herself
> wholly to her art. She made wonderful progress and those who
> heard her prophesied that she would be the greatest singer in the
> world. Meanwhile, her father died; and, suddenly, she seemed to
> have lost with him her voice, her soul, and her genius. She retained
> just, but only just enough of all this to enter the Conservatoire,
> where she did not distinguish herself at all. (p. 73)

She was, however, successful enough to get a job in the chorus of the
Paris opera, where she was also an understudy for the role of
Margarita in Gounod's *Faust*.

Raoul, by now a handsome young man of twenty-one, recognised
Christine at the Opera and was charmed by her beauty and the sweet
images of their childhood which it evoked. He tried to attract her
attention, but she did not see him. She appeared, for that matter, to
see nobody. And then he attended a gala performance when Carlotta,
the prima donna, fell unaccountably ill. Christine replaced her in the
role of Margarita and the heavens were torn asunder as an angel's
voice was heard upon earth for the delight of mankind and the utter
conquest of his heart (p. 73).

Raoul goes backstage and overhears a man's voice – a miraculously
beautiful voice – talking to Christine in her dressing room. The voice
said: 'Christine, you must love me!' She answers: 'How can you talk
like that? When I sing only for you?' The voice spoke again: 'Are

you very tired?' and she answers, 'Oh, tonight, I gave you my soul and I am dead!' She leaves the room alone, and Raoul, who now knew what love meant and jealousy, burst into the dressing-room to confront his rival, but found no one there (pp. 46-7).

In the meantime, the new managers of the Opera (one of them does not know one key from the other, but has all the right social connections) keep receiving notes from what seems to be a prankster signing himself the 'Opera Ghost' who demands their absolute obedience to his every command. The retiring managers who were themselves 'relieved at leaving behind a domain where that tyrannical shade held sway', warn the new managers that they had better take the Phantom's orders very seriously indeed. For every time his commandments had been disobeyed or disregarded some fantastic or disastrous event had occurred.

The Opera House is of course the domain of the Angel of Music (p. 160) who declares total warfare on its Philistine administrators whenever they dare to compromise the standards of excellence required in its charter, whereby 'The management of the Opera shall give to the performances of the National Academy of Music the splendour that becomes the first lyric stage in France' (p. 51). And of course the Opera Ghost himself had arranged for Carlotta to fall ill on the night of that gala performance and demands that the management henceforth replace the adequate but comparatively mediocre and uninspired prima donna with his own beloved protégée, Christine, 'whose genius is certain' (p. 56). In the context of Leroux's fable, Christine is to Carlotta as Mozart is to Salieri in Peter Shaffer's *Amadeus*; that is, the chosen instrument of the Angel of Music.

When Christine emerges as the greatest singer ever heard on the stage of the Paris Opera, the young Vicomte dismisses any problems posed by the difference in their social positions and determines to marry her. But when he goes to see her, he is told by the kindly old woman who had looked after her since her father's death that Christine has gone away with her 'good genius':

'What good genius?' exclaimed poor Raoul. 'Why, the Angel of Music!' 'Didn't you know? . . . did you think that Christine was free?' 'Is Christine engaged to be married?' asked the wretched Raoul, in a choking voice. 'Why no! Why no! . . . You know as well as I do that Christine couldn't marry even if she wanted to!' 'But I don't know anything about it! . . . And why can't Christine marry?' 'Because of the Angel of Music, of course!' 'I don't follow.' 'Yes, he forbids her to!' 'He forbids her . . . without forbidding her. It's like this: he tells her that, if she got married, she would never hear him again. That's all . . . . And that he would go away for ever! So, you understand, she can't let the Angel of Music go.' (pp. 100-1)

Lon Chaney's Phantom in the 1925 silent film.

Now as anyone familiar with perhaps the most famous of all silent movie stills from the film starring Lon Chaney will know, when Christine is taken down to the secret regions below the Opera by the Phantom, and when she rips off the mask to see the face of the Angel of Music, she is confronted with a hideous apparition: with the face of a corpse, a skeleton, a living death's-head. 'Imagine if you can' (Christine thus describes the unmasking to Raoul) a death's-head that had been dried and withered by the ages suddenly coming to life 'in order to express, with the four black holes of its eyes, its nose and its mouth, the extreme anger, the mighty fury of a demon' (pp. 140–1). And so the visage of Leroux's Phantom provides us with the most dramatic – or, rather, with the most melodramatic – of all examples of the supernatural image of 'life-in-death, death-in-life, which [within the Romantic and symbolist traditions] characterises the perfect being of art' and which is so vividly described throughout Frank Kermode's historical study of the *Romantic Image* (Kermode (1957),

p. 88; see also Mario Praz's pioneering study of *The Romantic Agony* (1933) Oxford).

In the case of Leroux's Christine, as in the case of the Romantic poet who sees the immortal face of Moneta in Keats's *Hyperion* ('deathwards progressing/towards no death was that Image'), the artist granted access to art's death-like, yet deathless Image must pay a terrible price in estrangement, isolation and alienation from everyday life. Like Christine, who must not marry lest she lose her privileged access to the Angel of Music Incarnate, the male artist who desires access to the Romantic Image must live 'without wife or child or friend. . . . His is the solitude of the soul' (Kermode, pp. 7–9). So far as the late-late-Romantic tradition is concerned, in the case of a gifted female such as Leroux's Christine or George du Maurier's Trilby, her artistic genius-daemon *is* her Demon Lover, the most jealous lover of all, just as in the case of the male artist, his art is his *belle dame sans merci*, the ultimate *femme fatale*. Thus seen as a 'grand death-rattle of romantic agony', Leroux's penny-dreadful has it all: the morbidity; the Gothic horror; the mask; the divine or demonic lover or muse or image; the conflict between perfection of the life or of the art; the contrast between the dark, subterranean domain of the Phantom of the Opera and the sunshine of common day and so on. Here, for instance, are the terms of the choice that Leroux's young *diva* must make.

As the instrument, the beloved, the chosen consort of the Angel of Music, Christine reigned over 'an empire which was artificial but immense, covering seventeen storeys and inhabited by an army of subjects'. Conversely, however, 'It was as though the real sky, the real flowers, the real earth were forbidden her for all time and she had been condemned to breathe no other air than that of the theatre.' When Christine invited Raoul to come for a walk, 'he thought that she would propose a stroll in the country . . . but she took him to the stage and made him sit on the wooden curb of a wall, in the doubtful peace and coolness of a first scene set for the evening's performance.' 'On another day, she wandered with him, hand in hand, along deserted paths of a garden whose creepers had been cut by a decorator's skilful hands. She took him to the property rooms, took him all over the empire where she moved among her subjects like a popular queen' (pp. 122–3). By now, Raoul is as jealous of and threatened by the Phantom as the Phantom is jealous of and threatened by him: 'He no longer doubted the almost supernatural powers of the Angel of Music in the domain of the Opera where he had set up his empire' and he henceforth 'detested the opera house as a prison whose jailer he could feel walking within the walls.' And so the battle-lines of the contention for the heart and soul and body of the young singer are as clearly drawn as the lines of contention between the demonic and angelic forces that battle for the body and soul of the hero in a morality play, or in the legend of Faust. The difference here, as *Time* magazine's reviewer noted, is that it is not altogether certain which side we are supposed to root for.

In the end, of course (*why* 'of course' is a question we'll examine later on) the handsome young vicomte wins the girl. The Phantom finally relinquishes all his claims on her, and Raoul and Christine leave the world of the opera behind them forever. In contrast to the spectacular ending of Lloyd Webber's musical wherein the Phantom vanishes as if by magic, Leroux's Phantom dies after Christine leaves him (the Angel of Music cannot exist/survive without his human instrument?). Earlier on in the narrative, Leroux gives us a realistic explanation of the Phantom as a genius-freak, congenitally hideous, like the Elephant Man. But he stresses the Phantom's allegorical role yet again in the Epilogue to his original novel: 'What', Leroux's

Maximilian Schell as the Phantom in the
1982 television movie.

Herbert Lom as the Phantom in the Hammer version of 1962.

narrator asks, 'had become of that wonderful, mysterious artist of whom the world was never, never to hear again?' Raoul and Christine, he informs us, had 'retired far from the world' to find happiness, probably in her native Scandinavia. Possibly, the narrator concludes, 'I too shall take the train one day from the northern railway-station of the world' and perhaps 'someday I shall hear the lonely mountains of the north echo the singing of her who knew the Angel of Music' (p. 254).

I have outlined the fable of *The Phantom of the Opera* in some detail because it so unsubtly portrays the various conundrums and character types that recur in so many other depictions of essentially the same central conflict. Here as elsewhere, the character who embodies the heroine's artistic genius and aspirations is portrayed, if not as the outright villain of the piece, as sinister, abnormal, freakish, alien, foreign. The hideous Phantom's counterparts in *Trilby, The Red Shoes* and *The Bostonians* are the Jewish megalomaniac, Svengali; the tyrannical impresario Lermontov (who is himself described by the ballerina heroine as 'a monster'); and the 'morbid' old maid, Olive Chancellor, who functions as a kind of surrogate stage-mother to the 'gifted' Verena Tarrant. Looked at symbolically, these various characters in one form or another likewise serve to exemplify, and/or personify, the alien, sterile, monstrous, demonic abnormality of a woman's professional or artistic ambitions. For instance: Trilby's 'dread, powerful demon', Svengali, is described in turn as the greatest artistic genius who ever lived and as an egotistical, fawning bully, who thus serves to exemplify the kind of genius that will grovel, flatter, cringe, bully, browbeat and exploit anyone and anything necessary in order to further its art. By the same token, in George Eliot's *Daniel Deronda*, the Jewish stage-father, old Lapidoth, personifies the coarse, crassly commercial, glitzy side of show-business from which his angelic daughter, Mirah, recoils. To give yet another example, in the popular film starring Doris Day that was based on the life of the singer, Ruth Etting (*Love Me or Leave Me*, 1955), the obsessive, crippled gangster, Marty 'The Gimp' Schneider (who was brilliantly portrayed by James Cagney) most dramatically personified the obsessive, antisocial/abnormal nature of the pretty young heroine's professional ambition. This explains why, in order for her to maintain the sympathies of the audience, the sweet, virginal, heroine *has* to seem a kind of puppet in the hands of some power figure – of a Phantom, a Svengali, or some comparably (monstrously) ambitious stage-mother such as the one portrayed by Ethel Merman on stage and by Rosalind Russell in the film, *Gypsy*. For if a lovely young *ingénue* showed – of her own free will and volition – the same single-minded dedication to her vocation as an artist that, say, the Angel of Music demanded of Christine, then she herself would likewise be stigmatised as a freak as monstrous as the Phantom of the Opera himself. The portrayal of the Alcharisi (a portrait of the utterly dedicated artist as a woman young and old) by George Eliot can serve to illustrate these points.

THE PRIMA DONNA

'Every woman is supposed to have the same set of motives, *or else to be a monster*' [my italics], observes the great prima donna, the Alcharisi, who defiantly refuses to play the orthodox roles required of a dutiful Jewish daughter, wife and mother in *Daniel Deronda*. 'I am not a monster,' she tells her son, Daniel, 'but I have not felt exactly what other women feel – or say they feel, for fear of being thought unlike others':

> When you reproach me in your heart for sending you away from me, you mean that I ought to say I felt about you as other women say they feel about their children. I did *not* feel that, I was glad to be freed from you.
>
> (*Daniel Deronda* (1967), p. 691)

She thus goes on to tell Daniel the story of her life. As a young girl, she had hated living under the shadow of her orthodox father's strictness: 'He never comprehended me, or if he did, he only thought of fettering me into obedience . . . "this you must be," "that you must not be" – pressed on me like a frame that got tighter and tighter as I grew' (pp. 692–3).

> He hated that Jewish women should be thought of by the Christian world as a sort of ware to make public singers and actresses of. As if we were not the more enviable for that! That is a chance of escaping from bondage. (p. 694)

In spite of her father, she had enough training to bring out 'the born singer and actress' within her. And although she had 'wanted not to marry' she found a measure of freedom when she married Daniel's father, a man who not only promised to put no hindrance in the way of her becoming an artist (p. 695), but subsequently 'made it the labour of his life' to devote himself to her: 'As I loved the life of my art, so he loved me' (p. 696). When he died, she explains to her son, she resolved to have no ties 'but such as I could free myself from'. 'I was the Alcharisi you have heard of: the name had magic wherever it was carried' (p. 697). 'I acted as well as I sang. All the rest were poor beside me. Men followed me from one country to another. I was living a myriad lives in one. I did not want a child' (pp. 688–9). 'I did not wish you to be born. I parted with you willingly' (p. 697). 'Had I not a rightful claim to be something more than a mere daughter and mother?' she finally asks her son: 'Whatever else was wrong, acknowledge that I had a right to be an artist, though my father's will was against it. My nature gave me a charter' (p. 728).

For Daniel, this reunion with his long-lost mother proved painfully disillusioning. The Alcharisi's 'frank coldness' had replaced his 'preconceptions of a mother's tender joy in the sight of him' (p. 695) and made 'the filial yearning of his life a disappointed pilgrimage to a shrine where there were no longer the symbols of sacredness'. And so, 'It seemed that all the *woman lacking in her* [my italics] was present in him' as he said, with some tremor in his voice – 'Then we are to part, and I never be anything to you?' and she answered, 'It is better so' (pp. 723–4).

Some of the taboos violated by the Alcharisi in defiance of her father are explicitly Jewish:

> I was to be what he called 'the Jewish woman' under pain of his curse . . . I was to feel awe for the bit of parchment in the *mezuza* over the door; to dread lest a bit of butter should touch a bit of meat; to think it beautiful that men should bind the *tephillin* on them and women not. (pp. 692–3)

But the most sacred of all the patriarchal taboos she defied are by no means exclusively Jewish. If a gifted young woman portrayed within a comparable work of art in the context of virtually any other religious orthodoxy (Catholic, Protestant, or Islamic) had shown the same dedication to her own genius and likewise refused to serve any man (whether as his daughter or his wife or his mother) so as to enjoy reigning as a queen in the theatre, over a host of adoring admirers (*Daniel Deronda*, p. 702) she would consequently (the prospect otherwise might seem simply too attractive to other women?) *have* to be shown to suffer for her sins and/or deemed to be as monstrous, as unnatural, as 'lacking' in true 'womanhood' as La Alcharisi. By contrast, the young man of genius who heroically dedicates himself to his vocation – his God, his music, his poetry, his scientific research, his regiment – at whatever cost to his mother, wife, children, etc., has not, traditionally, been stigmatised (as unnatural, unmanly, etc.) to anything like a comparable degree. Why should this be the case?

Ever since Lilith, the desire to play the star part rather than a supporting role has been deemed anathema – an accursed thing – in woman. And it still is.[1] There are very rare violations of this taboo (see below, p. 97), but generally speaking, a woman who aspires to and achieves great artistic distinction and fame and glory independently of any mentor *cannot* be officially extolled as the most admirable and sympathetic female character in any novel, film or soap-opera designed for a mass-market audience. 'I am Mrs Norman Maine!' proclaims the heroine whose Hollywood career – as it were tragically – outshone her husband's, and she thus maintains the sympathies of the audience at the end of both the first and second versions of *A Star is Born* (starring Janet Gaynor and Judy Garland). For it is morally all right for a Great Man's widow to carry a torch of fame and glory for *him*. Likewise, it is all right if stardom is thrust or forced upon the heroine, as it is in *Gypsy*. Otherwise, a woman's professional fame and glory have, traditionally, been equated with personal suffering, with domestic tragedy, with drink, drugs, death. To bring us closer up to date, *A Star is Born* was remade with Barbra Streisand in 1976, while in recent years the heroine with star quality who outgrows or professionally leaves behind the male mentor/ husband who bought her first guitar or encouraged her to pose for *Playboy* or otherwise helped her on her way to stardom has been treated as the tragic, or potentially tragic subject of various films based on real-life case histories. See, for example, the sympathetic biography of Loretta Lynn, who is torn between the claims of her career and of her husband and children in *Coal Miner's Daughter*. And see also *The Death of a Centerfold: The Dorothy Stratten Story* and *Star*

80 – both films deal with the identical subject: '*Playboy* centerfold Dorothy Stratten was groomed for stardom by her possessive husband, and later murdered by her two-bit Svengali when fame began to pull her from his grasp' (Scheuer (1988), p. 746). Times have changed in other ways, but the equation of a woman's exceptional success in virtually any sphere outside the home, with extreme personal suffering, or doom, is still, ideologically speaking, axiomatic.

Generally speaking (today as yesterday) it is also axiomatic that, unless a female protagonist is clearly portrayed as a villainess, or as tragically wrong-headed, she must not be shown from the outset to have determined to achieve power or glory for herself. Or if she does seek professional glory and find it for herself, then she must finally find it wanting. Indeed, the more successful and brilliant and ambitious and glamorous and famous she is in her own right, *and the more she enjoys her success*, the more she must be morally anathematised as a *femme fatale*, a vampire, an unnatural monster, a superbitch. 'You are an improbable person, Eve,' says the critic to the ambitious actress in the film classic, *All About Eve*, 'we have that in common.' 'Also a contempt for humanity, an inability to love or be loved, insatiable ambition – and talent. We deserve each other' (Quinlan (1987), p. 101).

As Julie Burchill observes (*Girls on Film* (1986), p. 40), two of the most famous films ever made about female stars of stage and screen 'had the hatchet out for women in general and actresses in particular'. Both in *All About Eve* and *Sunset Boulevard* the female superstars portrayed by Bette Davis and Gloria Swanson 'recited man-made lines to comfort men' – that their fame was a sham, that all they really wanted was a man, that a woman was 'not a woman' who didn't wake up and find *him* in bed with her, and so on. In *All About Eve*, the hatchet was out not only for the great star Margo Channing (Bette Davis), as well as the immensely talented and ambitious Eve (who was brilliantly portrayed by Anne Baxter as an unctuous, scheming bitch if ever there was one), but also for the ambitious, albeit untalented show-girl Miss Caswell, who was sneered at as a graduate 'of the Copacabana school of Dramatic Art'. As it were with a cruel irony, Miss Caswell was radiantly portrayed by the naturally very witty and talented, albeit comparably ambitious, young Marilyn Monroe – who in real life was often sneered at in terms virtually identical to the ones that Miss Caswell was sneered at in the film. Still, as Burchill notes, one line from these fifties put-downs of Broadway stars and gorgeous chorus girls and film stars alike rings true. 'You were a big star once,' says William Holden to Gloria Swanson in

Sunset Boulevard. 'I'm still big,' she answers. 'It's the pictures that got small.' So was it ever thus?

In *Daniel Deronda*, with what I believe to be a profound ambivalence, George Eliot shows us the traditionally unacceptable, 'monstrous' side of a woman's artistic genius in her portrayal of the magnificent Alcharisi while giving us an acceptably 'feminine' – e.g. comparatively feeble and insipid – form of artistic accomplishment in sweet Mirah Cohen, whose voice, like its 'delicate' possessor, was really not strong enough, simply too pure, for public performances. Portrayed in dialectical opposition to the Alcharisi and her sternly orthodox father (it's a pity the two daughters couldn't have swapped fathers) Mirah's father, old Lapidoth, couldn't have cared less about her religious instruction and wanted nothing more than for his beautiful and talented daughter to achieve stardom as a singer and an actress, while Mirah herself wanted nothing whatsoever to do with the wicked stage and wanted nothing more than to practise her religion just as her mother before her had done. And so, in marked contrast to the Alcharisi, who loved the life of an international superstar, Mirah recoiled from the sordid world of show business and the 'coarse, ugly manners' of its denizens that seemed so hateful and repugnant to her ultra-genteel sensibilities: 'always there were men and women coming and going, there was loud laughing and disput-ing, strutting, snapping of fingers, jeering, faces I did not like to look at'; 'the clapping and sounds of the theatre were hateful to me'; 'I did not want to be an artist; but this was what my father expected of me' (pp. 252–3). Thus, as Mirah's case-history reminds us, the world of the professional performer (which for years offered the only careers for women outside of domestic service as maids, governesses, etc.) is alien to the nineteenth century ideal of a 'lady', of a sheltered 'gentlewoman', even as it has long been associated with the 'world's oldest profession' open to a woman: that of a prostitute. Women performing for pay in the commercial theatre (which itself smacks of trade), women 'living independent lives, not married unless it suited them to be, earning and spending their own money' (Miles (1988), pp. 134–5) – to what other women could they be compared but prostitutes? For that matter, when her sweet voice turned out not to be 'strong enough' for public performances, the angelic Mirah's no-account father tried to supply her with – that is, sell her off to – a rich protector. But Mirah, who preferred death to the fate of a kept woman, ran away to seek for her long-lost mother and brother in London, where she ultimately finds true love and happiness and a perfect husband of her own faith in Daniel Deronda and also delights everyone who hears her 'delicate' voice in the *private* performances for which she and it were perfectly suited. And thus does ideal feminine virtue receive its reward.

In dramatic opposition to Mirah, who is portrayed as ideally 'feminine' – e.g. as a religious, social, and sexually conventional conformist – the Alcharisi is portrayed not just as a subversive, but as an outlaw in impenitent defiance of orthodox religious, social and sexual values and assumptions. 'You may try,' she tells her son,

> but you can never imagine what it is to have a man's force of genius in you, and yet to suffer the slavery of being a girl. To have a pattern cut out – 'this is the Jewish woman; this is what you must be; this is what you are wanted for; a woman's heart must be of such a size and no larger, else it must be pressed small, like Chinese feet; her happiness is to be made as cakes are, by a fixed receipt.' That was what my father wanted. . . . I don't deny that he was good. A man to be admired in a play – grand, with an iron will. . . . But such men turn their wives and daughters into slaves. They would rule the world if they could; but not ruling the world, they throw all the weight of their will on the necks and souls of women. But nature sometimes thwarts them. (p. 694)

And so – again in marked contrast to Mirah's 'childlike beauty' (p. 228), sweet voice, and shrinking-violet sensibilities – the Alcharisi's 'force of genius' and ambition and dedication to her art obviously constituted (and, arguably, still do constitute) a formidable threat to the sexual hierarchy upheld as if it were a sacred hierarchy by orthodox Western European and Middle Eastern – to say nothing of Far Eastern – religious orthodoxies promulgated down through the ages by patriarchs from Moses to St Paul (see, for instance, *Genesis* 3: 16; 1 *Corinthians* 11: 3–10, 14, 34; 1 *Timothy* 2: 11–15) to the Ayatollah Khomeini and so on up to and including certain quasi-religious and pseudo-scientific doctrines concerning 'true' femininity expounded and upheld by Sigmund Freud and his successors. As the Alcharisi also observes, 'a great singer or actress is a queen', a *diva*, to whom all classes and races must bow, and so her artistic genius transcends, just as it overthrows, established sexual, social and racial hierarchies. By contrast, however, to be portrayed as an ideally 'feminine' heroine, a talented female character must pose no danger or threat whatsoever to any established social, religious, sexual or political order of things; for that is precisely what 'true femininity' traditionally means.

Therefore, as Rupert Christiansen observes, by the twentieth century, 'particularly in English', the term 'prima donna' itself had come to denote a powerful, pejorative stereotype of an overwhelmingly ambitious, selfish, egotistical, temperamental, 'impossible' woman and so has stuck in the language 'as a label of abuse on a level with virago, shrew, or bitch'. To be a prima donna was not so much to be a great interpreter of operatic music as to be an outrageous *grande dame*, autocratic, exacting, torrential and exasperating: 'A woman who wants her own way is a prima donna. A woman who makes a complaint is a prima donna. A woman who changes her mind is a prima donna' (Christiansen's *Prima Donna: A History* (1986), p. 9).

The fact is that such behaviour on the part of female performers might have been, and may still be, necessary for artistic survival. 'Acting the prima donna' could well have been the only way to avoid exploitation, while 'a prima donna's greed was often the hard-headed refusal to work for less than her market value'.

> Her celebrated whims, too, often had solid reasoning behind them: not only were there artistic standards to maintain, but the singing voice is a sensitive physical instrument which requires careful handling and husbanding. A woman who refuses compromises is a prima donna. A woman dedicated to her talent is a prima donna.

Moreover, many real-life prima donnas worked their way up from unprivileged backgrounds, fought tooth and nail to get a hearing in a male-dominated world of ruthless intrigue, braved enormous risk and accepted the necessary sacrifices. 'The rewards – fortune, independence, public acclaim, the chance for self-expression beyond the roles of wife and mother – were incomparably high, but so were the odds against success. . . . Given such a gamble in such circumstances, a woman had to be alert and aggressive to survive.' (p. 10).

As Christiansen also observes, prima donnas have always been adored as much as they have been anathematised. At the very same time that 'like the sirens of the *Odyssey*, their voices were [deemed to be] sexually and morally dangerous', in the nineteenth century 'a prima donna also became a *diva*, a goddess' (pp. 10–11). And the glamorous image of the *diva* with her 'flowers, diamonds, applause, flattery' is, likewise, still deemed as morally and sexually dangerous as it is potently alluring: compare, for instance, the gloriously threatening/alluring images of female stardom, economic success and sexual insubordination projected by cinematic, soap-opera and rock prima donnas such as Mae West, Joan Collins and Madonna.

These identical points about the prima donna and about the way a *diva's* 'force of genius' threatens established (class-based, racial and sexual) hierarchies are most dramatically emphasised in the distinctions George du Maurier makes between the 'two Trilbys' – the socially humble artist's model, Trilby O'Ferrall and the magnificent *diva*, 'La Svengali', to whom emperors pay tribute. Where George Eliot gave us diametrically opposite personalities in the gentle Mirah and the formidable Alcharisi, George du Maurier gives us diametrically opposite images of the same character, thus creating a totally split personality:

> *There were two Trilbys.* There was the Trilby . . . who could not sing one single note in tune. She was an angel of paradise. . . . a gentle martyr on earth, a blessed saint in heaven! . . . But all at once--pr-r-r-out! presto! *augenblick!* . . . with one wave of his hand over her – with one look of his eye – with a word – Svengali could turn her into the other Trilby, *his* Trilby. . . . I have heard her sing to kings and queens in royal palaces! . . . as no woman has ever sung before or since. . . . I have seen the horses taken out of her sledge and the pick of the nobility drag her home to the hotel . . . with torchlights and choruses and shoutings of glory and long life to her! . . . and serenades all night, under her window! *she* never knew! she heard nothing – felt nothing – saw nothing! . . . When Svengali's Trilby was singing . . . *our* Trilby had ceased to exist . . . *our* Trilby was fast asleep . . . in fact, *our* Trilby was *dead.*
>
> (*Trilby*, pp. 449–50)

What's interesting here is the way that the heroine's angelic, gentle, saintly, martyr-persona is described as 'dead' when her artistic genius/daemon takes over and transforms her into a *diva*. Conversely, however, as a brief outline of du Maurier's plot can demonstrate, what originally caused the martyrdom of Trilby's saintly-angelic-womanly persona were the traditional class distinctions that her artistic persona so dramatically overturns.

'A DREAD POWERFUL DEMON'

A great singer and actress is a queen.
The Alcharisi in Daniel Deronda

She took him to the property room, took him all over her empire where she moved among her subjects like a popular queen.
Gaston Leroux, The Phantom of the Opera

Ah monsieur . . . that Trilby of Svengali's! I have seen emperors and grand-dukes kiss her hand, monsieur – and their wives and daughters kiss her lips, and weep . . . and she bowed to them right and left, like a queen.
George du Maurier, Trilby

*   *   *   *

As an artist's model in Paris, the merry and beautiful Trilby

' "Himmel! The roof of your mouth" '.Svengali examining the voice and soul of Trilby, original illustration by George du Maurier from his novel, Trilby.

O'Ferrall is loved by a young English art student, 'Little Billee' Bagot, whom she in turn adores. But Billee's middle-class mother does not consider Trilby socially acceptable enough to marry her son:

> Mrs. Bagot was just a shrewd little conventional British country matron of the good upper-class type, bristling all over with provincial proprieties and respectabilities, a philistine of the philistines. (p. 426)

Thus she emotionally blackmails Trilby into humbly/heroically renouncing her beloved Billee on account of the differences in their social stations: 'Will you ruin him by marrying him; drag him down; prevent him from getting on in life; separate him from his sister, his family, his friends?' (p. 312). Having promised Mrs Bagot that she will not marry her son, poor Trilby leaves Paris in despair while

Billee, who becomes seriously ill as a result of losing her, returns to England with his mother.

Earlier in the novel Billee's acquaintance and ultimate rival, the Jewish mesmerist-musician, Svengali, had discovered that although Trilby was tone-deaf, she had the most wonderful vocal chords in the world. Back then, Trilby had been terrified of the sinister-looking Jew, who was initially introduced to us as a freeloading reprobate of the worst sort, albeit a musical genius. If there *were two Trilbys'* there were also two Svengalis. As a man he was 'about as bad as they make 'em': 'walking up and down the earth seeking whom he might cheat, betray, exploit, borrow money from, bully if he dared, cringe to if he must'. But as a musician, Svengali 'was as one of the heavenly host' (p. 249). To Trilby, he at first seemed 'a dread powerful demon' who haunted her dreams 'like an incubus'. For she dreamed of Svengali even more often than she dreamed of her adored Billee (p. 286). It's as if Billee, along with his friends, relatives and associates, embodies the daytime – external – pressures and forces at work on Trilby while Svengali embodies the internal pressures (artistic genius, ambition, dreams of glory) subconsciously at work on and within the same person. In the end, Trilby's dying words are *'Svengali. . . Svengali. . . Svengali!'*. For after he died of a heart attack, and 'La Svengali' could no longer sing, it is as if Trilby herself can no longer live. And so Billee reports that

> She d-d-died with Sv-Sv-Sv. . . damn it, I can't get it out! that ruffian's name on her lips! . . . it was just as if he were calling her from the t-t-tomb! She recovered her senses the very minute she saw his photograph – she was so f-fond of him she f-forgot everybody else! She's gone straight to him, after all – in some other life! . . . to slave for him, and sing for him, and help him to make better music than ever. (p. 440)

To return to the plot outline: after her break with Billee, Svengali becomes Trilby's mentor and protector and husband-in-art, 'whose love for her seems to have been deep and constant and sincere; none the less so, perhaps, that she could never return it' (p. 434). Since George du Maurier doesn't seem to like the idea of the marriage between Svengali and Trilby being physically consummated, he informs us that Svengali remained legally married to someone else, while Trilby's heart still belonged to Billee. It is therefore as an artist and only as an artist that Trilby belongs, body and soul, to Svengali, whose influence over his 'wife, slave, and pupil' (p. 404) is compared to that of 'a demon', 'a magician', 'a god' (p. 446). When she sings, as he tells her, she shall 'hear nothing, see nothing, think of nothing, but *Svengali, Svengali, Svengali!'* (p. 379). While thus mesmerised, Trilby is transformed into the magnificent *diva* known as 'La Svengali', the like of whose voice had never been heard, nor ever will be again: 'A woman archangel might sing like that, or some enchanted princess out of a fairy tale' (p. 378).

When, several years later, Billee goes to a concert to hear the great singer and recognises his long-lost Trilby as 'La Svengali', their previous situation has, of course, been completely reversed: 'then and there his love for Trilby became as that of a dog for its master!' Hearing her sing, 'he felt a crushing sense of his own infinitesimal significance by the side of this glorious pair of artists, one of whom had been his friend and the other his love, – a love who had offered to be his humble mistress and slave, not feeling herself good enough to be his wife!' (p. 380).

And so – du Maurier goes on and on – the wretched Billee

> realised how hopelessly, desperately, wickedly, insanely he loved this woman, who might have been his, but was now the wife of another man; a greater than he, and one to whom she owed it that she was more glorious than any other woman on earth – a queen among queens – a goddess! for what was any earthly throne compared to that she established in the hearts and souls of all who came within the sight and hearing of her; beautiful as she was besides – beautiful, beautiful! And what must be her love for the man who had taught her and trained her, and revealed her towering genius to herself and to the world! . . . And the remembrance of them – hand in hand,

'*And the remembrance of them – hand in hand*'.
Svengali and Trilby, master and pupil, from Trilby.

master and pupil, husband and wife – smiling and bowing in the face
of all that splendid tumult they had called forth and could not quell,
stung and tortured and maddened him. (p. 387)

Billee would now give anything to be married to her himself –
although a question not clearly answered here is to *whom* does he so
desperately, hopelessly wish to be married? to 'his' Trilby? or to 'La
Svengali'?

> Ah! there'll never be an end of it for *me* – never – never – oh, never,
> my God! She would have married me but for my mother's meddling
> . . . . What a wife! Think of all she must have in her heart and brain,
> only to *sing* like that! And, O Lord! how beautiful she is – a goddess!
> Oh, the brow and cheek and chin, and the way her head's put on! did
> you *ever* see anything like it? Oh, if only I hadn't written and told
> my mother I was going to marry her! why, we should have been
> man and wife for five years by this time. (p. 390)

She now is also described as 'a siren': 'How dreadful these sirens are,
wrecking the peace of families!' (p. 401).

Trilby had, of course, posed no remotely comparable challenge to
the peace of families or to the class-system or to the sexual hierarchy
or to anyone or anything else back in those happy days when she
came 'to repair the Laird's linen, and darn his socks, and look after his
little comforts' (p. 265). Nor had she behaved in anything but an
appropriately docile manner when she 'gave way' to Billee's mother.
As Mrs Bagot herself puts it, Trilby 'behaved very well – she did her
duty – I can't deny that'. As another character wryly and pointedly
observes, 'She wasn't a siren then' (p. 401).

Throughout the novel, du Maurier's attitude towards 'good upper
middle-class' values is extremely ambivalent. He initially presents
them in opposition to happiness and art. Yet perhaps because he
finally wishes to divest his own novel of any siren-songs or threats to
the *status quo*, he ends the story of Trilby with a positive paean to the
'useful, humdrum, happy domestic existence' to which he consigns
his surviving characters, thus extolling 'that blessed harbour of refuge
well within the reach of all of us', if only we will leave off 'hankering
after the moon' (p. 453). Although there is no reason to doubt the
sincerity of the sentiments with which du Maurier ended a bestseller
written almost a hundred years ago (he himself was very happily
married and comfortably situated – see Daphne du Maurier's account
of her grandfather's marriage, p. xv), the identical kind of celebrity
tribute to humdrum domesticity, designed as it were to exorcise the
dread, powerful demon of a woman's artistic ambition, has resounded
in works designed for mass markets so often since then that by now
the message has come to sound all too obviously like propaganda.

Here, for instance, is an utterly typical example from a popular woman's magazine (*Woman's Journal* (1986), November, p. 68):

> Meryl Streep may be the greatest actress in the world, in a position to command an impressive three and a half million dollars for every picture. [Thus she sounds formidable – like a modern equivalent of La Svengali or the Alcharisi.] Yet she insists that her role as wife and mother means a lot more than any Oscar winning part. [And so the article immediately goes on to reassure us that she's really an unspoiled Trilby at heart.] One thing is certain: the woman of a thousand personalities, postures, hair colours and voices is quite probably at this moment changing [her youngest daughter's] nappies.

Query: What of it? If true, why should this fact seem of such *paramount* importance? *Answer:* one other thing is equally certain, today as yesterday, superstardom is generally deemed to be morally OK for a woman so long – *but only so long* – as her professional life comes second, or is publicly alleged to be relatively unimportant compared to her 'useful, humdrum, happy domestic existence'.

This particular public relations/journalistic formula does not seem to have changed very much over the years since the heyday of the 'feminine mystique' described by Betty Friedan in 1963. Then as now 'the one career woman' who was always welcome in the pages of popular magazines was the actress. 'But her image also underwent a remarkable change: from a complex individual of fiery temper, inner depth, and a mysterious blend of spirit and sexuality' (i.e. from the image of a prima donna, of 'the divine' Garbo) to a sexual object, a babyface bride or a housewife.

> When you wrote about an actress for a woman's magazine, you wrote about her as a housewife. You never showed her doing or enjoying her work as an actress unless she eventually paid for it by losing her husband or her child, or otherwise admitting failure as a woman.

For example, Friedan cites a *Redbook* article asserting that the award-winning actress, Judy Holliday, 'must find fulfilment in her career *because* [my italics] she is divorced from her husband, and has "strong feelings of inadequacy as a woman". . . . It is a frustrating irony of Judy's life, that as an actress she has succeeded almost without trying, although, as a woman, she has failed'. Once Betty Friedan herself wanted to write an article about an artist:

> So I wrote about her cooking and marketing and falling in love with her husband and painting a crib for her baby. I had to leave out the hours she spent painting pictures, her serious work – and the way she felt about it. You could sometimes get away with writing about a woman who was not really a housewife, if you made her *sound* like a

housewife, if you left out her commitment to the world outside the home, or the private vision of mind or spirit that she pursued.

(Friedan (1963), pp. 46–7)

The same traditional formula holds true for journalistic portrayals of brilliantly successful women in science: 'Grandmother Wins Nobel Prize!' proclaimed the popular press when Dorothy Crowfoot Hodgkin became a Laureate. And in sports, as Adrianne Blue has observed – see 'Women and sport: high-powered images', *Vogue* (1988), April, pp. 255–6 – 'the phoney issue of whether one is a woman or an athlete' has inevitably 'led to the phoney apology':

> Champions will speak passionately of their latest accomplishment, and then, *apropos* of nothing, throw in lines like 'But I like gentlemen to open car doors, and when I retire I'm going to devote myself entirely to my husband and children.' To be sure, many women champions are married, or get married after retirement, and some have gaggles of kids, but few sanguinely devote themselves *entirely* to nesting. . . . When it comes to retirement, these superstars evolve more naturally into top coaches, high-profile television sports reporters and chat-show guests than they do into single-purpose mothers. . . . If women athletes didn't play along with the image game – if they admitted the truth, which is that they are strong, self-centred, independent women, these champions might well lose some lucrative endorsements. But they would give young women, or women who are new to sport, more courage. As Judy Oates puts it, 'Naked ambition is not the prerogative of men. If women need it to win, why not show it?'

If (public-relations-and-propaganda-wise) it is virtually *verboten* for a woman frankly to acknowledge her own self-centred ambition (as Eliot's Alcharisi did), to likewise announce that she personally preferred not to have any children is, today as yesterday, to violate an ultimate taboo. So *de rigueur* is it for any and all childless female celebrities to express their abiding regret that they did not have any children of their own, that it is impossible to know whether any given assertions of this kind are genuine or phoney, true or false. Recently both Ann-Margret (age 47) and Claudette Colbert (age 85) were likewise reported as having expressed the mandatory regrets at not having had any children: 'Claudette Colbert regrets that she could not have children (it is a sadness she shares with Ann-Margret) but she never allowed herself to dwell on it. Her biggest enjoyment is travel. . .' (*TV Times*, 31 December 1988/6 January 1989, p. 9). And so, the article implies, the poor thing has bravely managed to soldier on between extended visits to her residences in Barbados and New York and her professional engagements on the London stage, where she starred opposite Rex Harrison in a drawing-room comedy when she was 80.

Query: Why not assume that a healthy woman with an income like Colbert's would have had, or could have adopted, a child if she had chosen to? The subtextual message of this journalistic harping on the real or imaginary sadness (by implication the inevitable consequence of their failure 'as women'?) allegedly shared by every childless female celebrity ever interviewed for a popular periodical (for some of them, surely, deliberately chose not to have children) is obviously that they are more to be pitied for their failure 'as women' than envied for any of their professional achievements. By the same token, the 'my husband and children come first' formula parroted by innumerable married female celebrities effectively informs any young girl seeking a role model that the *most* important thing to remember about a gifted female superstar such as Meryl Streep is that her professional career is nothing like as important to her personal happiness as her domestic role as a wife and mother changing nappies, etc. And these identical, useful, happy, humdrum domestic roles still afford 'that blessed harbour of refuge' well within the reach of all of us – if only we will leave off hankering after the moon.

By very much the same token, the insistence that even the most talented of women should never put her professional life before the man in her life and the identical warnings that professional ambition and success inevitably lead to failure and unhappiness 'as a woman' were bleated out from innumerable juke-boxes and radios in the late forties and the early fifties.

> Dance, ballerina, dance,
> And do your pirouette in rhythm with your aching heart.
>
> Once you said his love must wait its turn,
> You wanted fame instead, I guess that's your concern,
> We live and learn.
> And love is gone, ballerina, gone.
> So on with your career, you can't afford a backward glance.
> Dance on and on and on!
> A thousand people here, have come to see the show,
> As round and round you go,
> So ballerina, dance, dance, dance!

Written by Bob Russell (words) and Carl Sigman (music) and recorded by Vaughn Monroe, 'Ballerina' was in the US charts for 21 weeks in 1948, when it seemed to serve as a popular sermon on the theme of the cinematic ballet, 'The Red Shoes', as outlined in the same year by the impresario Lermontov and subsequently performed in the most famous of all films about the world of the ballet:

> LERMONTOV. 'The Ballet of the Red Shoes' is from a fairy tale by
> Hans Andersen. It is the story of a girl who is devoured by an

> ambition to attend a dance in a pair of red shoes. She gets the shoes
> and goes to the dance. At first, all goes well, and she is very
> happy. At the end of the evening she gets tired and wants to go
> home. But the red shoes are not tired. In fact, the red shoes are
> never tired. They dance her out into the streets, they dance her
> over the mountains and valleys, through fields and forests,
> through night and day. Time rushes by, love rushes by, life rushes
> by, but the red shoes dance on.
> CRASTER. What happens in the end?
> LERMONTOV. Oh! in the end she dies.

And so, too, in the end dies the ballerina who dances the role of the young woman whose red shoes wouldn't let her go home.

Before going on to discuss the primary similarities between the admonitory, propagandistic messages of various works directly or indirectly derived from Andersen's fairy tale – *all* of them associate a woman's professional life-as-a-dancer with her literal or figurative death-as-a-woman – it should be noted that the original tale is the most horrific of all. In Andersen's fable, which is a kind of inverse version of 'Cinderella', the command 'Thou shalt dance, dance' is a curse, and the humbly born young girl who aspires to dance at a ball in red shoes like those worn by a Princess is damned as well as doomed by her ambition.

'THE REAL RED SHOES'

> And if thy right hand offend thee, cut it off, and cast it from thee:
> for it is profitable for thee that one of thy members should perish,
> and not that thy whole body should be cast into hell. . . .
> No man can serve two masters; for either he will hate the one, and
> love the other; or else he will hold to the one, and despise the other.
> Matthew 5:30; 6:24

There was, Hans Andersen tells us, once a little girl named Karen who had to go barefoot in summer because she was poor and who, in winter, had to wear 'thick wooden shoes, so that her little instep became quite red, altogether red'. One day, Karen saw the Queen passing through the country with her little daughter, the Princess, who had neither train nor golden crown, but wore a splendid pair of red morocco shoes.

A nearly blind old lady who had befriended the recently orphaned Karen bought her a pair of red shoes that had been made for a Count's child, but had not fitted, and the delighted Karen went to confirmation in them, although the old lady would never have allowed that if she had known the shoes were red. During the confirmation, and on subsequent Sundays, Karen went to church in the red shoes, and having been complimented on her 'pretty dancing shoes' by an old soldier at the church door, she quite forgot to say her prayers. When all the people left the church and the old lady stepped into her carriage, Karen lifted up her foot to step in too, but just then the old soldier said 'Look what beautiful dancing shoes!' and Karen could not resist: she was obliged to dance.

> She danced round the corner of the church – she could not help it; the coachman was obliged to run behind her and seize her: he lifted her into the carriage, but her feet went on dancing, so that she kicked the good old lady violently. At last they took off her shoes and her legs became quiet. At home the shoes were put away in a cupboard; but Karen could not resist looking at them.

The old lady became ill and had to be nursed and waited on, and this was no one's duty so much as Karen's. But there was to be a great ball in town, and Karen was invited. She looked at the old lady who could not recover; she looked at the red shoes, and thought there would be no harm in it. She put on the shoes and went to the ball and began to dance. And of course she could not stop. When she danced into the churchyard there was no peace for her and when she danced toward the open church door she saw a stern angel who thus condemned her forever to dance: 'Thou shalt dance!' he said – 'dance in thy red shoes, till thou art pale and cold, and till thy body shrivels to a skeleton. . . . Thou shalt dance, dance!' 'Mercy!' cried Karen. But she did not hear what the angel answered, for the shoes carried her away – carried her through the gate on to the field, over stock and stone, and she was always obliged to dance. Finally, she danced up to the house where the town executioner dwelt and asked him to help her: 'Do not strike off my head,' said Karen, 'for if you do I cannot repent of my sin. But strike off my feet with the red shoes.' And then she confessed all her sin, and the executioner cut off her feet with the red shoes; but the shoes danced away with the little feet over the fields and into the deep forest. And the executioner cut her a pair of wooden feet, with crutches, and taught her a psalm, which the criminals always sing. 'Now I have suffered pain enough for the red shoes,' said she, 'Now I will go into church.' And she went quickly towards the church door; but when she came there the red shoes danced before her, so that she was frightened, and turned back.

At last, she went to the parsonage and begged to be taken in there as a servant. She promised to be industrious and to do all she could; she did not care for wages. The clergyman's wife pitied her and took her into her service. And she was industrious and thoughtful. Silently she sat and listened when in the evening the pastor read the Bible aloud to his family. All the little ones were very fond of her; but when they spoke of dress and splendour and beauty she would shake her head. Finally, when the others went to church, she went to her little room, which was only large enough to contain her bed and a chair, and there she sat with her hymn-book and as she read it with a pious mind, she lifted up her face, with tears, and said 'O Lord, help me!' Then the sun shone out brightly and before her stood the angel and it was as if her poor room had become a church and she was granted mercy: 'And her heart became so filled with sunshine, peace and joy, that it broke. Her soul flew on the sunbeams to heaven; and there was nobody who asked after the RED SHOES' (Andersen (1924), pp. 185–93).

And here we have, in their most elementary form, the series of minatory messages that have been and still are, constantly albeit more subtly, communicated to women in any number of differing ways.

The vain desires and ambitions that are signified by the Red Shoes stand in the way of salvation (e.g. in front of the church door) and the punishment for wanting and wearing them – damnation – is worse than mutilation or death. Therefore, if thy dancing feet offend, then cut them off, lest thy whole body should be cast into hell. Likewise, in both the movie and the ballet-within-the-movie, the dancer's dying request is that they 'take off the red shoes' as it were to avert her damnation.

Thou shalt not aspire beyond thy subordinate sexual/social station in life. Personal ambition in a woman and its twin sin, selfishness (for you can't have one without the other) are virtually unforgivable sins against God and Man, religion and society: Karen 'was condemned by the angel of God' so severely that even *after* having had her feet cut off and after being been taught a psalm 'which the criminals always sing' by the self-same executioner who cut off her feet, and after having humbly 'kissed the hand that held the axe' she *still* had not done anything like sufficient penance for her 'sin' (Andersen, p. 191).

Interestingly enough, in the ballet based on the fairy tale the girl is tempted to put on the Red Shoes by a diabolical shoemaker and so is portrayed more sympathetically than Andersen portrays Karen. For as a rule with very few exceptions, any female character like Andersen's Karen – or Flaubert's Madame Bovary – who 'selfishly' aspires to rise above her subservient social/sexual station and who has no Svengali or Phantom-figure to take the rap or the blame for her driving ambition, has been deemed to deserve whatever cruel and inhuman punishment she may get from Man or God for so aspiring.

The horrific warnings to women communicated by Andersen's original fairy tale fuse with the film's portrayal of the ultimate conflict between the heroine's vocation as a ballerina and her love for her husband, in the following definition of 'the real red shoes' from Margaret Atwood's novel, *Lady Oracle*:

> The real red shoes, the feet punished for dancing. You could dance, or you could have the love of a good man. But you were afraid to dance, because you had this unnatural fear that if you danced they'd cut your feet off so you wouldn't be able to dance. Finally you overcame your fear and danced, and they cut your feet off. The good man went away too, because you wanted to dance.
>
> (Atwood (1982), pp. 216-17)

Thus fairy-tales, films and melodrama alike occasionally come together to constitute our waking-dream-life's most terrifying forms of realism.

For although the heroine may not – as in the case of the ballerina portrayed by Moira Shearer in the film version of *The Red Shoes* – be sentenced to literal death, the fact remains that, time after time, as in 'Ballerina', the be-all of the heroine's life-as-an-artist *is* portrayed as the end-all, the renunciation, the death of her life 'as a woman' (in so far as 'being a woman' is defined as being a wife and mother). 'What do you want?' asks the impresario of the ballerina in *The Red Shoes*, 'To live?' And she answers, 'To dance.' Likewise, the Angel of Music forbade his Christine – without forbidding her – to marry by telling her that if she got married she would never hear him again, and that he would go away for ever. Conversely, however, the be-all of the heroine's marriage to her young lover may, with equal if not greater poignancy, be portrayed as the end – as the death – of her life as an artist, even as the voice of that 'wonderful, mysterious, artist' beloved of the Angel of Music was 'never, never heard of again'. And so, over and over again, the claims of a gifted woman's genius and the claims 'of a good man', of marriage, children, conformity and domesticity are shown to be – just as in real life they often obviously may be – profoundly at odds in so far as her vocation, her calling, her starring role as a dancer or singer or actress, and her supporting roles as a devoted daughter or wife or mother may likewise demand absolute dedication, total concentration and, above all, uninterrupted time. If, in the words of the Gospel according to St Matthew, 'No man can serve two masters' with equal devotion on a full-time basis, then surely no woman can either. And, as the impresario in *The Red Shoes* insists, it is virtually impossible to be a part-time *prima ballerina assoluta*. It is difficult to say whether art imitates life or vice versa in certain cases (the film impresario, 'Boris Lermontov' was based on

Serge Diaghilev – Powell (1986), p. 639), but the real-life director of the New York City Ballet, George Balanchine, was evidently just as adamant on this point as Lermontov is in *The Red Shoes*. According to the ballerina Gelsey Kirkland, even 'to have a boyfriend' jeopardised the possibility of dancing for Balanchine. 'Marriage was thought to be the kiss of death' (Kirkland (1987), p. 41).

It will by now – we'll come back to the real-life issues later on – seem far too obvious to need saying that the conflicts I have been describing lend themselves perfectly to portrayal in art. They are fundamentally dramatic. The various conundrums portrayed can be resolved in differing ways or left unresolved, and the ending wherein, say, the heroine finally renounces art for love can be depicted as happy or as tragic or as profoundly ambivalent. What's especially interesting about so many of these parables (Andersen's unequivocally minatory fairy tale is the only major exception) is that their ultimate message can be interpreted in diametrically opposite ways. On the one hand, they can, likewise, be read as propaganda for the sexual and social *status quo* – or, on the other hand, they can all be seen to subvert it. Here, for instance (I am indebted to Paula Volsky for this reading) is one way of interpreting the various novels and films dealing with the relationship between Christine and the Phantom, Svengali and his Trilby, the impresario and the ballerina in *The Red Shoes* and between Olive Chancellor and Verena Tarrant in *The Bostonians*.

To a lesser or greater degree, in all these works you get the same idea of a power-figure, who is usually an older man, often a kind of surrogate father (Olive Chancellor plays this sort of role as a kind of surrogate parent to Verena in *The Bostonians*), who moulds and controls the talent of a young and beautiful girl who is miraculously gifted but passive. *Very* passive. For instance, independently of their gifts as a speaker and singer, Henry James's Verena Tarrant and George du Maurier's Trilby are portrayed as lively, charming, indeed charismatic, young women. But so far as their own talents are concerned, they are described as near-inanimate objects in the hands of their mentors and manipulators. As we have seen, this passivity in the hands of a powerful male mentor effectively exonerates the talented *ingénue* from any prima-donna-like, Alcharisi-type sins such as ambition, aggression, selfishness and insubordination. And so it is, for instance, the egocentric, aggressive, arrogant, overbearing and demanding Phantom of the Opera and not the fair young heroine herself who browbeats the managers into letting her sing the prima-donna parts. Yet the heroine's dependence on, and subservience to, a male mentor not only serves to keep her 'femininity' intact. It simultaneously identifies the source of her artistry – indeed, the very 'force of genius' itself – with a male. In *Daniel Deronda*, the Alcharisi herself made exactly the same identification (see above, p. 57) while likewise equating the status of a girl with that of a slave: 'you can never imagine what it is to have *a man's force of genius* in you, and yet to suffer *the slavery of being a girl*' [my italics].

The same associations – girl=slave, man=genius – are verbally underscored in *Trilby*. As we have seen, the heroine who originally offered to be Billee's humble 'mistress and slave, not feeling herself good enough to be his wife', is subsequently described as Svengali's 'wife, slave, and pupil', whom he summons from beyond the grave to 'slave for him, and sing for him, and help him to make better music than ever' in another life. Likewise, in Lloyd Webber's musical the Phantom of the Opera insists to Christine, 'Your chains are still mine – you will sing for me!' (Perry, p. 157). Paradoxically, however, the heroine's service to her artistic daemon effectively serves to liberate her from her lowly position in the social pecking order as the daughter of a peasant, an artist's model, a *grisette*. What looks like the exchange of one form of subordination for another, when the relationship between the girl and her Svengali-figure is interpreted literally, looks like a form of liberation when the relationship is interpreted allegorically, as an artist's service to the Angel of Music or as a woman's service to her own artistic genius.

The feminist and anti-feminist implications of these and other related issues and arguments are ironically underscored, qualified and dramatised in Henry James's portrayal of the triangular relationship between the talented *ingénue* (Verena Tarrant), her mentor (Olive Chancellor) and her suitor (Basil Ransom) in *The Bostonians*. There is no numbering how often James uses the word 'gift' and its derivatives ('a gifted being', 'give up', 'give herself', etc.) with reference to Verena, who must finally decide how she will use her 'gift', to whom or to what cause she will 'give herself' and whether or not to 'give up' the man she loves for the sake of her talent or to renounce her career for the sake of her love.

Very like the tone-deaf Trilby, who must be mesmerised by Svengali before she can sing, James's wonderfully gifted young orator, Verena Tarrant (whose surname sounds like a kind of pun on 'talent') is first introduced to us as a kind of puppet in the hands of her mesmeric father. 'She has to have her father to start her up', says one observer, while another observer can't decide whether she is 'a parrot or a genius' (*The Bostonians* (1967), pp. 61, 72). She also seems 'like a moving statue' (p. 66), as if she were a pretty Galatea to her mesmeric father's Pygmalion. Subsequently, in the case of Verena (as in the case of Leroux's Christine), a new mentor takes over from the heroine's real parent. In *The Bostonians*, the passionate feminist Olive Chancellor buys the charming and talented Verena from her natural parents and thereafter acts as a surrogate mother-and-father figure as well as a professional and ideological mentor. Olive is also Verena's most adoring admirer:

> Verena, for Olive, was the very type and model of the 'gifted being'; her qualities had not been bought and paid for; they were like some brilliant birthday-present left at the door by an unknown messenger to be delightful forever as an inexhaustible legacy. . . . For her scrutinizing friend Verena had the disposition of the artist, the spirit to which all charming forms come easily and naturally. (p. 121)

But then, of course, a rival claimant for the girl's heart and soul and body, an ardent young suitor – in this case Olive's Southern cousin, Basil Ransom – as it were inevitably appears upon the scene.

And so one could argue that *The Bostonians* henceforth follows a standard pattern according to which the gifted *ingénue* is primarily portrayed as the object of contention between a powerful mentor who ostensibly desires her for the sake of her talent (although elements of sexuality generally underlie the love, the jealousy, the power-plays involved in the relationship between the mentor and the girl) and – on the other hand – a straightforward, hardy, wholesome, handsome young suitor who quite simply desires the girl as a love object and has little if any use for her artistic gifts although, perhaps significantly, they may be what attracted him to her in the first place. Albeit the artistic mentor may be far more fascinating and more sympathetically portrayed than the young lover, it is essential for the sake of a stable society that he-or-she must lose. By contrast, the young lover is portrayed as the natural winner and his triumph can be regarded as the girl's 'rescue' from the monster. The traditional values that he represents offer sanity, normality, health and stability in place of (say) the Phantom's alluring but barren artistry and the girl's ultimate destiny as contented wife/mother (by implication *sans* career) can therefore be seen as the happiest of all possible endings. The girl may grieve from time to time for her lost Svengali but she, like society in general, is best served by her acceptance of the traditional feminine role. A Freudian analyst could, of course, go on to argue that the heroine's progress symbolically enacts a feminine rite-of-passage as the influence of her father (living or dead) gives way to a kind of adolescent fantasy of stardom embodied in a surrogate parent, an artistic mentor or teacher (or a kind of tenacious father-spectre who will not let her go), whose influence is finally and rightly renounced by the heroine for the sake of true feminine fulfilment in the traditional, domestic role, etc., etc., etc.

By exactly this token, as Leon Edel observes in the Introduction to his edition of *The Bostonians*, critics have made much of the idea that since Basil Ransom offers Verena marriage, he speaks for 'normality' and 'morality' in contrast to the latent lesbianism they discern in Olive's feelings for Verena. The catch here, as Edel goes on to observe, is that the young lover's desire for possession and dominance is every bit as single-minded as Olive's. The radical feminist and the reactionary male chauvinist are equally ruthless and possessive in their pursuit of the identical goal: 'the absolute control of the young girl' (*The Bostonians* (1967), p. 8). And Edel is certainly right. There is no question that Olive seeks complete control over Verena and above all else wants her protégée as it were voluntarily to renounce, refrain, abstain, from marriage: 'Do you understand German? Do you know "*Faust?*" ' Olive asks Verena: ' "*Entsagen sollst du, sollst entsagen!*" ', ' "Thou shalt renounce, refrain, abstain!" ' (p. 93):

> 'I hope with all my soul that you won't marry. . . . Priests – when they were real priests – never married, and what you and I dream of doing demands of us a kind of priesthood. . . . You must be safe, Verena – you must be saved; but your safety must not come from your having tied your hands. It must come from . . . your feeling that for your work your freedom is essential, and that there is no freedom for you and me save in religiously *not* doing what you will often be asked to do – and I never!' Miss Chancellor brought out these last words with a proud jerk which was not without its pathos. 'Don't promise, don't promise!' she went on. 'I would far rather you didn't. But don't fail me – don't fail me, or I shall die!' (pp. 142-3)

It was an inspired idea of James's to make Olive's antagonist an unreconstructed Southerner and former slave-holder, whose firmest conviction is that woman's place is in the home. In dialectical opposition to Olive, Ransom insists that Verena must forever renounce, refrain and abstain from work, from feminism, and from everything and everyone else having to do with her career as a public speaker. '[He] wants me to give up everything, all our work, our faith, our future, never to give another address, to open my lips in public', Verena tells Olive.

> 'How can I consent to that?' Verena went on, smiling strangely.
> 'He asks you that, just that way?'
> 'No; it's not that way. It's very kindly.' (p. 370)

And so James draws the line of battle in the civil war waged both within and about Verena herself, as Olive Chancellor and Basil Ransom battle for absolute possession of the talented young orator:

'The situation between them . . . was war to the knife, it was a question of which should pull hardest' (p. 381). Ransom knew that Olive 'would fight him to the death, giving him not an inch of odds' (p. 389), and he in turn gives no quarter: 'Not for worlds', he tells Verena – who is just about to speak on behalf of the feminist movement, before the 'most magnificent audience ever brought together' in Boston – 'not for millions, shall you give yourself to that roaring crowd. Don't ask me to care for them, or for anyone! . . . You are mine, not theirs' (pp. 438–9). When Olive begs him to let Verena appear on stage for just one hour, he refuses on the grounds that 'An hour is as bad as ten years! She's mine or she isn't, and if she's mine, she's all mine' (p. 440).

Although a hallelujah chorus of male critics has proclaimed that Ransom's elopement with Verena is a consummation devoutly to be wished (for detailed criticism of their arguments see Fetterly (1978), pp. 101–53, and Culler (1983), p. 54 *ff.*), the fact is that Verena's future is described with manifest apprehension by Henry James himself.

> 'Ah, now I am glad!' said Verena, when they reached the street. But though she was glad . . . she was in tears. It is to be feared that with the union, so far from brilliant, into which she was about to enter, these were not the last she was destined to shed. (pp. 446–7)

Likewise, in the film of *The Red Shoes* the traditionally happiest of all endings underwritten by social and romantic conventions ('they got married and lived happily ever after') does not turn out to be happy at all. Acting in defiance of her artistic mentor the gifted ballerina, Victoria Page, elopes with her handsome young lover Julian Craster, who turns out to be a petulant, egotistical, selfish young sod if there ever was one, and she's miserable. Although Julian finds his own work as a composer far more interesting than he finds her, he is so furious, so chagrined, when Vicky chooses to star in Lermontov's revival of *The Red Shoes* in Monte Carlo instead of returning to London to applaud when *he* conducts his new symphony, that he comes to Monte Carlo to demand that she choose once and for all between the world of the ballet and her role as his wife. Vicky (very like James's Verena) pleads to be allowed to dance in *The Red Shoes* just one more time, but Craster (like Ransom) insists that if she does there can be no going back – it will be 'too late'. Lermontov, in turn, urges her to forget Craster and dance. And so, here as elsewhere, the conflicting characters correspond to the forces that contend on the psychological level of action. In their final confrontation, the husband (embodying her love/marriage) and the impresario (embodying her art) both demand the heroine's *absolute* allegiance, and the only resolution to the internal/external conflict lies in her destruction.

Why can't there be a compromise? Why can't the heroine combine a happy marriage with a brilliantly successful public career? In *The Bostonians* Henry James offers a compromise choice of this kind only to reject it. A rich young New Yorker, Henry Burrage, who prizes Verena 'for her rarity, which was her genius, her gift', is eager to marry her. In an effort to further the match, his wealthy mother tells Olive that she and her son alike will do everything in their power to promote the feminist cause, as well as to promote Verena's career. Moreover, as Olive observes, Henry Burrage 'was of so soft and fine a paste that his wife might do what she liked with him' (p. 309). By contrast Olive had long realised 'that there was no menace so great as the menace of Basil Ransom' (p. 316), for once he got hold of Verena he would 'shut her up altogether' (p. 313). And Olive is right. Like a compromise marriage, a compromise career for Verena is inconceivable to the absolutist Basil Ransom, because there *can* be no compromise between the forces of feminism and male supremism. Therefore, although – or precisely because? – the comparatively impecunious young Southerner realised that Verena 'might easily have a big career, like that of a distinguished actress or singer' (p. 320) and although he personally 'felt ashamed of his own poverty',

> it was no possible basis of matrimony that Verena should continue
> . . . the exercise of her remunerative profession; if he should become
> her husband, he should know a way to strike her dumb. (p. 321)

In *The Bostonians*, as in *The Red Shoes*, the either/or conflict whereby the heroine *cannot* serve two masters, *cannot* split herself between them and must finally choose which one will have her total allegiance – to whom will she (?) to what should she (?) choose to give herself (?) – is, obviously, far more suspenseful and dramatic than a conflict amenable to a compromise solution in which, say, Verena decided to marry Henry Burrage and subsequently enjoyed a happily married life in fashionable New York society while occasionally making wonderful speeches on behalf of the feminist cause. But whether these power-struggles and/or these mutually exclusive alternatives are looked at sexually or psychologically or politically or all three ways at once, the reasons for the either/or conflicts here portrayed seem ideologically, as well as dramatically, crucial. They even seem theologically crucial. For that matter, the heroine's choice is constantly compared to a 'Faustian' choice between diametrically opposite masters and destinies – between God and Lucifer, Heaven and Hell – as if the choice between her vocation as an artist and her duty as a wife were, for a woman, of comparable, ultimate magnitude: a matter of salvation or damnation.

THE FAUSTIAN CONFLICT

BAD ANGEL. Go forward, Faustus, in that famous art.
GOOD ANGEL. Sweet Faustus, leave that execrable art.
> Christopher Marlowe, *Dr Faustus*

[John Milton] was a true Poet, and of the Devil's party without knowing it.
> William Blake, *The Marriage of Heaven and Hell*

*   *   *   *

Time after time, the Svengali-Phantom-impresario-figures who are associated with supreme artistic creativity are also portrayed as demonic tempters. As proselytisers for a rival religion in opposition to the true faith, they are comparable to the diabolical Mephostophilis in Marlowe's *Dr Faustus* who lures the protagonist away from God with beautiful illusions, 'vain fancies' and 'castles in the air' (comparable to the 'unreal' domain of art in our works). Thus it's as if, like the Evil Angels in a morality play or the Red Shoes in Andersen's cautionary fairy tale, these characters allegorically represent vain fantasies and ambitions (the pursuit of phantoms?), inordinate aspirations, selfishness, egocentricity and desire for acclaim that eternally tempt young girls away from their true, 'womanly', religion-vocation-salvation in service to God and man, home and children in the 'real world' ('*Kinder, Kirche, Küche*', etc.). For these tempters markedly differ from other literary seducers in that they are not primarily concerned with the sexual seduction of the heroine. On the contrary: they are associated with sexual sterility, with physical celibacy, with a willed renunciation of sexuality-as-fertility. Thus the Phantom, the impresario and Olive Chancellor likewise implore their protégées to 'renounce, refrain, abstain' from marriage to their virile young suitors. For that matter in the realm of art, *regardless* of the biological sex of its inhabitants, their creative energies are primarily directed towards music, ballet, painting and performing rather than towards the begetting and nurturing of children, and so it would seem by definition 'artificially' creative, 'unnaturally' barren (a domain congenial to homosexuals?) – albeit fabulously alluring, invested with a divinity of its own.

Here, chosen from any number of equally obvious examples, are some differing illustrations of these identical points about the sterility and divinity of art. Although the marriage between Trilby and Svengali is spiritually and, by implication, eternally consecrated (she is, as it were, both literally and symbolically 'wedded to her art'), it is never *physically* consummated. By the same token, before Christine Daaé leaves his 'artificial but immense' empire behind her forever to elope with her vicomte, she returns the ring of the Phantom that had betokened her consecration as a votaress of the Angel of Music who had taken a vow renouncing all earthly loves. 'The divine voice', she tells Raoul, 'told me plainly that if I must bestow my heart on earth, there was nothing for the voice to do but to go back to Heaven.' 'I feared nothing so much as that I might never hear it again, and I swore to the voice that . . . my heart was incapable of any earthly love' (*The Phantom of the Opera*, p. 130).

Of course Christine's Angel behaves like the most jealous of all Demon Lovers later on. And so does the impresario in *The Red Shoes* who frankly admits to Vicky (the ballerina) and Julian (her husband) that he is jealous – but in extra-sexual ways that a mere husband could never understand. Lermontov goes on to challenge Julian's right as her husband to demand that his wife give up the kind of ultimate achievement as an artist that she would never have dreamed of asking *him* to give up for *her* sake. And he also jeers and sneers at Vicky's future role as a hausfrau looking after screaming children, in contemptuous comparison to the brilliant future he can offer her as a prima ballerina. In these speeches the impresario sounds like Satan tempting Eve away from Adam. Indeed, Lermontov, Svengali and the Phantom alike are ubiquitously associated with the demonic as well as with the abnormal in their opposition to the orthodox assumptions that a truly virtuous woman's place is in the home playing second fiddle to her husband, and that only an 'unwomanly' or immoral one would choose any other destiny.

For as George Eliot reminded us in *Daniel Deronda* the world of art has, traditionally, also been sexually identified with promiscuity and with prostitution in so far as it is associated with commercial show business and smacks of trade. Thus, it's as if a woman's artistic vocation, as opposed to her 'natural' (i.e. her only sexually *and* socially sanctioned) vocation as a devoted wife-and-mother, *inevitably* necessitates a sexual identification outside the pale, as a whore or as a celibate (an Old Maid or a Nun). On the one hand, these assumptions seem to reflect an atavistic fear that the whole 'natural' scheme of things would collapse if women like the Alcharisi could freely choose not to marry or have children so that they could go on to achieve other goals. Thus, when she was asked to comment on Grover Cleveland's dictum that 'a woman's place is in the home', the American prima donna Emma Eames pleaded that even if it 'might be appropriate for 80 per cent of women' that would be 'no reason to stifle the other 20 per cent' (Christiansen (1986), p. 10). For surely the fact is that it does seem most unlikely that the human race would come to an end even if far, *far*, fewer women felt obliged to propagate it than are likely to – i.e. even if women like the Alcharisi could choose not to do so without being made to feel guilty – or reviled as monstrous, unwomanly freaks. But apart from any atavistic terrors that it would, ultimately, lead to the extinction of the species, or (on the other hand) from a male supremacist desire to keep women confined to their supporting roles, it is hard to see any logical reason why a *woman's* free decision to say 'no' to marriage-and-family has traditionally been stigmatised as 'unwomanly' to the very same degree that a woman's autonomous decision to have sex with any man *she* chooses has been anathematised as immoral.

For even as our artistic-mentor figures are identified with the freakish, the alien, the abnormal and the monstrous, as well as the demonic, an Alcharisi-like refusal on the part of an autonomous female character, to subordinate herself to any man, has, traditionally, not only been anathematised as 'unwomanly', unnatural and monstrous: it is also deemed to be demonic and ultimately damnable in so far as it is comparable to Satan's own defiant refusal to serve God the Father Himself. '*Non serviam!*' would seem to be the motto of Lucifer, Faustus, Lilith and the Alcharisi alike. This is the primary reason why, in order to save her immortal soul, Hans Andersen's Karen is required to do such horrific penance for her 'sin': woman's salvation lies in serving others – her elders, her betters, her husband, her children. Thus, in Andersen's fable even a little girl's desire to wear a pair of pretty red dancing shoes (which causes her selfish failure to serve her benefactress) is treated as damnably comparable to the aspirations of Faust or of proud Lucifer himself.

Happily, however, some of our parables themselves seem to be 'of the devil's party' in so far as they – in effect if not intent – join forces with their devilishly attractive Svengalis, Phantoms and impresarios by positively encouraging artistic ambition, pride and insubordination in any young girls that fall under *their* spell. For the world of art as it is most often portrayed in these works not only tends to be associated with the demonic in some gloriously tempting, attractive and compelling and positively alluring ways: it is also dramatically associated with sublime achievement, with 'divine' as well as earthly glory, transcendence and triumph. The hours during which the

voice of the Angel of Music taught her to sing, says Leroux's
Christine,

> were spent in a divine frenzy, until, at last, the voice said to me, 'You
> can now, Christine Daaé, give to men a little of the music of
> Heaven!' I don't know how it was that Carlotta did not come to the
> theatre that night nor why I was called upon to sing in her stead; but
> I sang with a rapture I had never felt before and I felt for a moment as
> if my soul were leaving my body. (p. 130)

Looked at as romantic fictions, like the fantasies of Emma Bovary,
these dreams of glory can be condemned, but even the most
melodramatic of the works surveyed here differ from most if not all
other romantic fictions in that they demand an acknowledgement of a
woman's abilities and emotions in areas other than sexual or romantic
love. And viewed from this perspective they seem positively liberating. Personally speaking, among the most vivid of my own
childhood memories is, still, the radically unconventional ending of
the 1943 film adaptation of *The Phantom of the Opera* starring Claude
Rains as the heroine's violinist father-figure. This is the only version
of the fable that I know of where the forces embodied in the Phantom
triumph in the end, when the heroine leaves her two handsome
suitors behind to greet the throng of admirers clamouring at her
dressing-room door to acclaim the newest and greatest of all prima
donnas. By contrast to this ending, it would have seemed a terrible
let-down if she had betrayed her own genius, to say nothing of the
faith the Angel of Music had placed in her, to marry either a baritone
or a policeman (or a vicomte or a millionaire). Looked at from this
angle, Leroux's original Phantom still seems, to my mind, most
accurately described as the heroine's 'good genius', while Svengali, as
a musician, remains 'as one of the heavenly host'. Similarly, far from
discouraging any young girls who saw the film from aspiring to
dance – as the lamentable fate of its heroine might appear ideologically contrived to do – *The Red Shoes* caused an unprecedented rush
to enrol in ballet classes. So striking was this historical phenomenon
that it is communally remembered by various characters in the
musical *A Chorus Line* (see the lead-in to the number, 'Everything
was Beautiful at the Ballet') and explicitly cited as a matter of
historical record in Mikhail Barishnikov's introduction to the ballet
section of the film anthology, *'That's Dancing!'*. As practically every
female who saw it can attest, in effect the film actively inspired the
desire to 'put on the Red Shoes' and dance into the ballet-world of
fame and art, and public accomplishment and competition and
collaborative endeavour, and strenuous effort – to say nothing of
evoking the very dreams of 'beauty and splendour and dress' that

Andersen's minatory fairy tale piously exhorted young girls like
Karen to *renounce*.

But be all that as it may. The fact remains that, just as our various
works all involve an either/or conflict between the gifted heroine's
artistic career and her life 'as a woman', the 'Faustian' nature of the
contention for the heroine's body and heart and soul is explicitly or
implicitly alluded to in every one of them. For instance, the director
of *The Red Shoes*, Michael Powell, thus describes the filming of the
'big *Faust*-like scene' wherein the impresario, Boris Lermontov, and
the husband, Julian Craster, fight for the ballerina's heart and body
and soul. In the course of shooting the contention, it was as if 'the
selfishness and cruelty of the two men who loved and killed Vicky
Page' had 'suddenly flared into reality'.

> Anton Walbrook and Marius Goring [the actors playing Lermontov
> and Craster] were both very accomplished and neither of them was
> particularly inclined to let the other steal the scene. . . . They
> mishandled Moira Shearer, who played the ballerina, as if she were a
> beautiful thoroughbred, pulling her head savagely this way and that.
> Because the two men were both refined and cultivated artists, the
> brutality of the scene was all the more disturbing. This was no
> longer acting. Moira turned blindly from one man to another like a
> broken doll.
>
> *(A Life in Movies* (1986), p. 656)[2]

Comparable references to Faustian conflicts and choices pervade our
other works. As we have seen, in *The Bostonians* Olive Chancellor
pointedly quoted the lines about renunciation from Goethe's *Faust* to
Verena (*'Entsagen sollst du, sollst entsagen'*). In *Trilby* (p. 380),
George du Maurier informs us that none other than Charles Gounod,
the composer of the opera, *Faust*, was present in the audience when
'La Svengali' sang his *'Chanson de Printemps'* to an enraptured
audience. And that self-same Charles Gounod himself was *also* in the
audience at the Paris Opera on the night of that gala when Christine
Daaé, under the tutelage of the Angel of Music, 'revealed a Margarita
of a splendour, a radiance hitherto unsuspected'. Subsequently,
Christine was carried off by the Phantom immediately after, 'with
her arms outstretched' and 'the glory of her hair falling over her bare
shoulders', and with her throat filled with divine music, she sang the
lines from *Faust* that seemed to be addressed 'to that demon's soul':
'Holy angel, in Heaven blessed,/My spirit longs with thee to rest!'
(pp. 40–1, 153, 161).

As in the case of their ubiquitous allusions to Faustian conflicts and
bargains, to angels and demons, to salvation and damnation, to
heaven and hell, these differing works are likewise pervaded by

images of death and burials; and not only by images of the Phantom's death-in-life, but also by symbolic images of the death of talent, of art, of the burial of genius, as well as by images of the literal death of a talented woman who cannot live without art. Thus, when (through his portrait) Svengali seems to summon her from beyond the grave 'to help him make better music than ever', Trilby/La Svengali sings, divinely, one last time – '*Encore une fois? bon! je veux bien!*' (p. 436) – before she dies with his name on her lips.

Far more subtly, but just as pointedly, in perhaps the most moving and memorable lines in *The Bostonians*, we have references to the burial of Verena's talent that echo John Milton's scriptual allusion in his great sonnet on his blindness, to 'that one talent which is death to hide' (*Milton: Poetical Works*, p. 190). When Verena Tarrant's victorious suitor, Basil Ransom, demands that she quit speaking in public forever and henceforth devote herself and all her abilities to the domestic sphere – to love, to privacy, to him – Verena in turn asks him, why, then, 'should this facility have been given me':

> 'Why should I have been saddled with a superfluous talent? I don't care much about it – I don't mind telling you that; but I should like to know what is to become of all that part of me, if I retire into private life and live, as you say, simply to be charming for you. I shall be like a singer with a beautiful voice (you have told me yourself my voice is beautiful), who has accepted some decree of never raising a note. Isn't that a great waste, a great violation of nature? Were not our talents given us to use, and have we any right to smother them and deprive our fellow-creatures of such pleasure as they may confer? In the arrangement you propose' (that was Verena's way of speaking of the question of their marriage), 'I don't see what provision is made for the poor, faithful, dismissed servant. . . .' (p. 387)

In raising these questions, Henry James, by way of Verena, is clearly alluding to the most famous, the most terrifying and certainly the most profound of all parables of any human being's talent. Indeed, our very use of the term 'talented' to describe a specially 'gifted' individual derives from Christ's parable of the three servants who were given – or, rather, to whom were entrusted – certain valuable sums of money known as 'talents' by their Lord.

THE PRIMAL PARABLE

Here is the original 'Parable of the Talents' as it appears in the Gospel according to Matthew (25: 14–30):

For the kingdom of heaven is as a man travelling into a far country, who called his own servants, and delivered unto them his goods.

And unto one he gave five talents, to another two, and to another one; to every man according to his several ability; and straightway took his journey.

Then he that had received the five talents went and traded with the same, and made them other five talents.

And likewise he that had received two, he also gained other two.

But he that had received one went and digged in the earth, and hid his lord's money.

After a long time the lord of those servants cometh, and reckoneth with them.

And so he that had received five talents came and brought other five talents, saying, Lord, thou deliveredst unto me five talents: behold, I have gained beside them five talents more.

His lord said unto him, Well done, thou good and faithful servant; thou hast been faithful over a few things; I will make thee ruler over many things; enter thou into the joy of thy lord.

He also that had received two talents came and said, Lord, thou deliveredst unto me two talents; behold, I have gained two other talents beside them.

His lord said unto him, Well done, good and faithful servant; thou hast been faithful over a few things, I will make thee ruler over many things: enter thou into the joy of thy lord.

Then he which had received the one talent came and said, Lord, I knew thee that thou art an hard man, reaping where thou has not sown, and gathering where thou hast not strawed:

And I was afraid, and went and hid thy talent in the earth: lo, there thou hast that is thine.

His lord answered and said unto him, Thou wicked and slothful servant, thou knewest that I reap where I sowed not, and gather where I have not strawed;

Thou oughtest therefore to have put my money to the exchangers, and then at my coming I should have received mine own with [interest] usury.

Take therefore the talent from him, and give it unto him which hath ten talents.

For unto every one that hath shall be given, and he shall have abundance: but from him that hath not shall be taken away even that which he hath.

And cast ye the unprofitable servant into outer darkness; there shall be weeping and gnashing of teeth.

And so, as allegorically applied to whatever talent has been given to us, the moral 'Use it or lose it' is here enforced with a vengeance. This parable is the obvious source of Verena Tarrant's reference to that 'poor, faithful dismissed servant' and its merciless message may provide the answer to her questions about what will become of that part of herself if she marries Basil Ransom. As Henry James and the parable both predict, 'there shall be weeping'. Looked at from this perspective, works as different as *The Bostonians, The Phantom of the Opera* and *The Red Shoes* likewise associate the loss or forfeiture or burial of a woman's talent with weeping, with the outer darkness, with various forms of death and with fates worse than death itself. In so far as they do so, they are subversive of the very ideology they might officially seem designed to affirm. For so far as conventional wisdom – and that, in this case, *is* patriarchal ideology – is concerned, the dire message of the original parable of the talents has consistently been considered applicable to men only. Had Verena Tarrant's questions been raised with reference to a talented *man*, the answers to them, today as yesterday, would be, unequivocally, 'Yes'. 'It would be a great violation of nature to bury's one's talent.' 'Yes.' 'Our talents were given us to use, and we have no right to smother them.' Note, for instance, the masculine pronouns used, as it were necessarily, in Thomas Wolfe's poem on precisely this subject (quoted in Riese and Hitchens (1988), p. xiii):

> If a man has a talent, and cannot use it,
> he has failed.
> If he has a talent and uses only half of it,
> he has partly failed.
> If he has a talent and learns somehow
> to use the whole of it,
> he has won a satisfaction and
> a triumph few men ever know.

Then note the comparable way that well-nigh exclusively masculine pronouns are employed by the distinguished American psychologist, A. H. Maslow, in order to make exactly the same points (Maslow (1962), p. 6):

> He who belies his talent, the born painter who sells stockings instead, the intelligent man who lives a stupid life, the man who sees the truth and keeps his mouth shut, the coward who gives up his manliness, all these people perceive in a deep way that they have done wrong to themselves and despise themselves for it.

These people have all violated what Maslow describes as an 'intrinsic conscience' that is based on the unconscious or pre-conscious perception of one's own nature, one's own destiny or one's own 'call' in life. It insists that we be true to our calling and not deny it 'out of weakness, or for safety, or for advantage, or for any other reason'. According to Maslow, our capacities – or if you will our God-given talents – clamour to be used, and if they are not put to use they will fester: 'Theologians used to use the word "*accidie*" to describe the sin of failing to do with one's life all that one knows one could do' (p. 5).

As we have seen, the built-in ambivalences of various works portraying talented heroines suggest that these psychological insights, as well as the original parable of the talents from which they were derived, are of equal relevance to women. Looked at from this angle, these parables collide head-on with traditional arguments that the opposite moral holds true for women, and therefore the gifted female artist who buries her talent for the sake of her private 'life as a woman' is going to be psychologically *better* off leading a happy, humdrum, domestic existence than she would have been had she made the opposite choice. '*Of course*,' Maslow insists [my italics] 'femalehood is preponent over personhood, i.e., it calls for prior gratification, yet its gratification brings the claims of personhood into the foreground of the motivational economy' (p. 121). Maslow may well be right in arguing that the gratification of certain basic desires leads to the emergence of different desires and needs, and so the grass starts looking greener on the other side of a married woman's, or a successful career woman's, fence. Yet he certainly overstates his case when arguing that 'femalehood' is *necessarily* 'preponent over personhood' and 'calls for prior gratification'. This may hold true for some women, but not for every woman, in fact as well as in fiction. For instance, the claims of 'femalehood' never came first for the Alcharisi. 'I never wanted to marry again', she tells the son she had never wanted and had left to be raised as a gentile-gentleman by an English admirer:

> I meant to be free, and to live for my art. I had parted with you. I had no bonds. For nine years I was a queen. I enjoyed the life I had longed for. But something befell me. . . . I began to sing out of tune. . . . It was horrible to me. . . . It drove me to marry. . . . It was a resolve taken in desperation.

Although her second husband was a prince, by whom she had five children (of all things usually deemed to constitute the dreams-come-true of 'femalehood'!) her never-ending regret was that she left the stage and married him: 'I could not make myself love the people I have never loved – is it not enough that I lost the life I did love?' (p. 702).

> I made believe that I preferred being the wife of a Russian noble to being the greatest lyric actress of Europe; I made believe – I acted that part. . . . I repented [leaving the stage]. . . . That singing out of tune was only like a fit of illness; it went away. I repented; but it was too late. I could not go back. All things hindered me. All things.'
>
> (*Daniel Deronda*, p. 730)

But did she not, asks Daniel, love her other children?

> 'Oh yes,' she answered, as to a question about a matter of course, while she folded her arms again. 'But', . . . she added in a deeper tone, . . . 'I am not a loving woman. That is the truth. It is a talent to love – I lacked it. Others have loved me – and I have acted their love.'
>
> (p. 730)

Thus the Alcharisi makes the crucial, almost invariably suppressed (or repressed) points that to be a devoted wife and loving mother may require special talents that not all women possess, that she herself did not possess and that it was wrong for her to pretend to possess.

Literary imitations, Dr Johnson once observed, give us pleasure or pain, not because they are mistaken for realities, but because they bring realities to mind. Arguably, anyway, in allowing rebellious characters such as the Alcharisi to challenge conventional thinking, to upset stereotypes, to say the unsayable and violate sexual (and sexist) taboos, both classic and popular literary fictions – that are not mistaken for realities, but bring realities to mind – may provide us with some of our best defences against certain ideological fictions that have, historically, been passed off on us as scientific fact, as reality itself.

RESISTING IDEOLOGY

> Women must sacrifice all their life if they [accept that] behind his destiny woman must annihilate herself.
>
> Florence Nightingale

> I have yet to hear a man ask for advice on how to combine a career and marriage.
>
> Gloria Steinem

> A woman not only marries a man, she marries into a way of life – a job.
>
> Prince Charles

*   *   *   *

In a book entitled *Resisting Novels: Ideology and Fiction* (1987) the author, Lennard J. Davis, draws on psychoanalytic theory to warn us that novels can weaken the bonds that anchor us to the real world, and bind us to the ideological: 'Novels do not depict life, they depict life as it is represented by ideology' (p. 24). But so, one might argue, does a good deal of critical commentary on novels. And so, for that matter, does much psychoanalytic theory which could itself be defined, even as Davis defines ideology (p. 15) as 'a system of illusory beliefs, false ideas or false consciousness as contrasted with true or scientific knowledge'. Indeed, so far as their treatments of women are concerned, one could argue, *pace* Davis, that whereas psychoanalytic theory and practice alike have, historically, bound women to the ideological (Friedan (1963), pp. 95–173 and Miles (1988), pp. 215–18) various novels, films and plays may well afford us with our best defence against certain tenets of sexist ideology. Through their actual portrayals of individual women, differing works of art may, whether in intent or in effect, dramatically and/or emotionally serve to challenge, deconstruct and ultimately defy the ideological orthodoxies that they might at first glance seem designed to uphold. Although this phenomenon has tended to go unnoticed by male critics, it has perhaps inevitably seemed of obvious importance and of special interest to women young and old, while watching films or reading novels inside or outside of the classroom.

For instance, as Judith Fetterly has demonstrated, it is a cohort of male commentators on *The Bostonians* who, in a series of ideologically dictated arguments quite at odds with the emotional impact of the novel itself, proclaim the victory of the male supremacist Basil Ransom to be a triumph of 'normality' and 'morality': "The criticism of *The Bostonians* is remarkable for its relentless sameness, its reliance on values outside the novel, and its cavalier dismissal of the need for textual support' (p. 113). Thus, the fact that the 'far from brilliant' union into which Verena is about to enter will in all probability give her cause to shed more tears seems, as one such commentator observes, a small price to pay for achieving a normal relationship. Faced with a threat to what they regard as normalcy, male critics outdo each other in finding reasons to disparage Olive Chancellor, the character in whom James shows the greatest interest. Not surprisingly, the views of these commentators are virtually identical to Ransom's own views concerning the proper role of women, which in turn are virtually identical to those of Sigmund Freud and the Alcharisi's father – not to mention other male supremacists, such as Torvald Helmer (Nora's paternalistic husband in Ibsen's *A Doll's House*) or those all-powerful members of the Stepford Men's Association who turned women into domestic house-pets in Ira Levin's allegorical novel, *The Stepford Wives*. For instance, when Verena observes that Ransom's ideal social system has 'no place' for women, Ransom answers: 'No place in public. My plan is to keep you at home and have a better time with you there than ever' (p. 323):

'[In domestic life] we shall find plenty of room for your facility, it will lubricate our whole existence. . . . Think how delightful it will be when your influence becomes really social. Your facility, as you call it, will simply make you, in conversation, the most charming woman in America.'

(p. 376)

The comparably charming ideal of gentle, sweet, tender, adorable womanhood which Freud also describes as the most delightful thing in the world (we women really are such stuff as dreams are made on) is, likewise, dependent on a woman's renunciation of active aims, ambitions, interests of her own and necessitates a retreat from all activity directed outward to the world. Compare, for instance, Freud's derision of John Stuart Mill's essay advocating the emancipation of women, which is posited, in a letter to his own fiancée, in *exactly* the same terms as Ransom's reiterated arguments to Verena deriding Olive Chancellor's feminist views and extolling domesticity:

[John Stuart Mill] finds the suppression of women an analogy to that of Negroes. Any girl, even without a suffrage or legal competence, whose hand a man kisses and for whose love he is prepared to dare all, could have set him right. . . .

[*Query*: precisely how many men in Freud's time or since have actually been required to 'dare all' for love? Arguably, anyway, the ideals expressed in this letter by Freud are no less romantic, and of no more or less scientific validity than Madame Bovary's – or Barbara Cartland's.]

If, for instance, I imagined my gentle sweet girl as a competitor, it would only end in my telling her, as I did seventeen months ago, that I am fond of her and that I implore her to withdraw from the strife into the calm, uncompetitive activity of my home. It is possible that changes in upbringing may suppress all a woman's tender attributes . . . and that she can then earn a livelihood like men. It is also possible that in such an event one would not be justified in mourning the passing away of the most delightful thing the world can offer us – our ideal of womanhood. [But] I believe that all reforming action in law and education would break down in front of the fact that, long before the age at which a man can earn a position in society, Nature has determined woman's destiny through beauty, charm, and sweetness. Law and Custom have much to give women that has been withheld from them, but the position of women will surely be what it is: in youth an adored darling and in mature years a loved wife.

(Jones (1953), Vol. I, pp. 176–7)

Like most theorists who are primarily concerned with what they believe that women, essentially, ought to be like, Freud here describes a species (by definition adorable darlings who are happily house-bound) to which only certain members of the sheltered class of women on which he is basing his theory actually belong. Significantly, however, although Freud makes the points in gentler, kinder and far more romantic terms than the Alcharisi's stern father, the underlying message is identical: 'This is what you must be,' 'that you must not be'; 'this is what you are wanted for; a woman's heart must be of such a size and no larger, else it must be pressed small, like Chinese feet; her happiness is to be made as cakes are, by a fixed receipt' (*Daniel Deronda*, pp. 693–4).

But what about women who do not genetically or psychologically fit the ideal pattern, in so far as they are not particularly adorable and beautiful, or for that matter any more inherently sweet or gentle or charming than – say – their fathers or brothers or husbands or sons? What about women like George Eliot herself? And what about all the women, such as Trilby, who have had to earn their own livelihoods and to support dependants just like men? And what if woman's nature does not follow *any* 'fixed receipt'? 'Natural' talents for singing, acting, writing novels, doing mathematics, etc., are not biologically sex-linked characteristics: 'Acknowledge that I had a right to be an artist, though my father's will was against it' pleads the Alcharisi: 'My nature gave me a charter' (p. 728).[3] Perhaps (*pace* Maslow) 'femalehood' is not inevitably 'preponent over personhood' and therefore does not necessarily 'call for prior gratification' and it is, in fact, only socially and/or psychologically enforced gender-conditioning that makes it preponent over everything else to do with an individual woman's nature or destiny.

Moreover, given the complex operation of the Double Helix, it seems inevitable that apart from biological gender, some women, such as the Alcharisi herself, will inherit at least as many, if not more, characteristics from their fathers than their mothers, just as some men resemble their mothers and/or grandmothers more than their fathers and/or grandfathers, and so on. Given the 100,000 or so genes involved, the hereditary combinations and permutations are virtually infinite. In *Daniel Deronda* George Eliot seems particularly interested in the complex interactions between nature and nurture, heredity and environment. For instance, although she is portrayed as an artist in bitter opposition to her father, the Alcharisi nevertheless describes herself, psychologically, as his counterpart: 'My father had no other child than his daughter and she was like himself.' And the fact is that, in so far as they are equally self-willed, autocratic, imperious and impressive characters, the formidable Alcharisi can be best described in the identical terms which she herself used to describe her father – 'grand', 'with an iron will', 'to be admired in a play' (p. 694). If he enslaves women ('such men turn their wives and daughters into slaves' – p. 694), she enslaves men ('I was never willingly subject to any man. Men have been subject to me.' – p. 730). And so on. Thus, throughout *Daniel Deronda*, George Eliot (Mary Ann Evans) suggests that, independently of biological gender, individual men and women (such as herself and George Henry Lewes?) sometimes have a great deal more in common with each other – in personality, temperament and 'force of genius' – than with other members of their own sex. The Alcharisi, for instance, has much more in common with her father and – as a dedicated artist – with the comparably gifted musician, Elijah Klesmer, than with sweet, gentle, delicate Mirah, who is 'not ambitious', not 'one who must have a path of her own' (p. 728). Perhaps significantly, the only thing the Alcharisi has in common with Mirah 'as a woman' is that, as comparably rebellious daughters they were likewise browbeaten and pressured, if not finally forced, to do or to be what they, personally, did not want to do or be – on the one hand a wife and mother, on the other hand a professional artist. It is also perhaps significant that George Eliot portrays the one as most wanting to do or be whatever the other most desires not to do or be. Temperamentally speaking, Mirah, who so perfectly fits the conventional gender-stereotype of ideal *womanhood*, in turn has far more in common with the Alcharisi's tender and sensitive *son*, Daniel, who is explicitly portrayed by George Eliot as possessing the 'talent to love' that his mother lacked. Indeed, it is as if 'all the woman', i.e. all the loving, nurturing, traits traditionally associated with ideal womanhood that are lacking in the Alcharisi, are here portrayed as 'present' in her son (pp. 723, 730).

Time after time, both 'high' and 'popular' works in the artistic tradition surveyed here likewise tend, whether explicitly or implicitly, to be far more subversive of gender-stereotypes, and far closer to feminism in their sympathies for the aspiring women artists portrayed than *either* the (masculinist) critical tradition or the (Freudian) psychoanalytic tradition. For that matter our 'major' and 'minor' works most dramatically tend to glorify the very women that they might, ideologically, appear designed to suppress. For instance, as Judith Fetterly has observed, although the male supremacist views posited by Ransom and Freud alike were once encoded as truth itself in the critical tradition (as exemplified in a remarkably repetitive series of sexist commentaries on *The Bostonians*), and although it is unlikely that Henry James himself identified very much either with Olive Chancellor or with Basil Ransom – he treats militant feminism and male chauvinism with equal degrees of irony – the fact remains that 'it is Olive who interests him: it is she who claims his attention, and it is she who achieves stature'. 'For better or worse, *The Bostonians* is Olive Chancellor's book' (p. 118).

For another example, in a remarkably perceptive discussion of *Trilby* (*Woman and the Demon* (1982)) Nina Auerbach stresses the surprising fact that George du Maurier's 'put-upon heroine' is 'not fragile, as her role in the plot would lead one to assume, but a virtual giantess'. The original independent Trilby, who, as an artist's model, earns her own living and supports her little brother, is constantly described as a 'big' heroine with a cavernous throat and positively majestic feet, as well as a voice that was not only twice as big, but could also range far higher and lower than the voice of the celebrated singer, Madame Alboni (p. 233). Trilby is also an unconventional *ingénue* in other ways. Uninhibited, droll, free-spirited, funny and jolly, she exhibits her magnificent body without shame when she poses 'in the altogether' for her artist friends and employers. Moreover, as Auerbach also observes, 'reinforcing Trilby's size is her seemingly boundless capacity for metamorphosis'. 'She is a different woman in English and in French' and 'when she becomes a great singer, the essence of her artistry lies in its virtually endless variations' (Auerbach, p. 20). By contrast, the thoroughly nice boy Trilby loves is always referred to as 'Little Billee' Bagot (the diminutive is from Thackeray's ballad) and in virtually every other way but biological gender he seems a far more conventionally 'feminine' character than she does: 'He was young and tender, was Little Billee; he had never been to any school, and was innocent of the world and its wicked ways'. He was small and slender, very graceful, with very small hands and feet and very handsome ('in his winning and handsome face there was just a faint suggestion of some possible very remote Jewish ancestor'). As an art student, he was gifted with 'a sense of all that was sweet and beautiful in nature' and his 'almost girlish' purity of mind amused and charmed his friends (pp. 224–5).

Throughout du Maurier's novel, in what seem clear cases of consistent (yet refreshingly unselfconscious) gender-bending, Trilby's voice and personality, like Little Billee's sweetness, are explicitly described as attractively androgynous. Her voice was so 'rich and deep and full as almost to suggest an incipient *tenor robusto*; and one felt instinctively that it was a real pity she wasn't a boy, she would have made such a jolly one' (*Trilby*, p. 229). Thus, like Shakespeare's Rosalind and Viola, du Maurier's Trilby is portrayed as possessing qualities of spirit and personality that would be just as attractive and charming had they been 'incarnated' in a member of either sex:

' "*Et maintenant dors, ma mignonne!*" ' *Svengali's glorification of his*
'*goddess and empress*', *from* Trilby.

> She was one of those rarely-gifted beings who cannot look or speak
> or even stir without waking up (and satisfying) some vague longing
> that lies dormant in the hearts of most of us, men and women alike;
> grace, charm, magnetism – whatever the nameless seduction should
> be called that she possessed to such an unusual degree. (p. 419)

This raises an interesting question as to precisely what qualities of
personality and spirit that are genuinely attractive in members of one
sex are not equally attractive in both. As Janet Richards has observed,
a little consideration and comparison of attractive people of each sex
shows that there are almost none: independence, strength, gentleness,
charm, grace, wit, intelligence and the like are admired wherever they
occur (for further discussion see Richards (1982), p. 193). But be that
as it may: regardless of their sex or age, every character who gets to
know Trilby – up to and finally including Billee's mother –
ultimately comes to love her and to agree that the world would have
been a far better place if only there had been even more, ever more,
'incarnations of Trilbyness' in it.

Moreover, as Nina Auerbach also demonstrates, 'the potent
essence of each new "incarnation of Trilbyness" ' that simultaneously counterpoints and in effect contradicts 'her passive and
stupefied role in the plot is emphasised in the author's own illustra-

tions of his novel'. Du Maurier's drawings consistently reinforce our sense of Trilby's stature (p. 18). Even when she is depicted singing under the spell of her mentor-magus-master, the Trilby of the illustrations looms, monumentally, over the figure of Svengali himself:

> As with George Eliot's noble, outsize heroines, she seems cramped by the setting and action of her story; underlying her sacrificial destiny (like Dumas's Marguerite Gautier she repudiates her true love at the instigation of his snobbish parent and thus falls under Svengali's fatal power) is the hint that the novel's world is too small for her to live in.
>
> (Auerbach, pp. 18–19)[4]

In ways comparable to du Maurier's glorification of Trilby, various works in this tradition likewise tend, dramatically, to glorify the misfit characters (Jews, freaks, 'unwomanly' women such as the Alcharisi) who, looked at in terms of reigning social, racial, psychological and sexual assumptions would generally be anathematised as losers, outcasts, and/or social pariahs. Like James's unforgettable Olive Chancellor, du Maurier's Svengali, Leroux's Phantom and Eliot's Alcharisi are all endowed by their creators with a stature, with an imaginative grandeur and with a dramatic appeal unrivalled by the more conventionally proper and respectable characters. There are, I believe, several reasons why this is the case.

In *Daniel Deronda* (by way of the absolutely committed musician, Elijah Klesmer) George Eliot eloquently describes artistic endeavour as a kind of 'freemasonry' – a secret society whose members 'are all vowed to the service of Art, and to serve her by assisting every fellow-servant' (p. 304). This is precisely the kind of collaborative dedication to art that Michael Powell wanted to portray in *The Red Shoes*. He wanted the men and women portraying the impresario, the choreographer, the leading male dancer, the conductor and the ballerina to have 'enough genius' to enable them 'to create a recognizable group of eccentric and talented individuals' all in the service of artistic excellence. So successfully did they achieve this goal that Powell himself was impressed by the way members of the audience joined forces with them and felt that the creative, co-operative artistic endeavour portrayed in *The Red Shoes* made the world of art seem worth living and even dying for (Powell (1986), pp. 640, 660). Looked at in terms of George Eliot's freemasonry-of-artistic-endeavour, it seems virtually inevitable that artists depicting other talented artists, regardless of their sex or race or social origins, are going to join forces with their brother-and-sister servants of Art – of the Alcharisi, of Svengali, of the Phantom of the Opera – in opposition to the very formidable and generally victorious forces that are ranged against them.

Thus, whatever choice the doomed (to-death-or-to-domesticity) *ingénue* might make, individual members of the audience may finally end up preferring the domain of art and its misfits to its opponents and rivals: that is certainly what I, personally, did as a child and then as a teenager – and still do. This imaginative, emotional, sympathetic preference on the part of individual members of the audience as well as authors and other artists alike can be most dramatically demonstrated by citing the obvious fact that all of the best 'parts', all the *real* starring-roles in the novels and films and plays cited here are, without exception, the freakish, alien, misfit-artist parts. What actor who had the chance would choose to play 'Little Billee' if he could play Svengali? What actress would portray Mirah if she could play the Alcharisi? If, as Fetterly has observed, *The Bostonians* is Olive Chancellor's book, the movie version belongs to Olive Chancellor-as-portrayed-by-Vanessa-Redgrave in what is perhaps the greatest of that great actress's film performances to date. The gifted singer/actor/stunt-man, Michael Crawford, starring as the Phantom of the Opera, took all the awards for the best actor in a musical offered both in London and in New York. By the same token, Lon Chaney's performance as the Phantom in the original movie is still remembered as a classic, while no one remembers who played the ostensible winner/hero Raoul. And so on and on.

It is because art's impact on the passions, aspirations, admirations, sympathies and desires of individual members of an audience *cannot* be controlled by ideology and is as often as not at odds with it (Hawkins (1985) and Habicht (1989)) that totalitarian governments have historically been suspicious of art. For this very reason, one could argue that imaginatively and emotionally exciting literature, high and low, serves as a far more potent challenge to and/or critique of reigning ideologies than virtually anything else. For in marked contrast to, say, a theology or a Freudian methodology that interprets everything in accordance with its own reigning dicta, differing works of literature may 'allow us to size up a given situation' in altogether different ways and 'in keeping with correspondingly various attitudes' and, by doing so, as Kenneth Burke has persuasively argued, literature may in fact provide us with the best 'equipment for living' in the real world that we are likely to get (Burke (1964), pp. 100–9). Here, in illustration of Burke's points, are just a few of the differing ways in which we may 'size up' the situations portrayed in the various works just surveyed.

LIFE AND ART

The following points are all derived from conversations and informal interviews with women professionally active in the arts.

1. Certain conflicts portrayed in these fictions are painfully real. The choice confronting the heroine is all the more difficult because it is not a choice between good and evil, but a choice between differing goods, or Gods or goals which are so opposed that, as you approach one, you must recede from or renounce the other. One can, of course, have a lot of differing things in life, but one cannot do or be, two altogether different things at the same time: you can no more be at home with your husband and children and on tour dancing in *The Red Shoes* than you can, simultaneously, fill your cup from the source and from the mouth of the Nile.

2. Even in this so-called 'post-feminist' era, some of the external forces ranged against the Alcharisi still confront her great-granddaughters: it is, for instance, still generally considered an unnatural thing for a woman to be ambitious,[5] and the taboo against a woman's publicly stating that she personally never wanted to have children has only very recently been challenged.[6]

3. It may well be true that artistic geniuses such as the Alcharisi do not make the best of wives and mothers, not because they are monsters or demons, but because they are dedicated to the kind of vocation that, rather like a religion, requires their primary if not their absolute devotion. For the same reasons, male geniuses in the arts and sciences may not make the best of all husbands and fathers. After all, to do anything – say, to dance professionally – even competently well, requires considerable effort on the part of most people, and to do anything supremely well apparently requires unremitting concentration, uninterrupted time and strenuous effort from even the most talented of artists. And precisely because it so rarely gets said, perhaps it should not go without saying that the same may hold true of parenthood as well – the number of male and female non-geniuses (to say nothing of the geniuses) who have made deplorable parents is virtually infinite. Or, as Gore Vidal cruelly puts it, 'parenthood is a gift', a talent, 'which most parents find out too late, and most children find out right away' and for this if for no other reason, we should stop continually brainwashing every woman into thinking that 'motherhood must be her supreme experience' (Vidal (1977), p. 277).

Another cruelly tyrannical dogma – less often propounded now-adays, but not yet replaced – is that all women ought to excel at all things at once and so be the ideal wife and mother as well as a superstar. Yet the fact remains that very few of us can do more than one thing at once and well. This is why the conflicts posed in these older works of fiction remain active. It is also why one implicit message of these works, 'You pay your money and you take your choice' may not be quite so depressing or objectionable as at first glance it might appear to be. When, in a recent interview, the great ballerina Alicia Markova said that she had 'One regret, maybe – I didn't marry and have a family', but immediately added that 'I think I've been fortunate in life in other ways by achieving so much', the very tentative regret expressed seems no more painful than a retrospective glance back at a road not taken. On the other hand, the grandmother of a woman I interviewed, who gave up a brilliant career as a musician to marry and have children, never ceased to regret it. The difference seems to be the bitter regret evoked at a socially or ideologically or otherwise enforced choice. The catch is that, today as yesterday, it is sometimes hard to tell which is which.

For it is during exactly the same time required for an arduous professional apprenticeship that a young woman is most impelled by the physical and emotional desires for love, sex, marriage and children; to say nothing of being most tempted by some suitor such as Ransom or Freud to 'withdraw from the strife into the calm, uncompetitive activity' of his home. And this may very well seem an offer she cannot refuse. At certain times, to be domestically housebound or to remain, professionally, in a subordinate position as it were for ever after, may seem a small price to pay for getting out of the rat race – however much it may come to rankle later on. Looked at from this angle the problems of timing, of turning points and points of no return as underlined by the now-or-never, go-forward-or-give-up ultimatums issued to our heroines are also crucial in real life. In the performing arts, as in sports, age and timing alike may be of the utmost importance. For instance, if you don't move (at the right age and when the opportunity arises) out of the *corps de ballet* and on into solo parts and instead take time off to have a baby, you may not even be able to get back into the *corps de ballet* later on. Or, as the Alcharisi puts it in a terrible expression of utter regret, when she so desperately wanted to go back on stage, 'it was too late.' 'I could not go back. All things hindered me – all things.'

Certainly a central point that emerges from our fictional parables of a woman's talent is that the forces of convention – such as the pressures on a woman to conform to the traditional feminine role –

are among the most formidable forces that there are. Looked at from this point of view, the full power and glory and terror of the Angel of Music incarnate seems nothing like as oppressive, demanding and selfish as the forces of sexist orthodoxy not unattractively embodied in Henry James's Basil Ransom. It seems to me that, so far as a talented woman is concerned, the militant male supremacist Ransom is the ultimate oppressor. By contrast, there is a lot to be said for sympathetic professional mentors, such as Svengali and the Phantom. After all, as George du Maurier reminds us, there are times when supreme artistic accomplishment requires a joint or team effort, 'it takes two to sing like La Svengali, monsieur – the one who has got the voice, and the one who knows what to do with it' (p. 449). For that matter (I am indebted for this point to Evert Sprinchorn), the greatest stars have often had a kind of 'shadow person', somebody who brought them out, in a sense. For instance, Greta Garbo had Maurice Stiller (who was described by *Life* magazine as a veritable Svengali – 'an hypnotic director who made over even her very soul' – Scherman (1979), p. 13), while Marlene Dietrich had Josef von Sternberg and Duse had some young wastrel who told her she should act without make-up so that her facial expressions, so subtle, could be seen. One could go on and on. Monroe had Johnny Hyde; Bardot had Vadim; Elvis Presley had Colonel Parker; the Beatles had Brian Epstein – and so forth (Rogan (1988)). This may be as natural as it is necessary. Since everyone can't do everything, it could be very useful to a young soprano to have a supportive Phantom, even as many men have found it extremely helpful to have supportive wives.[7]

Society, however, is dead set against those Svengali-types who urge its humble Trilbys on and up. Its full support is with Basil Ransom by way of the incessant insistence that no other female achievement 'quite matches reproduction and the skills of home-making' and that 'no matter how great a woman's talent', if she 'wanted to feel *really* whole, she would have to find a man, develop her housekeeping abilities and bear children of her own' (Archer and Simmonds (1986), p. 96).[8] So strong is this view, still, that the interpretation posited in the blurb on the back of the Virago Press edition of *The Song of the Lark*, Willa Cather's story of the development of a prima donna – which is one of the very rare works wherein a woman who aspires to and achieves artistic fame and glory for herself is sympathetically and indeed triumphantly portrayed – insists, not on the magnificent accomplishment involved, but on the price the heroine paid for her success.

> This is the Cinderella story of Thea Kronberg, who becomes a great opera singer, but learns on the way that to be a true artist she must make the most bitter sacrifices of all.

This interpretation is, however, absolutely refuted by the primary message of the novel itself, which is that, for the true artist, the bitterest sacrifice of all would be the burial of that one talent it is death to hide. Unlike the various works by male authors (and *auteurs*) wherein a male mentor embodies the artistic genius of an extremely passive young prodigy, the female author of *The Song of the Lark* stresses the hard work, the relentless effort, required of the talented heroine. When told that her daughter, Thea, has 'talent', the heroine's mother 'comprehended perfectly' what that word meant: 'Mrs. Kronberg knew it meant that Thea must practise four hours a day' (*The Song of the Lark*, p. 30). For that matter, Willa Cather never ceases to remind us that Thea not only has spirit and brains and exceptional talent, she also has 'power of application', 'rugged will' (p. 37). Nevertheless, to do what she wants to do artistically takes even 'more than these – it takes vocation' (p. 263). Predictably, therefore, at a turning point in her career, Thea (like Verena Tarrant and Vicky Page) faces a crucial conflict between her vocation as an artist and the claims of love. And Thea chooses art. When she has an unhoped-for opportunity to sing a major part in an opera at Dresden, Thea stays in Germany, even though her beloved mother is ill and wants more than anything to see her. Thea, in turn, 'wanted to go to her mother more than she wanted anything in the world'. But she 'could not', she 'absolutely could not' leave Dresden.

> It was not that she chose to stay; she had to stay – or lose everything. The next few months would put her five years ahead, or would put her back so far it would be of no use to struggle further. (p. 491)

And so Mrs Kronberg dies without seeing her beloved daughter again; but, years later, Thea reincarnates her mother's great strength and love in an original interpretation of the 'unrewarding' part of Fricka, Wotan's resentful wife and queen, in *Rheingold*. As A. S. Byatt observes (introduction to *The Song of the Lark*, pp. xvi–xvii) 'it is perhaps Willa Cather's crowning moment of inventiveness when she makes Thea play Fricka as golden and generous.' 'It is there in the music' and in the theme of women's love ('weibliche Wonne'), which Wagner himself 'sets against the heroism and trickery of Wotan and Siegfried's world':

> But Thea has created the role out of the knowledge of her own mother and wears her hair for the part as her mother – a strong and complex and earthy woman – used to wear it. Yet the same Thea could refuse a summons to her dying mother's bedside out of devotion to ambition, or art – a chance to sing Elizabeth in *Tannhauser* that would not come again.

It seems to me that Willa Cather herself finally implies that Thea made the right choice and honoured her mother in the best way she could. It is hard to see that the alternative choice would have been better, and given the context of the heroine's struggle, there seem obvious reasons why it would have been worse. 'I've always felt', one friend of Thea's observes to another, that 'Thea made a mistake, not coming home when Mrs Kronberg was ill, no matter what it cost her.'

> Ottenberg moved about restlessly. 'She couldn't, Archie, she positively couldn't. I felt you never understood that, but I was in Dresden at the time, and . . . could size up the situation for myself. It was by just a lucky chance that she got to sing *Elizabeth* that time at the Dresden Opera, a complication of circumstances. If she'd run away for any reason, she might have waited years for such a chance to come again. She gave a wonderful performance and made a great impression. They offered her certain terms; she had to take them and follow it up then and there. In that game you can't lose a single trick. She was ill herself, but she sang. No, you mustn't hold that against her, Archie. She did the right thing.' (p. 485)

In certain instances, as Thea herself observes,

> Your work becomes your personal life. You are not much good until it does. It's like being woven into a big web. You can't pull away, because all your little tendrils are woven into the picture.
>
> (p. 546)

Thus, by the end of the novel, there seems no question that Thea's choice is vindicated. 'Take it from me', says her long-standing friend and admirer, 'No matter what she pays, or how much she may see fit to lie about it, the real, the master, revel is hers' (p. 512). And the great prima donna herself concludes, 'It's taken me a long time to do anything, of course, and I've only begun to see daylight. But anything good is – expensive' (p. 557). If fame costs, art costs, excellence costs, so does everything else worth having.[9]

Moreover, looked at allegorically, the fictional heroine's once-for-all choice either to excel professionally or to abandon her given vocation altogether – to either use her talent to the fullest or to lose it, seems a dramatic portrayal of the difference between doing one's best – going all the way – with a given talent and not developing to the limits of one's capacity. Which is all the difference in the world. This seems an important point, given the fact that women are constantly being conditioned to believe that playing second fiddle is really better, more feminine, more ladylike and a lot less work than playing first violin, or conducting the orchestra. This is a fallacious belief, in so far as doing routine, unchallenging, second-level work is *more*, not less, onerous and arduous and certainly more thankless than doing one's best at what one most wants to do. Perhaps significantly, virtually identical points about the profound emotional need (comparable to the scriptural imperative) to do one's best have been most emphatically stressed, with reference to both sexes, by very different women writers.

'It is terrible and unbearable' wrote Karen Blixen, for an artist 'to be encouraged to do, to be applauded for doing, his [or her] second best. . . . Through all the world there goes one long cry from the heart of the artist: "Give me leave to do my utmost!" ' ('Babette's Feast' in *Anecdotes of Destiny* (1958), p. 68). 'There is only one real sin,' concludes a perceptive female character in a novel by Doris Lessing, and that is to persuade yourself that 'second-best is anything but the second-best.' It is not so terrible, she adds, or rather, it may be terrible, but 'it is not damaging, not poisoning', to say 'My work is not what I really want. I'm capable of something bigger.' 'What's terrible is to pretend that the second-rate is first-rate' (*The Golden Notebook* (1973), pp. 266, 622). What may be even more terrible, as the Alcharisi observed, is *having* to pretend, *having* to make-believe to yourself as well as to others that second-best is really first-best. 'I made believe that I preferred being the wife of a Russian noble to being the greatest lyric actress of Europe; I made believe – I acted that part. It was because I felt my greatness sinking away from me, as I feel my life sinking now' (*Daniel Deronda*, p. 703). Thus (or so it seems to me), the composite message of all our parables would seem to be a variant on the Arabian proverb, whereby to 'take what you want and pay for that' is better than being forced to take what you don't want and paying for *that*. If you can't do, have and be everything, you can choose what you most want to do, have and be. The cost of the alternative will not be any lower.

Looked at from one angle, these various portrayals of talented women could serve to demonstrate that, like virtually everything else created by human beings, works of art inevitably tend to reflect the sexual, social, psychological and theological traditions and taboos of the cultures that produced them. Yet unlike most other modes of discourse, literary fictions also allow their misfits, outcasts, and outlaws (such as the Alcharisi) to plead their own cases, to have their say about the way things are, and in doing so they often evoke sympathies and raise questions that challenge reigning orthodoxies. This is most conspicuously true in the drama. And by all odds the most dramatically sympathetic portrayals of monsters, misfits, criminals and women entered the mainstream of the Anglo-American popular tradition through the plays of William Shakespeare. There were monsters such as the Gorgon and the Cyclops, and Grendel and the Dragon, in Western literature long before Caliban. But he is the very first beauty-loving beast to enter the dramatic tradition upstage-centre. Thus Caliban – the original King of Prospero's desert island, who heard musical sounds, 'and sweet airs, that give delight, and hurt not', and sometimes heard voices,

> That if I then had wak'd after long sleep,
> Will make me sleep again; and then, in dreaming
> The clouds methought would open and show riches
> Ready to drop upon me, that, when I wak'd,
> I cried to dream again
>
> (*The Tempest* III, ii, 138)

has subsequently peopled the island of art with an impressive succession of comparable monsters in popular genres up to and including Kong (the King of all the Beasts that Beauty killed) and the Creature from the Black Lagoon who evoked such sweet sympathy from Marilyn Monroe ('I think the creature just needed love and affection') in *The Seven Year Itch*.

The next chapter is devoted to Shakespeare's influence on modern genres for the obvious reason that no other individual talent has had anything like such a ubiquitous impact on the Anglo-American artistic tradition 'high' and 'low'. 'Brush up your Shakespeare,/Start quoting him now!' urged Cole Porter, and here are some representative works in which a single play, *The Tempest* (you could obviously make a comparably eclectic list for *Hamlet*) has been brushed up and quoted: W. H. Auden's *The Sea and the Mirror*; Aldous Huxley's *Brave New World*; John Fowles's *The Collector* and *The Magus*; Rachel Ingalls's 'Mrs. Caliban' (by way of *The Creature from the Black Lagoon*); Karen Blixen's 'Tempests', and Robertson Davies's *Tempest-Tost*. The phenomenally successful television series, *Star Trek*, was inspired by *The Forbidden Planet* (1956), a classic science-fiction film based on *The Tempest* that has in turn been revived on the London stage as a 'long-lost rock musical by William Shakespeare'. Even more obvious examples include the television series, *Fantasy Island*, John Cassavetes's *Tempest,* and Derek Jarman's film adaptation that climaxed in a wonderful appearance of the living goddess, Elisabeth Welch, surrounded by sailors and singing 'Stormy Weather' in what George Melly has described as 'arguably the campest, most sparkling moment in the history of cinema' (Melly (1989), p. 44). The astonishingly eclectic nature of Shakespeare's influence on modern genres thus raises some interesting and important questions about popular, as well as academic and critical, 'canons' of art.

CHAPTER THREE

From 'King Lear' to 'King Kong' and back

Shakespeare and popular modern genres

IN GENERAL

There is nothing either good or bad, but thinking makes it so.

Hamlet

TROILUS. What's aught but as 'tis valued?
HECTOR But value dwells not in particular will:
It holds his estimate and dignity
As well wherein 'tis precious of itself
As in the prizer.

Troilus and Cressida

*   *   *   *

To what degree is 'good' – or 'bad' – literature an artificial category? Are there any good – or bad – reasons why most societies have given high status to certain works of art and not to others? Could Hamlet be right in concluding that there is nothing either good or bad but thinking (or critical or ideological discourse) makes it so? Or are certain works of art so precious, so magnificent, or so trashy, that they obviously ought to be included in the canon or banned from the classroom? So far as I know, there is not now any sign of a consensus on the correct answers to these questions either in Britain or in the United States. From the conservative right in America (Bloom (1987), *The Closing of the American Mind*) and from the liberal centre in England (Gardner (1982), *In Defence of the Imagination*), you have differing, often contradictory, arguments in favour of the value of traditional canons of literature and of traditional literary studies. On the other hand, there are critical arguments that what counts most is not what you read but the way that you read it. You might as well study *King Kong* as *King Lear*, because what matters is not the script involved but the critical or ideological insights emergent from your reading of whatever it is you are reading. Reviewing a ground-breaking collection of essays arguing in favour of cultural studies (Widdowson (1982), *Re-Reading English*), the poet Tom Paulin gave the following account of the central issues involved in the debate:

> The contributors are collectively of the opinion that English liter-
> ature is a dying subject and they argue that it can be revived by
> adopting a 'socialist pedagogy' and introducing into the syllabus

105

'I thought you said King Lear . . .'

'other forms of writing and cultural production than the canon of literature' . . . it is now time to challenge 'hierarchical' and 'elitist' conceptions of literature and to demolish the bourgeois ideology which has been 'naturalised' as literary value. . . . They wish to develop 'a politics of reading' and to redefine the term 'text' in order to admit newspaper reports, songs, and even mass demonstrations as subjects for tutorial discussion. Texts no longer have to be books: indeed, 'it may be more democratic to study *Coronation Street* [England's most popular soap opera] than *Middlemarch*'.
                    (*The London Review of Books* (1982), 17–30 June, p. 14)

However one looks at these arguments, it seems indisputably true that the issues involved are of paramount critical, pedagogical and social importance. There are, however, any number of different ways to look at the various arguments. So far as I am professionally concerned, they raise the central question, 'Why should any of us still study, or teach, Shakespeare's plays (or *Paradise Lost* or *The Canterbury Tales*)?' After all, there are quite enough films, plays, novels and poems being produced today, to say nothing about 'other forms of writing', including literary criticism, to satisfy anyone interested either in 'high literature' or in popular genres, or any form of 'cultural production' whatsoever. They also raise the obviously reflexive question, 'Assuming that all traditionally "canonised" works were eliminated, overnight, from the syllabus of every English department in the world, would not comparable problems of priority, value, élitism, ideological pressure, authoritarianism and arbitrariness likewise arise with reference to *whatever* works, of whatsoever kind and nature, were substituted for them?'

If, for instance, the place on the syllabus currently assigned to *King Lear* were reassigned to *King Kong*, those of us presently debating the relative merits of the Quarto, the Folio or a conflated version of *King Lear* would, *mutatis mutandis*, have to decide whether to concentrate classroom attention on Merian F. Cooper's original version of *King Kong* (1933) or to focus on the 1976 remake, which by now has a cult following of its own (Scheuer (1988), p. 425): 'While this version doesn't deliver the thrills and the suspense of the original, it remains an oddly effective fable with a romantic sweep and lushness not attempted in the action-oriented classic of 1933. More a bizarre love story than an epic adventure.' Although classroom time might not allow the inclusion of both, a decision to exclude either version might well seem arbitrary or authoritarian and so give rise to grumbles about the 'canon'. Moreover, comparable questions of 'canonisation' might well arise with reference to other films excluded from a syllabus that included either, or both versions, of *King Kong*. For example, why assign time to *King Kong* and not to a comparable film, *Slave Girls of the White Rhinoceros* (compare also the classical legend of the Minotaur) wherein a beast is likewise worshipped in the jungle and beautiful girls are offered up to him (see Medved and Medved (1986), p. 164): 'In a civilization dominated by sadistic brunettes, all blondes become the helpless Slave Girls of the White Rhinoceros'. According to its *auteur*, the tragic conflict between blondes and brunettes was intended as an allegory on 'the futility of racism'. Although the Medved brothers did not award *The Slave Girls* their prize for the worst male chauvinist fantasy ever filmed, it was an obvious contender. Yet who, if any one of us, ultimately has the right to decide whether *King Lear, King Kong* or this film should, or should not, be included on or excluded from the syllabus? And can the decision to include or exclude any one of them be made by any one of us, on any grounds whatsoever that do *not* have to do with comparative aesthetic merit or comparative value judgements, or with special interests – that is, with the ideological priorities, personal preferences and prejudices of the assigners of positions on whatever syllabus there is? And in so far as most, if not all our judgements and preferences are comparative, are they not inevitably hierarchical?

Like sports, all arts can be seen as democratic in so far as artistic ability, like athletic ability, knows no class distinctions. On the other

hand, sports and arts alike can be seen as profoundly élitist, as genetically determined, and thus in one sense hereditary aristocracies, since
some people are born with great natural talent or ability and others
are not. No amount of effort or training or wealth could make
Florence Foster Jenkins sing like Kiri Te Kanawa. Looked at from
this angle, it is hard to see how 'great' literature is any more or less of
an artificially imposed category than the superstar status afforded by
people who especially enjoy the kind of thing they do to certain
athletes and composers and artists (like Hank Williams or Bob Dylan
or Miles Davis or Elvis Presley or Loretta Lynn). And what about
the canonisation of certain critical theorists as opposed to others?
Arguments objecting to the canonisation of Shakespeare and to the
tyranny of 'author-ity' often contain appeals to the critical authority
of surnames intoned like those of saints: instead of, say, 'just
Marlowe' we have 'just Lacan', or 'Derrida' or 'Foucault'. So what
else is new?

Is there, in fact, any form of endeavour or accomplishment known
to the human race, from sport to ballet to jazz to cooking, wherein
comparative standards of status comparable to certain 'hierarchical'
and 'élitist' conceptions of literature are non-existent? Comparable
degrees of connoisseurship are involved in the ranking accorded jazz
performers by jazz buffs, critical theorists by theory buffs and
country and western singers by their fans, just as successive
audiences, actors, playwrights and directors have acclaimed the
comparatively low-born Shakespeare above the aristocratic authors
of *Gorboduc*; and successive musicians, conductors, and audiences
have preferred the works of the foul-mouthed Mozart to those of the
genteel Salieri. Even bad film buffs find certain bad films more
gloriously awful than others. And, perhaps significantly, given its
comparatively short lifetime, the cinema has, by now, produced
snobs to rival the most élitist literary critic who ever lived, such as the
one who thus puts down a friend who likes ordinary Hollywood
films:

> Ah that's all right for you. I know the sort you are, but give me a
> private job that's shot on faded sepia sixteen millimetre stock with
> non-professional actors . . . no story and dialogue in French *any day
> of the week*.
>   (*The Best of Myles*, by Flann O'Brien, as quoted by Griffen
>   (1982) in *The Small Oxford Book of Snobs*, p. 59)

What is striking about the snobbish assumption parodied here is how
characteristic it is of a long tradition of critical élitism that has
consistently sneered at popular genres (e.g. romance fiction, soap
operas, horror films, westerns, etc.) as well as works popular with

'bourgeois' audiences, that are tainted by the profit motive and tend to 'give the public what it wants' in the way of sentimentality, sensationalism, sex, violence, romanticism and the like. And, dramatically speaking, the fact is that Shakespeare's art can be critically categorised as 'good' or 'bad' – or attacked and defended – in the same ways and for the same reasons that virtually any popular Hollywood film, such as *King Kong*, can be categorised as 'good' or 'bad' in comparison with that 'private job' shot on faded sepia sixteen-millimetre stock.

These and other related issues will get more detailed discussion later on, but it should be stressed here that the crucially important questions why certain works of art should, or should not, be forced on our students cannot really be answered by flinging charges of élitism back and forth at each other. For that matter, one could posit the argument (as Gore Vidal does in his essay on the Oz books) that the surest way to destroy the popular status of any given work might well be to put it on the syllabus and thus create an instant hostility to it on the part of unwilling students: 'Is it possible that Baum's survival is due to the fact that he is *not* taught? That he is not, officially, Literature? If so, one must be careful not to murder Oz with exegesis' (Vidal (1983), p. 76). You could likewise argue that one major distinction between 'popular' art forms and academically 'canonised' works could be that fans of popular art and artists engage in their connoisseurship or scholarship voluntarily, and not in school. But the energies that go into the voluntary reading and writing of journals such as *Station Gamma One* (devoted to *Star Trek*), *Elvisly Yours* and *Downbeat* are the same ones that go into (or once went into) the reading and writing of books and articles devoted to the most popular authors in the canon – as labours of love. But in any event, very like the status of an athlete, the comparative ranking of an individual artist or work of art in the hierarchy of admiration is determined by the kind of people who most enjoy watching or performing in or practising or reading about the same kind of thing – whether that thing be sport, or jazz, or dramatic literature. And of course the kind of things that we may, subsequently, most enjoy watching or reading or writing about in later years may well depend on what we most vividly remember having enjoyed as children or adolescents whether watching films such as *King Kong*, or TV shows such as *Star Trek*, or videos such as *Thriller*, or while reading stories such as the Oz books, or *Lord of the Rings* for no other purpose but pleasure.

Conversely, in his biographically based book on the way 'higher education has failed democracy and impoverished the souls of today's students' (*The Closing of the American Mind* (1987)), Allan Bloom argues that, in an America 'where tradition is not privileged' and the 'Great Books' are no longer reverently read, there *is* no 'relation between popular culture and high culture', since 'the former is all that is now influential on our scene' (pp. 322, 353). Given the political as well as the educational reverberations of these and other assertions in Bloom's ultra-conservative bestseller, it is worth stressing the historical fact that Shakespeare entered the mainstream of the American literary tradition not at the top – with the Founding Fathers or in the élite, Eastern centres of learning that Bloom extols – but from the bottom. For that matter, as Alistair Cooke has observed,

> There is no need to wonder what the Founders of New England thought about Shakespeare. They didn't. In all the Colonial literature of the seventeenth century there is not, I believe, a single allusion to him. Harvard College showed its usual enlightenment by acquiring its first copy of Shakespeare in 1723, 87 years after its founding. . . . New England as a Shakespearean desert may well be explained by the Puritans' intense obsession with theological literature, by their moral authoritarianism, which banished plays and players as summarily as Cromwell had done. As late as 1686, Cotton Mather was alarmed by what he called 'much discourse of beginning stage plays'. . . . It took, indeed, about sixty years for the Republic to welcome Shakespearean productions, and not until the mid-nineteenth century did it spawn its first native Shakespearean actor (the son of an immigrant London actor) in Edwin Booth. Even then, Mrs Trollope was shocked to find that in the more civilized cities, Shakespeare was thought to be obscene; which is not surprising now when you consider that for the thirty years or so before the Civil War, literate Americans were brought up on Noah Webster's authorized version of the Bible, in which 'to go whoring' was replaced by 'go astray'.
>
> ('Shakespeare in America', pp. 18–19)

'It comes then', Cooke notes, 'as a surprise – to me, at any rate – to find that the first *popularization* of Shakespeare happened far from the Eastern cities or seats of learning.' It came from strolling players who followed the flatboats floating down the Allegheny and rode into the rowdier pioneer towns springing up around and across the Appalachians: 'Actors . . . were generally regarded as vagabonds, chronic debtors, and sexual fly-by-nights. And the expanding frontier was a wonderful wide place to perform in, pick up the box-office receipts, and get lost before descending on another settlement that could be counted on to be gullible – for one night.'

But where did these vagabonds get their knowledge of Shakespeare? The real infusion of Shakespeare's art into the American literary tradition began around 1835, when a schoolteacher named

William Holmes McGuffey published two school readers designed to
introduce children in rural schools to the best models of their own
language.

> They were bought in job lots and used as basic English textbooks in
> the very elementary schools of the empire of the Mississippi and the
> South. In the sixth edition there were 138 selections from over a
> hundred authors, and Shakespeare was the preferred author of choice
> with nine extracts. Time and time again the memoirs of pioneers
> across three thousand miles are studded with saws and instances
> from the Bible, *Pilgrim's Progress*, and Shakespeare. Children in log
> huts who could only imagine New York or London and who, unlike
> the divines of New England, had never heard of Rousseau or
> Goethe, could – unlike the divines of New England – yet quote
> Hamlet and recite the Fall of Wolsey. For the distribution of the
> McGuffey readers stopped short of New England. Everywhere else,
> the readers sold, at the last count, something like 200 million copies.

And so, 'while Boston and Philadelphia were honouring Shakespeare
in the breach', the Republic's enduring association with the Bard was
established by 'such genteel, florid scoundrels as the type of W. C.
Fields', or the king and the duke in *Huckleberry Finn*, who were
always one step ahead of the bailiffs. And who had shrewdly
observed that their audiences on the rivers and the prairie quite
naturally wanted to know where Wolsey had fallen from and why
Henry V got so excited at Agincourt. They also made the crucial
discovery that, once Shakespeare had been thoroughly dinned into
everybody's mind 'as the grandest figure of the literary Establishment, he was – like other grandees of the Establishment – fair game
for burlesque' (Cooke, pp. 19–20). And so you can track send-ups of
Shakespeare through the comic tradition in America from Mark
Twain to Thurber's 'The Macbeth Murder Mystery' to Jack Benny
(in 1942) and Mel Brooks (in 1984) who, in turn, presented
'Highlights from Hamlet' as the ham actor-manager in *To Be Or Not
To Be*.

As Bloom observes, it is obviously true that most American
students today are not, from early childhood, very well schooled in
the Greek and Roman classics, the Bible and Shakespeare. Yet neither
were very many of their forebears, whose experience of the Great
Books, as such, was limited to whatever wise saws from Shakespeare
and Bunyan they remembered from McGuffey's readers, and/or
more pleasurably derived from popular performances and burlesques
of Shakespeare's scripts, of which the following soliloquy, so
unforgettably rendered by 'the duke' that it 'just knocked the spots
out of any acting that ever *I* see before' is, of course, the perfect
amalgam (*Huckleberry Finn*, 1955 [first published 1884] pp. 158–9):

To be or not to be; that is the bare bodkin
That makes calamity of so long life;
For who would fardels bear, till Birnam Wood do come to
                                                    Dunsinane,
But that the fear of something after death
Murders the innocent sleep,
Great nature's second course,
And makes us rather sling the arrows of outrageous fortune
Than fly to others that we know not of.
There's the respect must give us pause;
Wake Duncan with thy knocking! I wish thou couldst;
For who would bear the whips and scorns of time,
The oppressor's wrong, the proud man's contumely,
The law's delay, and the quietus which his pangs might take,
In the dead waste and middle of the night, when churchyards
                                                    yawn,
In customary suits of solemn black,
But that the undiscovered country from whose bourne no
                                              traveller returns,
Breathes forth contagion on the world,
And thus the native hue of resolution, like the poor cat
                                                i' the adage,
Is sicklied o'er with care,
And all the clouds that lowered o'er our housetops,
With this regard their currents turn awry,
And lose the name of action.
'Tis a consummation devoutly to be wished. But soft you, the
                                              fair Ophelia;
Ope not thy ponderous and marble jaws,
But get thee to a nunnery – go!

Nor were students very much more meaningfully versed in the works of Shakespeare in the fifties, which Bloom describes as a golden age in American education. If he was there then, so was I, and (biographically speaking) the foundations of my subsequent interest in Shakespearian drama and 'high' art generally were laid, not by prescribed texts, but in the comparable imaginative pleasures derived in the extra-curricular time I spent reading fantasies such as the Oz books and going to shows. In terms of chronology, this chapter would be most accurately entitled 'From *King Kong* to *King Lear* and back' since I loved, and wept while watching, the majestic and terrifying African King enchained and humiliated, then defying the airplanes and trying to save the little heroine, years before I had ever heard of *King Lear*. Yet it was upon watching the original film of *King Kong* that I first felt I was seeing 'A sight most pitiful in the meanest wretch,/Past speaking of in a King!' (*King Lear* IV, vi, 204–5). And that is not the worst way for a ten-year-old to experience, firsthand, what Aristotle meant when he described the combined emotions of pity and terror characteristic of high tragedy. By now, I cannot remember the original version of *King Kong* without thinking of *King Lear* ('Howl, howl, howl, howl'). And today I can't think of either King without remembering the connection Karen Blixen made between Shakespeare's tragedy and the real-life tragedy of the natives and animals she describes in *Out of Africa* (1964), pp. 404–5:

> All my life I have held that you can class people according to how they may be imagined behaving to King Lear. You could not reason with King Lear, any more than with an old Kikuyu, and from the first he demanded too much of everybody; but he was a king. It is true that the African Native has not handed over his country to the white man in a magnificent gesture, so that the case is in some ways different from that of the old king and his daughters; the white men took over the country as a Protectorate. But I bore in mind that not very long ago, at a time that could still be remembered, the Natives of the country had held their land undisputed, and had never heard of the white men and their laws. . . . Some of them were carried off by the slave-traders and were sold at slave-markets but some of them always remained. . . . The old dark clear-eyed Native of Africa, and the old dark clear-eyed Elephant, – they are alike. . . . Either one of the two might find himself quite perplexed by the sight of the great changes that are going on all around him, and might [like King Lear] ask you where he was, and you would have to answer him in the words of Kent: 'in your own kingdom, Sir'.

The insights that works deemed 'high' art (such as *King Lear*) or popular films (such as *King Kong*) or memoirs (such as *Out of Africa*) give us into other works of art would seem to fade to insignificance in comparison with their extensions of our sympathies or the insights they afford us into life. But they can also illuminate each other. It is not the artistic tradition but the academic tradition that has erected barriers between 'high art' and popular genres, even as it has erected barricades between art and life. The artistic tradition (popular as well as exalted) tends to break all such barriers down, even as in the last analysis it is the artists (popular as well as exalted) who create the extra-generic, extra-curricular, extra-temporal and international canons of art.

For instance, in the middle of Cole Porter's *Kiss Me, Kate*, a couple of tap-dancing gangsters stop the show to give the following advice to male members of the audience:

> Brush up your Shakespeare,
> Start quoting him now.
> Brush up your Shakespeare
> And the women you will wow.

Rather like Kenneth Burke (see p. 94 above), Cole Porter's hoods clearly see 'high' literature as an eminently practical equipment for living. And this is a view with which Shakespeare himself would certainly concur: 'Learning is but an adjunct to ourself,/And where we are our learning likewise is' (*Love's Labour's Lost*, IV, iii, 310–11). He would also have concurred with the gangster's view about rhetorically wowing the ladies – see *The Two Gentlemen of Verona*, III, i, 104–5 – 'That man that hath a tongue I say is no man/If with his tongue he cannot win a woman.' But so far as both 'high' art and popular genres are concerned, what is especially interesting here is that the advice, 'Brush up your Shakespeare', seems equally applicable to anyone who wants to 'wow' the women (just as Richard III wowed Lady Anne) and to someone who wants to wow an audience at a Broadway musical. Cole Porter, for instance, obviously took his own advice. He not only brushed up his Shakespeare in the writing of his Broadway version of *The Taming of the Shrew*; he started quoting him at the outset, in the title *Kiss Me, Kate*. And of course the same process occurs throughout the Bernstein–Robbins–Sondheim *West Side Story* of *Romeo and Juliet*, wherein their teenage heroine derives her best-known lyric, 'Tonight, tonight, I'll see my love tonight' from Juliet's own most lyrical lines, 'Come night, come Romeo . . . come loving, black-browed night.' The same feelings are felt, and communicated, in both – and so is the same rhythmical heartbeat.

As Leonard Bernstein observed in a television interview some years ago, the pulse of the mightiest lines of English verse – the iambic pentameter of Marlowe, Shakespeare, and Milton – also throbs through Dixieland jazz (as well as the song from *West Side Story*). Any regular iambic pentameter line can be set to 'St. Louis Blues':

> Ĭ hàte tŏ sèe tℎe eˇv'nĭng sùn gŏ dòwn.
> Tonìght, tonìght, I'll sèe m̌y lòve tonìght.
> Cŏme gèntle nìght, cŏme lòving, blàck-brŏwed nìght.

T. S. Eliot, of course, caught the jazz connection in his own line, 'Ŏ Ŏ Ŏ Ŏ thăt Shàkespĕheriăn Ràg.'[1] Walt Disney, along with Michael Jackson and Vincent Price (in 'The Thriller Rap'), apparently preferred the four-beat line that Shakespeare had, for once and for all, both rhythmically and dramatically associated with magical incantations. Compare, for instance:

> Whèn shăll wè thrĕe mèet ăgàin?
> Iň thùndĕr, lìghtnĭng, òr iň ràin?

(Macbeth, I, i, 1–2)

> Aňd grìzzlў ghòsts from èvĕry tòmb
> Aře clòsiňg iň tŏ sèal yoŭr dòom.

('The Thriller Rap')

Whèn hĭs lȯve hĕ dotḣ ĕspẏ,
Lèt hĕr shìne ăs glòriŏusly
Ås thĕ Venŭs òf thĕ skẏ.

(A Midsummer Night's Dream, III, ii, 105-7)

Mĭrrŏr, ṁirrŏr oṅ thĕ wàll,
Ẇho's thĕ fàireṡt òf uŝ all?
Hĕr lìṗs lĭke blòod,
Hĕr hàir lĭke nìght,
Hĕr skìn lĭke sṅow,
Hĕr nàme, Snŏw Ẇhite.

(Snow White)

In Shakespeare's *Cymbeline*, the treatment of the fair heroine by her wicked stepmother, in turn, has obvious associations with the fairy tale, 'Snow White'. Visually, however (so goes the process of cross-breeding), the Wicked Queen in Disney's *Snow White* is a perfect cartoon-version of Lady Macbeth, while the recipe for the witch's brew that turned her into a hag was clearly inherited from her Shakespearian precursors. But the most amusing of all dramatic connections between Walt Disney and Shakespeare is described in Laurence Olivier's book *On Acting* (1986), p. 85. For his legendary performance as the wicked King, *Richard III*, Olivier based his makeup and mannerisms on an American theatre entrepreneur called Jed Harris, 'the most loathsome man I'd ever met'. Harris was 'apparently equally loathed' by the artist who had used him as the model for the Big Bad Wolf in the Disney cartoon of *The Three Little Pigs*. Thus, Olivier's Richard III bears an uncanny resemblance to the Big Bad Wolf – and vice versa – and so the loathsome Jed Harris has achieved a kind of immortality in art.

Nothing could be easier than to demonstrate on the basis of these and other examples that neither innumerable popular works, nor subsequent works of 'high literature', would exist as we know them if Shakespeare had never written. No other author has been the cause of so much wit in others. It's as if the nature – the subsequent evolution – of the Anglo-American artistic tradition, rather like the 'dyer's hand' in Sonnet 111, has been indelibly coloured by Shakespeare's art; or, rather, as if Shakespeare's hand has permanently coloured the multitudinous seas of subsequent art. For instance, the interrogation of Cinna the Poet in *Julius Caesar* seems, in its combination of absurdity and terror, to anticipate the interrogation of Stanley Webber by Goldberg and McCann in Harold Pinter's *The Birthday Party*:

1 PLEBEIAN What is your name?
2 PLEBEIAN. Whither are you going?

3 PLEBEIAN. Where do you dwell?
4 PLEBEIAN. Are you a married man or a bachelor?
2 PLEBEIAN. Answer every man directly.
1 PLEBEIAN. Ay, and briefly.
4 PLEBEIAN. Ay, and wisely.
3 PLEBEIAN. Ay, and truly, you were best.
CINNA. What is my name? Whither am I going? Where do I dwell?
 Am I a married man or a bachelor? Then to answer every man
 directly and briefly, wisely and truly; wisely, I say I am a
 bachelor.
2 PLEBEIAN. That's as much to say as they are fools that marry.
 You'll bear me a bang for that, I fear. Proceed directly.
CINNA. Directly, I am going to Caesar's funeral.
2 PLEBEIAN. As a friend or an enemy?
CINNA. As a friend.
4 PLEBEIAN. For your dwelling – briefly.
CINNA. Briefly, I dwell by the Capitol.
3 PLEBEIAN. Your name, sir, truly.
CINNA. Truly, my name is Cinna.
1 PLEBEIAN. Tear him to pieces; he's a conspirator!
CINNA. I am Cinna the poet, I am Cinna the poet.
4 PLEBEIAN. Tear him for his bad verses, tear him for his bad verses!
CINNA. I am not Cinna the conspirator.
4 PLEBEIAN. It is no matter, his name's Cinna; pluck but his name
 out of his heart and turn him going.
(Julius Caesar, III, iii, 5–33)

And the interrogation of the comparably hapless Stanley Webber in
turn just as eerily seems to echo the rhythms as well as the menace of
Shakespeare's one-liners:

GOLDBERG. Where was your wife?
STANLEY. In –
GOLDBERG. Answer.
STANLEY. What wife?
GOLDBERG. What have you done with your wife?
McCANN. He's killed his wife!
GOLDBERG. Why did you kill your wife?
STANLEY. What wife? .
GOLDBERG. Why did you never get married? . .
McCANN. Who are you, Webber?
GOLDBERG. What makes you think you exist?
McCANN. You're dead.
GOLDBERG. You're dead. You can't live, you can't think, you can't
 love. You're dead. You're a plague gone bad. There's no juice in
 you. You're nothing but an odour.
(The Birthday Party (1976), pp. 59–62)

'Which came first?' asks Goldberg. 'Chicken? Egg? Which came
first?', asks McCann. 'And which came first? Which came first?
Which came first?', they ask Stanley, together, in a single line (p. 62).

Asking whether Shakespeare seems to be dramatically anticipating Pinter in his Kafkaesque, Beckett-like interrogation scene, or whether Pinter is directly or unconsciously paying homage to Shakespeare (and/or Kafka and Beckett) in his, seem comparably moot questions given the way each brings the other to mind.

Given the current controversy about the academically established 'canon' of English literature, it seems of great importance to stress the obvious historical fact that Shakespeare's artistic place in the sun was – and still is – assured quite independently of any critical or ideological establishment. 'Shine forth, thou Star of Poets, and with rage,/Or influence, chide, or cheer the drooping Stage', wrote Ben Jonson in 1623, and by now there is no numbering the artists, from his own time to the present, who have acted under Shakespeare's influence. If, as John Dryden noted in the Prologue to *The Enchanted Isle* (his own adaptation of *The Tempest*),

> Shakespeare's Magick could not copy'd be,
> Within that Circle none durst walk but he.

that self-same circle has served as the point of departure for works as different as, for instance, Dryden's tragedy, *All for Love*; J. O'Keefe's comedy, *Wild Oats*; Shelley's 'Ariel to Miranda'; Browning's 'Caliban upon Setebos'; Verdi's operas, *Otello* and *Falstaff*; the 'happy-ending' version of *Romeo and Juliet* as performed by the Crummles in *Nicholas Nickelby* and the highlights from Shakespeare's plays that were performed by the king and the duke in *Huckleberry Finn*; the Broadway musicals *The Boys from Syracuse, Kiss Me, Kate* and *West Side Story*; Tom Stoppard's farce *Rosencrantz and Guildenstern are Dead*; the horror film *Theatre of Blood*; the gangster film *Joe Macbeth*; and Kurosawa's Japanese adaptations of *Macbeth* and *King Lear, Throne of Blood* and *Ran*. Indeed, the identical words that Jonathan Bate has used to describe Shakespeare's influence in the Romantic period – 'pervasive', 'ubiquitous' and above all 'Protean' (Bate (1986), pp. 6–21, and see above, p. 101) – are the only accurate words to describe his influence on popular genres as well as 'high' art in the twentieth century: Sting used 'Nothing Like the Sun' as the title of an album, and the Rolling Stones go on about Antony and Cleopatra in 'Blinded by Love'.

I have cited the most obvious examples of the way Shakespeare has influenced modern musicals and will give further examples from science fiction and horror movies, as well as works by Tom Stoppard, John Fowles and Woody Allen, in order to argue that it ought to be – although nowadays it often tends not to be – taken for granted that a firsthand knowledge of Shakespearian drama in particular (and indeed of 'high art' generally) might prove the best of all foundations for a successful career as a popular novelist, or playwright or lyricist, or film producer; and that, *mutatis mutandis*, a knowledge of popular plays and films and novels will inevitably enhance one's understanding and enjoyment of Shakespearian drama. For the fact is that the forces and energies and impacts that account for the status and indeed the survival of an 'immortal' masterpiece are pretty much the same forces and energies and impacts that assure commercial success at the box office in any age.

For that matter, the legendary producer-director, Cecil B. De Mille, looked at the Old and New Testaments themselves as ready made script factories. 'Give me any couple of pages from the Bible', said C. B., 'and I'll give you a picture'. Thus De Mille gave due credit to by all odds the holiest of all his ghost writers, adding, with becoming modesty, that he could neither take the credit nor the blame for his themes: 'I didn't write the Bible and I didn't invent sin' (Halliwell (1978), pp. 89–90). Of course, the Book of Judges will still be reverently read long after De Mille's film version of the story of Sampson and Delilah is forgotten. But the fact remains that the most – if by no means the only – significant difference between what is revered as a work of 'high', and even holy, literature and the latest bestseller or blockbuster hit at the box office is, surely, that the work deemed a classic of its kind has proved to be continuously or sporadically popular and meaningful to readers or audiences or other artists for centuries rather than for weeks, months, or years, just as the comedies and tragedies of Shakespeare have, so far so success-fully, stood and passed the acid test of time: they have been liked better than their competitors by the kind of people who like that kind of thing (audiences, actors, directors, subsequent playwrights, poets, etc.). The same would hold true of a 'classic' jazz recording or country and western recording or an opera. Whatever its kind, any work of art has to compete in an ongoing popularity contest in which its very survival, as well as its status, must finally depend on the quantity and quality of admirers it can attract and keep on attracting.

One can, therefore, predict with as much certainty as one can predict anything that if – for instance – the works of Woody Allen prove comparably popular with audiences and inspiring to other artists over four hundred years, they will inevitably be ranked as classics and studied alongside the works of William Shakespeare by our great-great-grandchildren's grandchildren (assuming, of course, that anyone is then around to study any art at all). Conversely, if or when Shakespeare's comedies and tragedies ever cease to appeal to audiences and readers and artists, they will finally cease to be

reprinted or staged and so they will perish; or perhaps be redis-
covered and reclassified as 'of historical, or academic interest only' to
the kind of scholar who in AD 3000 might publish a learned note on
'The Influence of a Little Known Comedy by William Shakespeare on
Woody Allen's *A Midsummer Night's Sex Comedy*'. In short, Shakespeare's works will be divested of their current status as formula-one
masterpieces precisely in so far as they cease to exert any appeal or
influence in their own right, and so prove unable to stand up to, or win
out against, or to outlast their competitors.

This is why it seemed so patronising, as well as demonstrably
erroneous when, at the International Congress devoted to Shakespeare
as a 'Man of the Theatre' that was held at Stratford-upon-Avon in
1981, several directors and academics stated, as if it were truth beyond
controversy, that because audiences nowadays are too sophisticated to
believe in ghosts, witches, spirits and fairies, modern productions,
necessarily, had to send up or put down or demystify or otherwise
update Shakespeare's supernatural beings in order to make them
palatable to modern theatregoers. For, surely, the idea that modern
audiences are incapable of crediting or enjoying imaginative portrayals
of witches, ghosts, demons, spirits, and magic can be proved false by a
glance at lists of film hits from *Snow White* to *The Wizard of Oz* to
Rosemary's Baby to *The Omen* and *The Return of the Jedi* – which would
seem to suggest that, far from being put off by them, modern audiences
are starved for magic, for mystery, for the paranormal, for demonic
and benevolent beings from elsewhere and, today as yesterday, will
willingly spend their hard-earned money at the box-office to watch
supernatural beings not a whit any less difficult to believe in than the
Ghost in *Hamlet*, the witches in *Macbeth* or Oberon, Ariel or Caliban.

There are, of course, lots of people who read bestsellers and enjoy
modern horror and science fiction films who do not read Shakespeare's
plays and do not go to see Shakespeare productions because they do not
have the chance, or because they find the language difficult, or because
they loathed having *Julius Caesar* force-fed to them in school. But the
reasons why certain people nowadays may not want to see or to read,
say, *Macbeth* or *Hamlet* or *A Midsummer Night's Dream* or *The Tempest*
surely have little, if anything, to do with the fact that these particular
plays have supernatural beings in them, since virtually identical types of
characters abound in films that they do go to see and, perhaps more
significantly, take their children to see. Indeed, by now the odds are
very good that, regardless of their education, their age or their class,
most people who make up the audiences at performances of Shakespeare's plays and at modern films alike have, so far as their enjoyment of
the drama is concerned, cut their teeth on horror films and science fiction

films, from the original *King Kong* and the Bela Lugosi *Dracula* on
through *Star Wars* and *E.T.* By now there are whole cohorts of
thoroughly modern playgoers and cinemagoers on both sides of the
Atlantic who spent their childhoods watching *Star Trek*; and heaven
only knows how many episodes of that ever-popular series – such as
'The Conscience of the King' (*Hamlet*), 'A Dagger of the Mind'
(*Macbeth*) and 'Requiem for Methuselah' (*The Tempest*) – were directly
or indirectly derived from Shakespeare's plays, along with other equally
fantastical classics of imaginative literature such as Swift's *Gulliver's
Travels* and Milton's *Paradise Lost* (see the episode entitled 'The Apple').
In *Star Trek* the ultra-rational Mr Spock is the Vulcanian counterpart of
a Swiftian Houyhnhnm lord, even as Darth Vader is a descendant of
Milton's Satan who was, after all, the one who started, and for all we
know may yet win, the most crucial of all '*Star Wars*'.

By very much the same token, Shakespeare's 'spirits of a gentler
sort', such as Puck and Ariel, have most recently been reincarnated as
R2D2 and C-3PO, just as Prospero is the prototype of Obi-Wan
Kenobi – 'The Force' is with them both. For that matter George
Lucas, the director, has most explicitly acknowledged his indebted-
ness to Joseph Campbell's *The Hero With A Thousand Faces* (first
published in 1949), a book surveying epics from differing cultures
that describes comparable heroes and parallel conflicts and episodes
(the call to adventure; supernatural aid; woman as temptress; the
magic flight; freedom to live; the hero as world redeemer; the hero as
warrior; and so on). This explains why the outline of *Star Wars* has as
many affinities with the story of King Arthur (with its 'chosen' hero,
saviour of the nation and the people, who is ostensibly of humble
birth, tutored by a magus with formidable powers and so on) as it
does with *The Tempest* or *Paradise Lost* – or with Alexander Korda's
classic adventure film *The Thief of Bagdad*, which was of course based
on *The Arabian Nights*, a work edited by none other than Joseph
Campbell. There are comparably obvious affinities between J. R. R.
Tolkien's tremendously popular *The Lord of the Rings* and works of
'high' literature which he himself had taught and edited and, consequently, had done a great deal to popularise, such as *Beowulf* – see
Tolkien's famous essay on 'The Monsters and the Critics' (1936) –
and *Gawain and the Green Knight*. Tolkien's friend, C. S. Lewis, was
likewise indebted to Milton and Spenser in his popular works such as
Perelandra and *That Hideous Strength*. And such are the ways of
retrospective influences, retroactive recognition and compound interest that modern students on both sides of the Atlantic who have
especially enjoyed *Star Wars*, *Star Trek*, *The Chronicles of Narnia* and
Lord of the Rings often find the 'original' works to which their

favourite modern authors (or *auteurs*) were so conspicuously indebted at least as, if not even more enjoyable than, their twentieth-century successors. Thus differing works of differing genres and differing eras tend, either directly or indirectly, to derive imaginative impact from, at the same time they pay artistic tribute to, each other.

One could go on and on about the processes of cross-fertilisation. For instance, John Fowles's 'Magus', Maurice Conchis, explicitly compares himself to his Shakespearian precursor: 'Prospero will show you his domaine', says Maurice to Fowles's antihero, Nicholas Urfe. 'Prospero had a daughter', observes Nicholas hopefully. 'Prospero had many things', replies Maurice. 'And not all young and beautiful, Mr. Urfe' (Fowles, 1966, p. 73). This Shakespearian allusion adds to Fowles's atmosphere of mystery, magic and suspense just as Bogart's allusion to *The Tempest* at the end of *The Maltese Falcon* haunts the memory of everyone who has seen Huston's film. In cases like these, all competition ceases and various works of art successfully collaborate with each other in enchanting or enlightening or amusing their audience. Thus, an appreciation and understanding of either one will tend to enhance an appreciation and understanding of what is going on in the other. And this holds true no matter which one was written first and no matter which one you, personally, saw or read first. Whichever way you look at them, it is equally easy to trace the relationship between, say, Woody Allen's *A Midsummer Night's Sex Comedy*, Ingmar Bergman's *Smiles of a Summer Night* and its musical version, Sondheim's *A Little Night Music* and Shakespeare's *A Midsummer Night's Dream*.

The chronological ordering of the title of this chapter, 'From *King Lear* to *King Kong* and back' was nevertheless mandated by the very same reasons why an American student, who was particularly interested in modern literature, said that he had been so impressed by Shakespeare. In so many forms of dramatic construction, character types and comic and tragic effects, 'He was the one who got there first'.

IN PARTICULAR

I wonder where my easy rider's gone,
Oh, I wonder where my easy rider's gone!
Mae West, singing 'Easy Rider' in *She Done Him Wrong* (1933)

CLEOPATRA.   O Charmian,
Where think'st thou he is now? Stands he or sits he?

Or does he walk? Or is he on his horse?
O happy horse, to bear the weight of Antony!
          Shakespeare, *Antony and Cleopatra*, I. v. 18–21 (*c.* 1606)

If one can imagine 'Macbeth', 'The Wolf Man', 'The Addams
Family' and 'Easy Rider' in one stew, this is it.
          Variety review of *Werewolves on Wheels* (1971)

*   *   *   *

By now we are so used to pitiable werewolves, sympathetic monsters
and compassionately portrayed criminals that it is worth noting that,
within the English dramatic tradition Shakespeare virtually initiated
the comparatively compassionate, as opposed to the simply ludicrous
or melodramatically villainous portrayals of aliens, outcasts, criminals, disreputable women and other traditionally anathematised
types. For the fact is that, whether or not characters such as Caliban
and Shylock were originally intended by Shakespeare to evoke
sympathy from the audience, as any actor knows (and Shakespeare
was a professional actor as well as a playwright) they can be played in
such a way as to compel it. Caliban, who had dreams so beautiful that
when he woke he cried to dream again, can thus be seen as a dramatic
precursor of countless beauty-loving monsters including the Hunch-
back of Notre Dame and the Phantom of the Opera as well as the
Creature from the Black Lagoon and Kong. Other archetypal
elements in Shakespearian drama likewise contribute to the enduring
appeal of his plays and so does the bravura treatment of sheer villainy.
Shakespeare's Richard III, 'the man you love to hate', who can smile,
and murder while he smiles and sets the murderous Machiavel to
school, is clearly the Elizabethan ancestor of J. R. Ewing, whose
seductions and connings of Sue Ellen, Bobby, Cliff Barnes and
everybody else in *Dallas* are directly analogous to the seductions and
connings of Lady Anne, Clarence and various other losers in *Richard
III*. So far as Shakespeare's most gruesome portrayals of cruelty are
concerned, it is hard to think of a critical or moral attack on the
sadism, mutilation and violence currently portrayed in X-rated films
and videos that could not be levelled against *Titus Andronicus*, which
(it could go without saying) was, in its own day, extremely popular.
And it could be that the stereotype of the ineffectual intellectual had
its origins in nineteenth century interpretations of Hamlet as a man
who could not make up his mind, just as Shakespeare's sparring
lovers, Kate and Petruchio, and Beatrice and Benedick foreshadow
the way Spencer Tracy and Katherine Hepburn work their way
through combat to kisses in so many films.

One could argue, on the basis of these and countless other examples, that Shakespeare's plays would necessarily have to be required reading for practically any course in the historical origins of popular modern genres. For that matter, some of Shakespeare's methods have proved of more obvious use to popular, than to élitist, writers. For although he, himself, never appears to have been inhibited by any considerations of due decorum and good taste, Shakespeare invariably knew a sure-fire dramatic situation when he saw one. 'Come to my bed', says Angelo to Isabella, 'or I'll have your brother killed.' 'Come to my bed', said J.R. to Sue Ellen in *Dallas*, 'or I'll have your innocent young lover jailed on a drug charge.'

As Julie Burchill has noted, the modern TV soap-opera is the '*nouveau riche*' relation of high drama, as 'vulgar and vital as all get out' (*Girls on Film*, p. 189). And anyone familiar with (for instance) *Measure for Measure* will know that nothing could be easier than to chart the lurid, cliffhanging, mission-impossible, how-will-the-characters-get-out-of-this-mess format of questions raised in (shall we say?) the continuing saga of '*Vienna*': Episode 1. Will Isabella yield her body up to Angelo? If not, will Claudio die? Episode 2. Will the bed-trick played on Angelo succeed? If so, will Angelo pardon Claudio? Episode 3. Since Angelo breaks his word and refuses to pardon Claudio, how will the Duke save poor Claudio from the executioner's axe? Will he allow Barnardine to die? Episode 4. When will the Duke make his power known? Will Isabella pardon Angelo for Mariana's sake? Will the Duke really have Lucio whipped and hanged? Will Isabella accept the Duke's proposal? Will Mariana find true happiness with Angelo? Will Isabella find true happiness as a Duchess? Although the action of *Measure for Measure* is condensed into under three hours and the action of a soap-opera can be extended *ad infinitum*, it is probably best to play each episode and each character in *Measure for Measure* for maximum dramatic impact as they would be portrayed in a soap-opera. After all, its dramatic life may depend as much on its sensational, lurid, cliffhanging qualities as the commercial success of a popular soap-opera. Or the success of the kind of episodic novel ('Will little Nell die?') from which the structure of the soap-opera descended to keep modern audiences coming back for more. It can thus be argued that the affinities – not the lack of affinities – between Shakespeare's plays and popular genres like romances, revenge-films and soap-operas account for their primary appeal to any audience. But, of course, Shakespeare's greatest plays have other qualities as well.

As I believe a brief account of the obvious similarities, and the most significant differences, between *Macbeth* and a justifiably famous horror film can serve to illustrate, whatever differences there are between a masterpiece that will live on for centuries to come and a TV potboiler whose impact will not outlast the night on which one watched it, these differences must, necessarily, have to do with the quality and validity of the insights they contain, as well as the power (the eloquence, the wit, the beauty, the terror) with which those insights are communicated to the audience. For the differences clearly have nothing whatsoever to do with their genre, their origins or their raw materials – or their subject matter – all of which may be identical.

An unforgettable experience of pity and terror shared by everyone who saw it at an early and impressionable age was evoked by the original werewolf movie *The Wolf Man* (1941), starring Lon Chaney, Jr, as a man who had been attacked by what appeared to be a wolf. Soon after, we in the audience, along with the horrified hero, were informed by an old woman that, ever after, when the moon was full, he would turn into a werewolf:

> Even a man who is pure at heart
> And says his prayers by night
> Can become a wolf when the wolfbane blooms
> And the moon is shining bright.

As the moon rose we – and he – watched with horror as the mutation began and the wolf fur started to grow on his hands and face. The force compelling the mutation was indeed inexorable and subsequently drove him to commit murder after murder. The only way the werewolf himself could be killed was with a silver-tipped cane displaying the head of a wolf and the design of a pentagon. This is essentially the same movement that occurs in *Macbeth*. But before going on to discuss the structural and thematic similarities, it should be observed that, as the *Variety* review of *Werewolves on Wheels* (1971) quoted on p. 122 so eloquently testifies, the line of succession between *Macbeth* and werewolf films moves on and on through time, even as the lycanthropic hero of *An American Werewolf in London* (1981) himself most vividly remembered having seen the original werewolf movie under discussion here.

At the beginning of Shakespeare's tragedy Macbeth is, as a result of the witches' prophecies, bitten and infected by the external–internal werewolf of ambition and inexorably mutates into a monster. Subsequently driven to commit murder after murder Macbeth, like the hero-victim-villain of *The Wolf Man*, looks on *himself* as if he were an alien creature:

> What hands are here? Ha! they pluck out mine eyes.

To know my deed, 'twere best not know myself.

Had I but died an hour before this chance,
I had lived a blessed time.

                Better be with the dead,
Whom we, to gain our peace, have sent to peace.
Than on the torture of the mind to lie,
In restless ecstasy.
                    (*Macbeth*, II, ii, 59, 73; II, iii, 89–90;
                                III, ii, 19–22)

Macbeth thus describes the fate worse than death familiar to all of us from countless horror movies depicting the state of the 'undead' who cannot find peace in life and envy the dead. For Macbeth himself cannot be killed save by the Shakespearian equivalents of a silver-tipped cane displaying the head of a wolf and the design of a pentagon. He cannot die until Birnam Wood comes to Dunsinane; only a man who was 'not of woman born' can kill Macbeth.

Like the werewolf movie, *Macbeth* can be seen as a nightmare image of the way human beings may be victimised, infected, altered and doomed by forces outside their control. Yet *Macbeth*, unlike the werewolf film, can also be seen in moral terms as a Dostoevskian portrayal of crime and punishment even as Macduff, who was 'from his mother's womb untimely ripped' finally avenges his dead wife and children with the force of nemesis. Moreover, Macbeth's tragedy has to do with natural, as well as supernatural forces and solicitations – with political, social, sexual and domestic pressures – as well as with the psychological proclivities of the individual that interact to determine all our destinies. Moreover, the word 'if ' occurs over and over again throughout the play (Rosenberg (1980), pp. 109–17) and the conditional frame of reference seems to imply that things might well have gone in an entirely different way. Without the influence exerted on him by his wife, Macbeth might not have acted on the promptings of the witches (Banquo did not). And if fate would have Macbeth king, it might have crowned him, just as it made him Thane of Cawdor, without his having treacherously murdered anyone. Thus Macbeth affords us, as the werewolf movie does not, a comprehensive account of the complex interaction between psychological, moral, social and domestic pressures and circumstances that, in real life, determine the way human beings actually do live and die. It also allows us to observe the way that prophecies and imaginings may play a part in bringing about their own fulfilment in so far as they incite us to act upon them. As the physical anthropologist Loren Eiseley put it in his essay on *Macbeth*, the play passes on to us 'the deadliest message' to be encountered in 'all of literature': 'what we wish will come' (Eiseley (1971), 'Instruments of Darkness', in *The Night Country*, pp. 47–55). What we imagine or are told that we are destined to be may influence the way we behave and thus determine the kind of person we turn out to be and the future we actually get, which may not be what we really wanted at all:

> My way of life
> Is fall'n into the sere, the yellow leaf;
> And that which should accompany old age,
> As honour, love, obedience, troops of friends,
> I must not look to have; but, in their stead,
> Curses not loud but deep, mouth-honour, breath,
> Which the poor heart would fain deny, and dare not.
> (*Macbeth*, V, iii, 22–8)

There is no more powerful reminder than the way things turn out for Macbeth of the tragic ironies with which fate may keep the word of promise to our ear, and break it to our hope.

Yet there is a sure way to defuse the dramatic impact of this tragedy and, in effect, kill *Macbeth* off for once and for all, on stage or in the classroom. And that is to divest it of the aesthetic and emotional qualities that made both it and the original werewolf movie unforgettable to audiences in the first place. One of the most boring theatrical performances in living memory was the production of *Macbeth* at Stratford-upon-Avon in 1982 where the witches were not witches – they were three perfectly ordinary young women passing a piece of cloth back and forth – and Macbeth was portrayed as a dimwit who delivered his lines in a flat monotone and at a snail's pace. Strip either *The Wolf Man* or *Macbeth* of all their metaphysical ramifications; take away their most dramatic 'instruments of darkness'; hold the tragic hero in complete contempt; divest the poetry or the cinematography or the soundtrack or the set of any emotional impact (see Scheuer on 'the mist-laden scenery full of those Universal Studio trees that grow straight into the ground – or floor – without any roots' in *The Wolf Man*), and you will assure that the audience spends a very boring time in the theatre. Brechtian alienation is alien to the spirit of Shakespearian tragedy in that, as in the werewolf movie or the original *King Kong*, the dramatic success of the work depends on evoking primal pity and terror and it is, therefore, designed to engage our emotions by every means at its disposal, including sentimentality, sensationalism and special effects. *Throne of Blood*, Kurosawa's Japanese film adaptation was truer to the spirit of Shakespeare's *Macbeth* than many recent stage productions, and in its wonderfully spooky portrayal of the mists surrounding 'Cobweb Castle' it was reminiscent of the original werewolf film as well.

Because so many stage productions, as well as the generally boring BBC television productions, have tended to desentimentalise, desensationalise, depoeticise, deromanticise and otherwise sanitise Shakespeare's plays in accordance with the ideological interpretations imposed upon them by critics and directors, it is immensely refreshing to have a professional playwright's perspectives on the issues here involved. In a lecture with a title well worth pondering, 'Is It True What They Say About Shakespeare?', Tom Stoppard raises some good questions about certain performances that have disputed Shakespeare's claim to fame as the creator of a 'theatrical event' and not just texts for critical or directorial commentaries. Here is Stoppard's account of a London production of *Hamlet* that de-externalised and updated the Ghost by having its lines come from Hamlet himself:

> In this Royal Court production . . . what happens is that, at the moment where he is brought to the pitch of confronting the Ghost of his father, and at the moment where Shakespeare was ready for the Ghost to utter, Hamlet sinks to his knees and appears to be about to be sick, and an awful retching noise starts coming from his stomach, and lo! the retching becomes the words 'Mark Me!' The duologue takes place between the actor playing Hamlet and a voice, his own distorted voice, being wrenched out of his guts. . . . One might reasonably ask: if the Ghost of Hamlet's father is being wrenched up from Hamlet's stomach, what happens to the scene where the ghost is first seen by Horatio, Marcellus and Bernardo? The answer is perfectly simple in this case: the scene is simply cut and the production begins with the second scene of the play. But this needs to be looked at more carefully. You all recall that first scene: there is a real theatrical excitement about the way the play just kicks off, it goes off like a motor-bike: 'Who's there?' – 'Nay, answer me!' 'Stand and unfold yourself!' 'Long live the King!' – the whole thing is so fast. . . . 'What! Has this thing appeared again tonight?' and, what thing?, we all say, what thing, what thing? But without that scene, we begin with a gathering together of the court, and there is Claudius saying: 'Though yet of Hamlet our dear brother's death/ The memory be green,' and so on. The scene misses that retroactive glance at what we have been shown and . . . I must say I was not surprised to read at least one commentator say that without the first scene the production gets off to a slightly tedious start.
>
> (Stoppard, pp. 5, 8–9)

Samuel Taylor Coleridge saw the first characteristic of Shakespearian drama as a preference for 'expectation over surprise': 'As the feeling with which we startle at a shooting star compared with that of watching the sunrise at the pre-established moment, such and so low is surprise compared with expectation' (Nichol Smith (1916), p. 236). Years later, Alfred Hitchcock made the same distinction between cinematic surprise and suspense. 'Surprise', said Hitchcock, 'is when you show a group of men playing poker in a cellar and a bomb suddenly goes off. Suspense is when you show the audience the bomb ticking away before you show the men sitting down to play poker.' 'There is no terror in a bang,' said Hitchcock. 'Only in the anticipation of it.' Hitchcock, by the way, was well versed in Shakespeare: he got the title *North by Northwest* from *Hamlet* and once caused consternation by muttering the following paraphrase of Lady Macbeth's famous line (V, i, 38) very audibly to a friend in a crowded elevator: 'I didn't think the old man would bleed so much' (Halliwell (1978), p. 90). And there is no question that Shakespeare's usual method is suspense. In effect, he shows the audience the bomb that will go off by having the witches meet the audience before they meet Macbeth, and by having the audience, as well as the soldiers, see the Ghost on the parapet at Elsinore before Hamlet does and so (as the song goes) sets up that 'Shakespearean scene' where 'A Ghost and a Prince meet/And everything ends up mincemeat' ('That's Entertainment').

Here, to illustrate some of these points, is Kenneth Burke's justifiably famous account of the way the master combines suspense with surprise in the dramatic crescendo that climaxes in Hamlet's confrontation with the Ghost:

> It is not until the fourth scene of the first act that Hamlet confronts the ghost of his father. As soon as the situation has been made clear the audience has been, consciously or unconsciously, waiting for this ghost to appear, while in the fourth scene this moment has been definitely promised. . . . Hamlet has arranged to come to the platform at night with Horatio to meet the ghost, and it is now night, he is with Horatio and Marcellus, and they are standing on the platform. Hamlet asks Horatio the hour.
>
> HORATIO. I think it lacks of twelve.
> MARCELLUS. No, it is struck.
> HORATIO. Indeed? I heard it not. It then draws near the season
>   Wherein the spirit held his wont to walk
>
> Promptly hereafter there is a sound off-stage. Hamlet's friends have established the hour as twelve. It is time for the ghost. Sounds off-stage, and of course it is not the ghost. It is, rather, the sound of the king's carousal. . . . A tricky, and useful, detail. We have been waiting for a ghost, and get, startlingly, a blare of trumpets. . . . But the trumpets announcing a carousal have suggested a subject of conversation. In the darkness Hamlet discusses the excessive drinking of his countrymen. He points out that it tends to harm their reputation abroad, since, he argues, this one showy vice makes their virtues 'in the general censure take corruption'. And for this reason, although he is himself a native of the place, he does not approve of the custom. Indeed, there in the gloom he is talking very intelligently on these matters, and Horatio answers, 'Look, my Lord, it comes.' All this time we had been waiting for a ghost, and it comes at the one moment which was not pointing towards it. This

ghost, so assiduously prepared for, is yet a surprise.
                              (Burke (1964), pp. 20–1)

These points are especially interesting with reference to the production of *Hamlet* at the Royal Court Theatre described by Tom
Stoppard. For whatever consistency and power that version of the
confrontation between Hamlet and the Ghost's voice coming from
his own stomach may have had, its impact on the audience had to be
altogether different from the Shakespearian fusion of suspense and
surprise in that every single one of the special effects described by
Burke and Stoppard alike would be lost. For there is no way that any
audience could ask 'What thing?' 'What thing?' during the opening
scene, or that Horatio could announce that it 'draws near the season/
Wherein the spirit held his wont to walk' immediately before the
cannon fires and those trumpets sound in the fourth scene, if the only
spirit in the play is confined to Hamlet's belly.

Discussing the technical problems involved in producing successful
film adaptations of popular novels and Broadway hits, the Hollywood producer David O. Selznick said that he took it for granted that
the audience knew the conventions of the cinema and would accept
the cuts and revisions necessary for a film adaptation of a well-known
novel like *Rebecca* or *Gone With the Wind*. But he warned his
scriptwriters against tampering with what he called the 'chemicals' of
a popular play or novel being adapted for the screen, on the principle
that 'the same elements that drew people to a classic or a Broadway
hit or a best-selling novel would attract them to the movie'. He
therefore vetoed major alterations to the original structure or characterisation, on the grounds that 'No one can certainly pick out the
chemicals which contribute to the making of a classic. And there is
always the danger that by tampering, you may destroy the essential
chemical' (Selznick, as quoted in Flamini (1978), pp. 197–9).

Certain successful works of high, and popular, art alike – whether
by design or by a chance combination of chemicals – do, somehow,
achieve the alchemical change that transforms or transmutes an
audience from witnesses to participants in the tragic or comic
recognition, even as these works transmute their raw materials, which
may be hackneyed old saws, into the pure gold of art. As Tom
Stoppard observed, the transformation of an audience from spectators
to participants was once achieved quite by accident in a production of
Hamlet, wherein 'the Ghost was supposed to be a bright light shining
from the back of the auditorium, and on the night I was there, some
member of the audience unfortunately having to leave the theatre at
that point, got in the way of this light – and a shadow passed over the

audience; and my blood, and I think everybody's blood, went cold' (Stoppard, pp. 4-5).

It is critical and directorial efforts to turn Shakespeare into some kind of non-popular, non-sentimental, non-sensational, anti-heroical, anti-romantic moralist or ideologue that have tampered with, to the point of destroying, the essential chemistry of the Shakespearian properties they are dealing with. By the same token, one could destroy the original *King Kong* or *The Wolf Man*, or a song by the Beatles or Hank Williams or practically any popular work, if one divested it of the rhythm, the sentiments, the special effects, the poetry, the pity or the terror that made it popular to begin with. For, as W. B. Yeats reminds us in a poem appropriately entitled 'The Circus Animals' Desertion', it is a fatal mistake to assume that even the most masterful images of art have their origins in, or make their primary impact on, 'pure mind' or that they can long survive independently of their energy sources in, and their power lines leading up from and back down to, the place where all artistic ladders start, in the 'foul rag-and-bone shop of the heart'. Arguably anyway, aesthetic and emotional impacts have more to do with artistic survival than ideological messages. For that matter, as Karl Marx observed, it is not at all difficult to see any work of art as the product of a given social, historical and technological stage of development or in terms of a reigning ideology. What Marx himself believed it was far more difficult – and far more important – to account for was why Greek art and Shakespearian drama have continued to give succeeding generations such great pleasure and why, to ages and nations in very different stages of social and technological development – as well as in states with dialectically opposite ideologies – they 'still prevail as standards and models beyond attainment' (*Grundrisse*, in *Karl Marx: Selected Writings*, ed. McLellan (1977), 360).

Although, in marked contrast to Shakespeare's plays, critical commentaries rarely outlast the generation for which they were written, Marx's points about seeing works as products of reigning social, historical and ideological premises are manifestly valid with reference to critical discussions of Shakespeare's plays. You can, generally and accurately, categorise a critical interpretation of any given play by Shakespeare according to the critical and ideological paradigms that were dominant at the time when it was written. It is, however, not so easy to see to what degree one's *own* interpretations and reactions to the plays are, likewise, historically determined by critical and ideological vogues. For the fact is that, so long as we disregard any evidence against our own partial view of Shakespeare's scripts (or any other text – see the anti-feminist critical discussions of

The Bostonians, cited by Judith Fetterly) nothing is easier than to re-interpret them in terms of whatever ideology we personally, or professionally or politically or theologically, find especially congenial. Some specific examples of reactionary, liberal and radical interpretations of *Othello* can best serve to illustrate these points.

SHAKESPEARE AND POLITICS

Interpretations of *Othello* well nigh invariably have to do with racial as well as sexual politics. The sexual taboos violated when the young, beautiful and pure white Desdemona deceives and defies her father to marry the black man she loves are so strong that the traditional, extra-textual message of past and present interpretations of this play by white male critics is that (on the one hand) Desdemona got just what was coming to her for desiring and marrying a black man and disobeying her father and/or that (on the other hand) Othello was so sexually insecure (or even impotent) that the marriage would not have worked out even if Iago had never existed. Elaborate attempts are made to defend the 'clear perception of reality' by the character Shakespeare here associates with absolute evil, because so many white male critics agree with Iago about the unsuitability of the match between the black man and the white woman whom Iago himself critically denigrates, in turn, as 'an erring barbarian' and 'a super-subtle Venetian' (I, iii, 354). Writing about *Othello* in his book on *Shakespeare's Politics*, Allan Bloom (for instance) concludes that

> Iago's speeches, read dispassionately, show that he is the clearest thinker in the play. 'Honest Iago' is not merely a tragically misplaced epithet. Iago does tell more of the truth than any character.
>
> (Bloom (1964), p. 63)

According to Bloom, it is only 'a human softness and sentimentality' – i.e. a fuzzy liberalism – and 'our natural partisanship with love and lovers' that 'causes us to see only Iago's wickedness in destroying the love of Othello and Desdemona; we like to believe that, without his intervention, all would have been well.' Therefore, Bloom insists that a 'defence can and must be made' for Iago; although it is hard to say why, *except* in so far as he speaks for a traditionally hierarchical (sexist and racist) ideology that sees Desdemona's defection as the result of a monstrous misconception. 'However indulgently we may look on her love for Othello, there is no question but that she is guilty of disobedience, and her love comes into conflict with most sacred duties.' Thus Bloom defends Iago as the clearest thinker in the play, and sees Desdemona as guilty of offences against 'civil society' that manifestly deserve punishment:

> Desdemona's death is in large measure due to her own errors. They were noble errors which elevated her above the level of ordinary humanity, but they deserved punishment. From the point of view of everyday life, Desdemona sins in deceiving her father. We take her side because she does so in the name of something higher. But perhaps, from a third and highest standpoint, we must come to the defense of civil society and see her defection as the result of a monstrous misconception. Perhaps the true cosmopolitanism can be attained only by renouncing the dearest hopes of practical life. . . [Desdemona] leads a noble life, but one that is against law and against reason.
>
> (Shakespeare's Politics, pp. 61–2).

Looked at historically, it is obvious that when he first published these assertions about *Othello* in 1964, Bloom was expressing the reigning social and sexual orthodoxies of the time in which his book was written. At the very same time that Bloom was making this case for the prosecution of Shakespeare's Desdemona, various courses in 'Mate Selection' were being used to transmit the identical, minatory messages to students in colleges and universities throughout the United States. See, for instance, the following arguments in favour of these 'functional' courses as propounded by one of the 'sex-directed educators' quoted by Betty Friedan in *The Feminine Mystique* (1963), p. 160:

> Kids tend in adolescence to be very idealistic. They think they can acquire a different set of values, marry a boy from a different background, and that it won't matter later on. We make them aware it will matter, so they won't walk so lightly into mixed marriages, and other traps.

As Friedan observed, 'exceptional' cases were 'of no practical concern' to ideologues of this ilk. Although they invariably (and thus as it were scrupulously) acknowledged that 'there are exceptions' ('only the exceptional woman can make a go of a commitment to a career') the 'exceptional' in the jargon of the time bore 'the connotation of handicap'. 'The blind, the crippled, the retarded, the genius, the defier of convention – anyone who is different from the crowd . . . bears a common shame.' They are all 'exceptional' – as 'a mixed marriage is "exceptional".' 'Somehow' Friedan wryly observed, 'the student gets the point that she does not want to be the "exceptional woman".'

Bloom uses the case history of Desdemona to make the very same points: she'd have been ever so much better off if only she had taken a course in Mate Selection, and consequently obeyed her father and stayed within the tribal-patriarchal-racial fold. But alas, Bloom concludes, 'Desdemona never recognizes her error'. 'Unlike Miranda she has no Prospero to guide her imagination and set her on the right course. Her untutored understanding spawns monsters.' Fortunately, however – or so it is strongly implied – enlightened mid-twentieth-century students have commentators such as Bloom to assure that Shakespeare's plays are 'properly read and interpreted' (p. 2). And so, even as Shakespeare's *Othello* is here offered as the Elizabethan equivalent of a crash course in 'Mate Selection', the case history of Desdemona can be used to tutor the imagination of young women, to set them on the right course and to make sure that they do not walk so lightly into mixed marriages and other traps. For that matter, in addition to 'the two major considerations' – 'colour and nation' – which made the match between Desdemona and Othello 'so unsuitable', 'there are age, wealth, and social station'. Their love-match thus disastrously 'differs from conventional marriages supported by money, beauty, and similarity of position and education' (Bloom, p. 43). And so forth and so on. Yet the ultimately overwhelming questions: 'What of it?' '*Apart* from offending the racist sensibilities and sexual prejudices of Brabantio and Iago and certain critical commentators, what conceivable harm, deserving punishment by death, is done to anyone, onstage or off, by Desdemona's love for Othello?' – are never finally answered by Bloom's ideological interpretation of a script which very strongly suggests that the answer to the second question is 'None'.

The fact is that the innumerable, and directly comparable, racist and sexist defamations of the play's hero and heroine alike by white male critics all boil down to facile arguments against miscegenation and for sexual apartheid. Here, for instance, are some historically representative put-downs of the play's black hero (for other examples and for excellent critical arguments against them see Martin Orkin (1987), *Shakespeare Against Apartheid*, pp. 105–17):

1. In 1693, Thomas Rymer jeered at the preposterous absurdity of the love-match between Othello and Desdemona being considered acceptable by the Venetians:

> This [play] may be a caution to all Maidens of Quality how, without their Parents consent, they run away with Blackamoors. . . . With us, a Black-amoor might rise to be a Trumpeter; but Shakespear would not have him less than a Lieutenant-General. With us a Moor

> might marry some little drab, or Small-coal Wench: Shake-speare,
> would provide him the Daughter and Heir of some great Lord, or
> Privy-Councellor; And all the Town should reckon it a very
> suitable match. . . .
>
> (Rymer as quoted in Dean (1961), pp. 107–8)

2. In his lectures on Shakespeare (*c.* 1818), Samuel Taylor Coleridge thought that Othello needed a whitewash in order to make Desdemona's love for him palatable:

> It would be something monstrous to conceive this beautiful
> Venetian girl falling in love with a veritable negro. It would argue a
> disproportionateness, a want of balance in Desdemona, which
> Shakespeare does not appear to have in the least contemplated.
>
> (Nichol Smith (1916), *Shakespeare Criticism*, p. 267)

3. In 1958, the editor of the influential Arden edition of the tragedy conceded that the colour of Othello should be adjusted so as not to offend a racist audience ('the rage is beige'?):

> I feel . . . that Othello should be imagined in reading, and presented
> on the stage, as coal-black, a negro, though not at all necessarily of
> the particular negroid type which Coleridge presumably had in mind
> when he spoke of a 'veritable' negro. But if it is thought that such a
> presentation on the stage will, with a particular type of audience (one
> with a stronger sense of colour-bar than we may suppose the
> Elizabethan audience to have had, say an audience in the southern
> states of America), evoke a reaction of *disgust* at Desdemona rather
> than one of startled sympathy and admiration, then the presentation
> had better no doubt be modified, since that reaction is certainly not
> what Shakespeare intended and knew would be evoked in his own
> audience.
>
> (Ridley (1958), p. liv)

4. On the other hand, in *Shakespeare's Politics* (1964, p. 41), Allan Bloom insists that 'Othello's color not only provides a visual contrast, but is meant to horrify the viewer . . . [since he so obviously] would not be considered a normal or appropriate choice for a young beauty's romantic interest.' Moreover, according to Bloom, it is crucially important to remember 'that Othello is born a stranger to Christianity as well as to Venice. In respect to both religion and race, he is by birth closer to the Turks' (p. 48). Thus, Shakespeare 'appears to tell us that it is not good to introduce influences that are too foreign, regardless of the guise in which they come'. In support of these arguments Bloom cites, as 'the most penetrating criticism of *Othello* that I have read', the Earl of Shaftesbury's assertions that 'the marriage of Othello is a mismatch, a monstrous union founded on the lying pretensions of a charlatan and the unhealthy imagination of a misguided young girl'. Not surprisingly, for Shaftesbury, as for Allan Bloom himself,

the tragedy is not the consequence of Iago's vile machinations, but the natural fruit of seeds that are sown in the characters of the heroes and in their relationship. The simple, citizen's moral of the story is . . . that such marriages between foreigners who have nothing in common other than their desire for novelty are to be avoided and condemned.
(Shaftesbury (1727), *Characteristicks*, London, Vol. 1, pp. 347–50, as quoted by Bloom on p. 36)

5. In 1970, K. W. Evans likewise argued that, to all intents and purposes, the marriage was doomed from the start on account of Othello's naïvety as well as the racial barrier, etc.

Desdemona dies . . . because of a naïvety that exceeds her own. . . . Considering the factors of age, race, and above all, the lover's simplicity, ordinary realism suggests this marriage was doomed from the start. . . .
(K. W. Evans (1970), 'The racial factor in *Othello*', *Shakespeare Studies*, **5**, pp. 124–40, also quoted in Orkin (1987), p. 109)

Nowadays, as Orkin has also noted, highly personal attacks on the adequacy of Othello as a tragic hero, as a general, and, ultimately, as a man (compare the personal attacks on Olive Chancellor by male commentators on *The Bostonians*) are now dominated by a critical concern with his sexual anxieties and sexual potency. For instance, Orkin cites an article on 'Othello's unconsummated marriage' by T. G. A. Nelson and Charles Haines (*Essays in Criticism* (1983), **33**, pp. 1–18) as yet 'another attempt to pin on Othello a *personal* accusation to account for the tragedy. The authors base their claim that Othello is sexually frustrated and sexually unsuccessful on his never having consummated his marriage with Desdemona' – an argument which is, at best, 'highly disputable' (Orkin, pp. 127–8).[2] Perhaps significantly, there is nothing like this much fussing and fuming over the *white* men in Shakespeare who are destructively jealous on the basis of circumstantial evidence even less telling than the proof produced by Iago (Leontes in *The Winter's Tale*, Claudio in *Much Ado About Nothing* and Ford in *The Merry Wives of Windsor*). No one goes on and on about how *their* marriages were doomed at the outset and/or for all time, about *their* lapsing into barbarism, etc.

The fact is that Brabantio's only objection to Othello as a son-in-law is his race: he invited Othello to dinner, and so on. And his racial objection to Othello – whether as a 'veritable negro' or a not-so-veritable negro – is ultimately sexual. He just didn't want his daughter to marry (have sex with) one. Otherwise, he and Othello could have got on just fine, as they had done in the past. It must have come as a shock to Othello, who thought her father loved him (I, iii,

129),· when Brabantio describes Desdemona's love for him as a monstrous aberration: she was either 'gross in sense' or induced by drugs to run to 'the sooty bosom/Of such a thing as thou – to fear, not to delight' (I, ii, 70–5). Comparably, although they might very well disapprove of any other form of racial apartheid, one has a feeling that past and present white male critics likewise most devoutly wish that the marriage between Desdemona and Othello had, somehow, remained *sexually* unconsummated. Bloom, for instance, describes this 'strange union' ('not an easy union to analyze'), between an 'old, black, foreign warrior' and a 'young, beautiful, innocent Venetian noblewoman' as 'completely beyond physical need' (p. 44). Presumably Iago is not as truthful as Bloom otherwise believes him to be when he says that Desdemona will realise the error of her choice 'when she is sated with his [Othello's] body' (I, iii, 340).

As opposed to the artistic tradition where, most notably in *Otello*, Verdi (like Shakespeare) treats the hatred embodied in Iago as the ultimate, negative evil, even as he lyrically infuses the love between the hero and heroine with sensual and romantic beauty, the critical tradition has joined forces with Brabantio and Iago in denigrating and destroying the love match. The very idea of a highly desirable white woman sexually preferring a black man to any white suitor, very like the idea of a black man being free to desire and court and marry and sexually enjoy as well as satisfy a white woman – and worst of all, the idea of the black man and the white woman together achieving glorious happiness in a love of the romantic and noble category in which there is no distinction between bodily and spiritual appetite or satiety (which is exactly the kind of mutual love expressed by Othello and Desdemona when his ship lands at Cyprus) has evoked comparable horror in male critics from the seventeenth century to the twentieth. Looked at from this angle, the most romantic interpretation of *Othello* is politically, sexually and racially the most radical.

For that matter, in a note on *Lolita* Vladimir Nabokov cited two subjects that, in the middle of the twentieth century, were likewise 'utterly taboo' as far as 'most American publishers' were concerned: 'a Negro–White marriage which is a complete and glorious success resulting in lots of children and grandchildren, and a total atheist who lives a happy and useful life and dies at the age of 106'. And in fact, as recently as 1987 the citizens of Alabama just barely voted that Negro–White marriages should not be *illegal*. Indeed, if a script for a tragedy showing a passionate and erotic and tender and romantic love between a black man and a white woman destroyed by a white man who embodied Evil Incarnate were *not* indelibly associated with

William Shakespeare's artistically canonised name, but had been written by a hitherto unknown modern writer, one wonders precisely when, or whether, it could ever get enough financial backing to be professionally staged in Alabama. Or in South Africa.

Underlying many arguments (pro and con) about the Shakespeare 'canon' is the demonstrably fallacious assumption that Shakespeare's plays necessarily uphold orthodoxy and invariably affirm the sexual, social, political and/or religious *status quo*. For even though they have been academically used as instruments of political, sexual, social and racial reaction – as have (what hasn't?) sociology, anthropology, history, psychoanalysis, and literary criticism – Shakespeare's scripts themselves more often than not tend to raise questions that challenge and, in certain cases, finally refute reactionary interpretations of them. *Othello* was, for obvious reasons, branded as 'racially unacceptable' in the Third Reich (Habicht (1989), p. 117); yet the official permission for 'true-to-score' (*Werktreue*) performances of the classics 'gave the theatres an opportunity unintended by the politicians'. 'In fact, theatre professionals in their turn increasingly adopted the credo of *Werktreue*, of staging Shakespeare "from within the text"; for they knew that it could be used as a shield for protecting original explorations and even oppositional touches.' In short, 'despite the dictatorial efforts at ideological appropriation . . . Shakespeare was vindicated, Shakespeare caused irritation'. His classic status thus served as a shield for artistic resistance.

In obviously comparable ways, Shakespeare's artistically sacrosanct status undoubtedly helped Janet Suzman stage her politically defiant, as well as theatrically triumphant, true-to-score production of *Othello* before mixed audiences in South Africa with a popular black actor as Othello, a beautiful and sensual white actress as a wonderfully loving and spirited Desdemona, and a *Werktreue* (if ever there was one) portrayal of Iago as a brutally sexist and racist liar. As televised in England over the Christmas holidays in 1988, this production could not have done more to affirm the validity of the title of Martin Orkin's book, *Shakespeare Against Apartheid*. Indeed, its 'Afrikaner' Iago came as close as any modern player could to evoking the ideal response described in the apocryphal story of the Chicago actor on tour in the West who played Iago so splendidly that one of the cowboys in the house, unable to endure the triumph of evil, pulled out his pistol and shot the bastard. 'There was nothing for the townspeople to do but hang the cowboy and bury him and the actor under one tombstone inscribed: *'THE PERFECT ACTOR AND THE PERFECT SPECTATOR'* ' (Sprinchorn (1968), pp. 201–10). The critical tradition to the contrary notwithstanding, in this play Iago dramatically embodies hate and evil that reinforce the barriers of sex and race that destroy love, just as Desdemona embodies the romantic and sexual love that surmounts all barriers of nationality, class, and race. And if the hatred he embodies cannot finally be killed off in the end, neither can her love for Othello or his love for her.

Significantly, in the same historical period when Bloom and other critics (notably F. R. Leavis) were going out of their way to find reasons to castigate them, one of the most sympathetic of all critical defenders of the love and marriage between Desdemona and Othello was a woman (see Helen Gardner 'The Noble Moor' (1955) for an eloquent refutation of arguments by male critics of the type cited above). For that matter, the most powerful critical arguments on these points published in the 1980s are by a woman. See Karen Newman's brilliant discussion of 'Femininity and the monstrous in *Othello*' (1987): Othello is 'represented as heroic and tragic' at a historical moment when (with the exception of Othello's precursor, Shakespeare's Morocco in *The Merchant of Venice*) the only black characters portrayed on the stage were villains of low status. Shakespeare's representation of Desdemona as 'at once virtuous and desiring', and her choice of love as 'heroic rather than demonic' is comparably radical. And, of course, the dramatically triumphant and politically daring South African production of the tragedy was directed by a woman with unequivocal sympathy for the hero and heroine. Which leads us to the questions of personal and sexual identities and identifications posed in the next chapter.

CHAPTER FOUR

Identities and identifications

BINARY OPPOSITIONS: SPLIT PERSONALITIES
AND WICKED WOMEN

There's never only one of any of us.

Margaret Atwood, *Cat's Eye*

She reminds me of *me*!
John Wayne as 'Rooster Cogburn' paying his ultimate tribute to the
heroine in *True Grit*

*   *   *   *

In the construction of her tales, Karen Blixen often used a special
projection technique that she had learned from Goethe and Shakespeare. According to this method, the major characters are 'formed in
the likeness of the passions they arouse' and thus designed to
correspond with 'the forces which contend on the psychological level
of action' while the 'seemingly fortuitous' events that occur in the
story serve 'to trigger latent forces in the persons whom they affect'
(Thurman (1982), pp. 118–19) Shakespeare himself may, in turn,
have derived this way of organising the characterisation and action of
a given drama from religious and secular morality plays wherein the
protagonist's soul is torn between good and evil, besieged by the
world, the flesh and the devil, and wherein component parts of the
psyche are split into separate characters. Looked at from this angle,
you could see Iago as the embodiment of hate (the passion he most
resembles and arouses) as well as the personification of jealousy,
malice and envy, who torments and infects and takes over the soul of
the hero ('Will you, I pray, demand that demi-devil/Why he hath
thus ensnared my soul and body?' *Othello* V, ii, 304–5), while
Desdemona represents mercy, fidelity, pity, love, forgiveness and
Emilia finally represents truth: 'Villainy hath made mocks with
love. . . . Moor, she was chaste; she loved thee, cruel Moor;/So come
my soul to bliss as I speak true.' (V, ii, 252–3). And so various forces –
love, hate, falsehood, truth – that interact in all of us contend with
each other on stage and in the end combine to arouse our pity and our
terror.

Comparably obvious projections of forces that contend with each
other within the hero (and the audience) occur in popular works

141

that split the individual protagonist into altogether different *personae*: Dr Jekyll and Mr Hyde; Tarzan of the Apes and Lord Greystoke; Superman and Clark Kent; David Banner and the Incredible Hulk. The same process occurs in George du Maurier's portrayal of the split between Trilby and La Svengali. But *Trilby* is an exception to the general rule governing most portrayals of women, whereby instead of splitting one character into two personalities, the usual practice is to isolate, segregate or split up virtues and vices between contrasting female characters defined with reference to the male protagonist, thus giving one trait to one female character and another to another, so as to imply that women must be either virtuous or vicious, either wives or mistresses, either angelically chaste or indiscriminately promiscuous. Indeed, the traditional literary as well as the theological segregation between the seven deadly sins and the seven cardinal virtues that implies a binary opposition between traits (such as Desdemona's sexual fidelity and her desire for Othello) that often *coexist* with each other in real life is endemic to the point of seeming a mirror of nature itself,[1] and not just a dramatically or melodramatically devised split such as the one between Trilby and La Svengali.

In any event, this parcelling out of traits between female characters competing for the love of the hero and/or for the approval of the reader, well-nigh inevitably triggers comparably competing responses within individual women reading the novel or watching the film. And so, for instance, reading *Daniel Deronda*, a young woman might well ask: 'Do I want to be like (am I anything like? ought I to act like?) the sweet, virtuous Mirah Cohen, who gets the man she wants in the end; or am I more like the ambitious Alcharisi, or most like the not altogether perfect, nor so single-minded Gwendolen Harleth?' Psychological responses and identifications may thus compete with each other just as the female characters themselves are traditionally portrayed as rivals competing for the hero's love or allegiance within the story itself: 'I may be most like character A, but she's not the one I'd really like to be like; and though Z is the character I morally approve of, X is the one I enjoy reading about most.' And so on. With lots of popular male characters, a male member of the audience could rest content with one name: 'I'd most like to be like Rick in *Casablanca*; I like Rick better than any other male character in the film; I am like him in once having loved and lost'.[2] With women, you often get a conflict and confusion: 'I'd like to *look* like Garbo in *Anna Karenina* and I'd love to have a passionate affair like the one she had with Vronsky, but I wouldn't want to suffer like that, and I don't like the way she left her little boy. It might

be better to be like sweet Kitty, but she isn't *wonderful* and Garbo is.'
You'd get the same sort of conflicting responses to, say, Scarlett
O'Hara as portrayed by Vivien Leigh in *Gone With the Wind*. But
perhaps the most obvious illustration of these points and surely one
of the most brilliant exploitations of traditional, fictional, female
identities and identifications is the portrayal of the narrator and the
eponymous heroine-villainess in Daphne du Maurier's *Rebecca*.
Where George du Maurier split his most famous female character into

*The second Mrs de Winter and Mrs Danvers from the 1940 Hitchcock screen version of
Daphne du Maurier's novel,* Rebecca.

two personalities, his granddaughter splits conflicting identifications – what the female narrator, or reader, would most like to be like (confident, beautiful, and loved), as opposed to what one fears one really is like (inadequate, nondescript, unwanted) – between two entirely different characters. At the same time, however, their counter-images seem photo-negative reversals of each other, or two sides of one coin, just as both characters are simultaneously known as 'Mrs de Winter', and both wear the same costume to the Manderley ball.

We never know the first name of the narrator. She is the young, innocent and adoring second wife of the brooding, romantic Maximilian de Winter who is the master of Manderley, a great estate in Cornwall. But the narrator and the reader alike soon become obsessed with and intrigued by, even as Manderley seems haunted by the ghost of Max's first wife, the fabulously beautiful, charming and accomplished Rebecca. Mrs Danvers, who came to Manderley as housekeeper 'when the first Mrs. de Winter was a bride', still rules the estate like a spectral projection of her adored mistress, whose ghost will not be laid to rest: 'Sometimes', Mrs Danvers tells the narrator, 'when I walk along the corridor here I fancy I hear her just behind me. That quick, light footstep. I could not mistake it anywhere. . . . It's almost as though I catch the sound of her dress sweeping the stairs as she comes down to dinner.' 'Sometimes I wonder if she comes back here to Manderley and watches you and Mr. de Winter together' (p. 205). In turn, the narrator herself subsequently wonders,

> Perhaps I haunted her as she haunted me; she looked down on me from the gallery as Mrs. Danvers had said, she sat behind me when I wrote my letters at her desk. That mackintosh I wore, that handkerchief I used. They were hers. Perhaps she knew and had seen me take them. Jasper had been her dog, and he ran at my heels now. The roses were hers and I cut them. Did she resent me and fear me as I resented her? (p. 280)

Sometimes Mrs Danvers seems to speak as much like a voice from within as a voice from without when she whispers in the narrator's ear:

> You'll never get the better of her. She's still mistress here, even if she is dead. She's the real Mrs. de Winter, not you. It's you that's the shadow and the ghost. It's you that's forgotten and not wanted and pushed aside. . . . He doesn't want you, he never did. . . . It's you that ought to be lying there in the church crypt, not her. It's you who ought to be dead. (p. 295)

The narrator herself had long since concluded that her husband would never love her 'because of Rebecca'. 'He did not belong to me

The shadow of Rebecca, from the Hitchcock film.

at all, he belonged to Rebecca. He still thought about Rebecca.' 'She was in the house still . . . her scent lingered on the stairs. The servants obeyed her orders still, the food we ate was the food she liked. Her favourite flowers filled the rooms.' 'Rebecca was still mistress of Manderley. Rebecca was still Mrs. de Winter.'

> I could fight the living but I could not fight the dead. If there was some woman in London that Maxim loved, someone he wrote to, visited, dined with, slept with, I could fight with her. . . . I should not be afraid. Anger and jealousy were things that could be conquered. One day the woman would grow old or tired or different and Maxim would not love her any more. But Rebecca would never grow old. Rebecca would always be the same. And she I could not fight. She was too strong for me. (pp. 279–80)

The female reader, it is generally assumed, will readily identify with the insecure narrator's sense of inadequacy in contrast to the unattainable perfection of the woman who had everything: 'brains, beauty, breeding'. And this assumption is obviously valid. Yet – *mutatis mutandis* – the character most female readers would most *like* to be like is, of course, the confident, the fearless, the popular, the accomplished, the adored, Rebecca. And Rebecca is, in fact, the woman who the comparatively mousy narrator herself wishes she were like and thus most profoundly identifies with.

For instance, sitting down to dinner in the dining room in her accustomed place, the narrator pictures Rebecca 'sitting in where I sat now, picking up her fork for the fish', answering a telephone call, talking to Max in 'a gay, careless way', telling him some story of her day, and of course he would be laughing, 'looking at her and smiling', putting out his hand to her across the table.

> 'What the devil are you thinking about?' said Maxim.
> I started, the colour flooding my face, for in that brief moment, sixty seconds in time perhaps, I had so identified myself with Rebecca that my own dull self did not exist, had never come to Manderley. . . . I wondered what he would say if he really knew my thoughts, my heart, and my mind, and that for one second he had been the Maxim of another year, and I had been Rebecca. (pp. 239–40)

Putting on the same costume that Rebecca wore at the last Manderley ball, the narrator is amazed at the transformation: 'I looked quite attractive, quite different altogether. Not me at all. Someone much more interesting, more vivid and alive' (p. 246). And in the last dream described in the end of the book, the narrator goes to the looking glass and sees a face that was not her own.

> It was very pale, very lovely, framed in a cloud of dark hair. The

eyes narrowed and smiled. The lips parted. The face in the glass stared back at me and laughed. And I saw then that she was sitting on a chair in the dressing-table in the bedroom, and Maxim was brushing her hair. He held her hair in his hands, and as he brushed it he wound it slowly into a thick long rope. It twisted like a snake, and he took hold of it with both hands and smiled at Rebecca and put it round his neck. (p. 456)

Earlier, as in a dream, she had identified with her husband when he told her he had killed Rebecca:

I had sat there on the floor beside Maxim in a sort of dream, his hand in mine, my face against his shoulder. I had listened to his story and part of me went with him like a shadow in his tracks. I too had killed Rebecca, I too had sunk the boat there in the bay. I had listened beside him to the wind and water. I had waited for Mrs. Danvers' knocking on the door. All this I had suffered with him, all this and more.

It is as if the character's identity is finally forged in and through successive, often contradictory identifications. At the same time Max told her about the murder, she was 'thinking and caring for one thing only, repeating a phrase over and over again, "He did not love Rebecca, he did not love Rebecca" ' (p. 342).

Yet the ideal image of Rebecca is never fully exorcised. 'It's not often you get someone who is clever and beautiful and fond of sport' (p. 148). 'She had an amazing gift, Rebecca I mean, of being attractive to people: men, women, children, dogs.' . . . 'Easy to like, I supposed, easy to love' (pp. 224–6).

The narrator is not only compared unfavourably to Rebecca by Mrs Danvers and numerous other characters in the novel, she is also, obsessively, contrasted unfavourably to Rebecca by herself. The second Mrs de Winter comes to think of herself primarily as a dull foil to the original Mrs de Winter and 'like to like' she therefore confides in the shy overseer at Manderley, Frank Crawley, whom everyone else dismisses as dull.

I liked Frank Crawley. I did not find him dull or uninteresting. . . . Perhaps it was because I was dull myself. We were both dull. We neither of us had a word to say for ourselves. Like to like. (p. 151)

'I realise every day', the narrator confesses to the sympathetic Crawley, 'that things I lack, confidence, grace, beauty, intelligence, wit – oh, all the qualities that mean most in a woman, – she possessed.'

'Tell me', I said, my voice casual, not caring a bit, 'was Rebecca very beautiful?'
Frank waited a moment. I could not see his face. He was looking

away from me towards the house. 'Yes,' he said slowly, 'yes, I
suppose she was the most beautiful creature I ever saw in my life.'
(pp. 157, 160)

By the way, the names of Rebecca and Frank Crawley well-nigh
inevitably bring to mind the most famous of all wicked females who
overshadow their comparatively dull foils in English literature:
Thackeray's own Rebecca (Becky Sharp) Crawley.

But be that as it may, in du Maurier's novel Rebecca's is the
inevitably enviable image of unattainable perfection in contrast to
which most women feel inadequate, but to which most aspire. Thus
the novel splits responses in narrator and reader alike between, on the
one hand, fascination, admiration, a profound desire to be identified
with the beautiful, accomplished Rebecca, who 'had a gift' of being
attractive to people and on the other hand, a sense of inadequacy
likewise shared with the (literally) nondescript narrator, who is not
very effectively reassured by Frank Crawley that 'kindliness, and
sincerity, and if I may say so – modesty – are worth far more to a
man, to a husband, than all the wit and beauty in the world' (p. 158).

When asked how he got away without ever being sued for
portraying deplorably flawed male characters who were clearly
identifiable as people he knew in real life, a witty author replied that
he always described them as irresistibly attractive to the opposite sex.
This does seem the ultimate way to flatter most people in real life
and/or to make a literary character enviable. Whatever else you
wrote about them, however scurrilous, would be tolerated if you also
put into print that although (say) Rebecca de Winter had every
known moral or sexual vice, she also had an amazing gift of being
attractive to everyone; to men, to women, to children, relatives, dogs
and casual acquaintances. Or that, although Scarlett O'Hara 'was not
beautiful', men 'seldom realized it, when caught by her charm as the
Tarleton twins were'. Regardless of their manifest lack of certain
ideally feminine virtues, by making Rebecca and Scarlett seem both
naturally and artificially and *always* exceptionally attractive to men,
Daphne du Maurier and Margaret Mitchell make them interesting
and enviable to most women[3] in very much the same way that a
character such as James Bond, who is portrayed as devastatingly
attractive to women, seems interesting and enviable to most men.

In any event, no matter how much one may sympathise with the
young narrator, the fact remains that whenever anyone mentions
'Rebecca' the character – or *Rebecca* the novel or *Rebecca* the movie or
Rebecca the TV mini-series – the primary thing everyone remembers
is the enduringly enviable, glamorous persona of the first Mrs de
Winter. And this holds true even after you have long known about

the surprise ending wherein it turns out that Rebecca was utterly wicked, definitely a nymphomaniac, 'not even natural' (there are suggestions of lesbianism in her relationship with Mrs Danvers) and that Maximilian de Winter himself killed her. And that he didn't kill her because he loved her. He hated her. Maxim hated Rebecca; and so the nameless narrator ultimately rejoices to learn that she had no cause to envy his love for her dead predecessor. Even so, Rebecca remains one of the most enviable women in fiction for the obvious reason that she is one of the few women in all the annals of literature who controls her own life and death in the way male heroes often do. Max killed her because she wanted him to. She chose not to die an agonising death from an incurable disease:

> 'Mrs. de Winter afraid?' said Mrs. Danvers. 'She was afraid of nothing and no one. There was only one thing ever worried her, and that was the idea of getting old, of illness, of dying in her bed. She has said to me a score of times. "When I go, Danny, I want to go quickly, like the snuffing out of a candle." ' (p. 414)

So she drove her husband to shoot her with the fiction that she was carrying another man's child as heir to Manderley. 'You'd like an heir, wouldn't you, for your beloved Manderley?' she had asked him. 'It would give you the biggest thrill of your life, wouldn't it, Max, to watch my son grow bigger day by day, and to know that when you died, all this would be his?' 'I'll be the perfect mother, Max, like I've been the perfect wife.' 'She turned around and faced me', he tells the narrator, 'smiling, one hand in her pocket, the other holding her cigarette.' 'When I killed her she was smiling still. I fired at her heart. The bullet passed right through. She did not fall at once. She stood there, looking at me, that slow smile on her face' (pp. 336–7).

There are, of course, hosts of male heroes in fiction who likewise control their own lives and deaths, but if you can name other women who do so in fiction, and who are *not* emotionally dependent for their happiness, to say nothing of their identity, their status or their livelihood, on a male character, the odds are very good that the ones you name will be 'wicked' women such as Rebecca's very own soap-opera successor, Blake Carrington's first wife, Alexis, as portrayed by Joan Collins in *Dynasty*.[4] Or the deliciously evil Madame de Merteuil, the quintessential villainess of the film *Dangerous Liaisons*, as well as the stage play by Christopher Hampton based on the notorious eighteenth century novel by Choderlos de Laclos, *Les Liaisons Dangereuses*.

Like Rebecca, Madame de Merteuil projects the image of the perfect woman as a mask for her sexual indulgences. And both characters, like male Don Juan types up to and including James Bond, discount their relationships with members of the opposite sex while managing simultaneously to seduce a whole lot of them. 'She was not in love with you, or with Mr. de Winter. She was not in love with anyone.' 'Love-making was a game for her, only a game', Mrs Danvers tells one of Rebecca's lovers. 'She had a right to amuse herself, hadn't she?'

> She did it because it made her laugh. It made her laugh, I tell you.
> She laughed at you like she did at the rest. I've known her come back
> and sit upstairs on her bed and rock with laughter at the lot of you.
> (p. 410)

The horrible possibility suggested here ('there was something horrible in the sudden torrent of words, something horrible and unexpected') is that any woman, in fact, might discount her relationships with men in exactly the same way that men often discount their relationships with women. But, as Madame de Merteuil asks in *Les Liaisons Dangereuses*, why shouldn't women use men as instruments of pleasure in the same way men use women? Like du Maurier's Rebecca, Laclos's Madame de Merteuil treats love as an amusing game as well as an exercise in power.

When the Marquise first entered society, she was 'like every other young girl, anxious to discover love and its pleasures'. So she deliberately made the most of every social opportunity to observe and to reflect. She was 'thought to be scatter-brained and absent-minded' and in fact she paid little attention to what everyone was so anxious to tell her, but was 'careful to ponder what they attempted to hide' (Laclos, p. 181). She also learned how to dissemble her own thoughts and feelings:

> Since I was often obliged to conceal the objects of my attention from
> the eyes of those around me . . . I tried in the same way to control
> the different expressions on my face. When I felt annoyed I practised
> looking serene, even cheerful; in my enthusiasm I went so far as to
> suffer pain voluntarily so as to achieve a simultaneous expression of
> pleasure. I laboured with the same care, and even more difficulty, to
> repress symptoms of unexpected joy. (p. 182)

Thus, from adolescence on, she had 'revealed to others' only what she 'found it useful' to reveal.

> [When] I was only fifteen, I already possessed the talents to which
> most of our politicians owe their reputation, [but] I had as yet
> acquired only the elements of the science I intended to master. . . . I
> had no wish to enjoy, I wanted to know, and the desire for
> knowledge suggested a means of acquiring it. (p. 182)

She then turned to works of fiction and non-fiction alike as sources of knowledge about how to act.

> I studied our manners in the novelists, our opinions in the
> philosophers; I went to the strictest moralists to find out what they
> demanded of us, so as to know for certain what it was possible to do,
> what it was best to think, and what it was necessary to seem to be.
> (p. 184)

To know what it is necessary to 'seem to be' – that is, to find out
what is 'demanded of us' – is the crucial imperative for a woman.

Like an actress creating a character on stage, the Marquise de
Merteuil created the image of an ideally virtuous woman, while
Rebecca created the image of a perfect wife as a façade behind which
she could do and be exactly what she wished. Her personal principles,
the Marquise tells her male counterpart and confidante, were not,
'like those of other women, found by chance, accepted unthinkingly,
and followed out of habit'. 'They are the fruit of profound reflection.
I have created them: I might say that I have created myself' (p. 181).

The one thing the young Marquise most wanted to know was how
to inspire love, but in order to do so she first had to learn how to
pretend to be inspired by it:

> In vain had I been told and had I read that it was impossible to feign
> the feeling; I had already observed that to do so one had only to
> combine an actor's talents with a writer's wit. I cultivated both, and
> not without success; but instead of courting the vain applause of the
> theatre, I decided to use for happiness what so many others sacrificed
> to vanity. (p. 184)

This emphasis on acting a part on the stage of the world would seem
to underscore the fact that what so many male moralists and theorists
up to and including Freud have traditionally ascribed to natural
femininity is socially constructed, like the role of the ideally virtuous
heroine in a play that 'wicked' female actresses simply play-act in.
The men have written the script to which the women are supposed to
adapt, assigning certain rights and privileges and powers and
pleasures to their own sex that they deny to women. But why
shouldn't women claim their fair share of pleasure and power?
Looked at from this angle, the Marquise de Merteuil is literally as
well as symbolically the man-made nemesis of man: 'I was', she tells
her partner in intrigue, 'born to revenge my sex and master yours.'[5]

In 'high' and 'popular' literature alike, as in the notorious *Liaisons
Dangereuses*, the most interesting and memorable portrayals of
women in literature involve a complex interaction between socially
prescribed ideals, dire necessity, genuine feelings and artful acting.
These interactions tend to give certain 'wicked' – or far from ideally
virtuous – women such as Gwendolen Harleth and Scarlett O'Hara, a
complexity, a vivacity, a sense of personality necessarily absent from

female figures of stereotyped virtue such as Mirah Cohen or Melanie
Hamilton, whose motives and actions are invariably pure. For
instance, after her second husband, Frank Kennedy, died Scarlett
(who is on the verge of a crying jag) confesses to Rhett how she had
lied to Frank and tricked him into marrying her and made him
unhappy and ultimately – albeit unwittingly – caused his death, and
how she wished she had *not* had to behave like that; and it is
interesting to note how a sense of genuine strain, a conflict between
multiple selves is here conveyed through a series of complex confusions between personal identity and the differing identifications and
relationships implicit in the use of the word 'like'.

> 'I don't see how I could have done it! Rhett, it doesn't seem like it
> was me who did all these things. I was so mean to him but I'm not
> really mean. I wasn't raised that way. Mother –' She stopped and
> swallowed. She had avoided thinking of Ellen all day but she could
> no longer blot out her image.
> 'I often wondered what she was like. You seemed to me so like
> your father.'
> 'Mother was – Oh, Rhett, for the first time I'm glad she's dead, so
> she can't see me. She didn't raise me to be mean. She was so kind to
> everybody, so good. She'd rather I'd have starved than done this.
> And I so wanted to be just like her in every way and I'm not like her
> one bit . . . but I wanted to be like her. I didn't want to be like Pa. I
> loved him but he was – so – so thoughtless. Rhett, sometimes I did
> try so hard to be nice to people and kind to Frank but then the
> nightmare would come back and scare me so bad I'd want to rush
> out and just grab money from people, whether it was mine or not.'
> (pp. 827–8)[6]

Thus a complex sense of personality is conveyed.

And so – or so it will be argued – however much a work in the
'great tradition' such as *Daniel Deronda* and a popular work such as
Gone With the Wind may differ in other ways, in the cases of
Gwendolen Harleth and Scarlett O'Hara, both George Eliot and
Margaret Mitchell likewise create what seem to be individual female
characters with distinct personalities emergent from the interactions
between self and society, heredity and environment, nature and
nurture, between real feelings and artful acting – and between what
happens to them and how they are driven to act.

'HIGH LITERATURE' AND *GONE WITH THE WIND*: THE STRESS ON SAMENESS

I have forgot much, Cynara, gone with the wind
Ernest Dowson, 'Cynara' (1896)

Gone with the wind. Hosts of Mullaghmast and Tara of the kings.
James Joyce, *Ulysses* (1922)

Was Tara still standing? Or was Tara also gone with the wind which
had swept through Georgia?
Margaret Mitchell, *Gone With the Wind* (1936)

Was she beautiful or not beautiful? and what was the secret of form
or expression which gave the dynamic quality to her glance?
(The opening sentence of *Daniel Deronda*)

Scarlett O'Hara was not beautiful, but men seldom realized it, when
caught by her charm as the Tarleton twins were.
(The opening sentence of *Gone With the Wind*)

*   *   *   *

James Joyce once observed that the classical hero, Ulysses, 'was the
most admirable of protagonists because he is known in so many
postures, as father, son, husband, lover' (Ellmann in *Ulysses*, p. 709).
Likewise, writing about *Daniel Deronda*, Barbara Hardy observes that
the villain, Grandcourt, seems 'horrifyingly real' because we see him
from so many points of view including those of his wife, his mistress,
his lackey, his children, his rival, his dogs and the author:

> Views of Grandcourt are impressed, wary, intimately horrified,
> ambitious, cowed, right, wrong, serious, frivolous, dismissive,
> contemptuous, and deeply critical. We see him on some occasions
> almost as a caricature, on others as a felt power.

On the other hand, the virtuous hero 'is a character we are told about
in one long breath of exposition'. It is not so much, Hardy concludes,
that 'we object to noble characters (though we do tire a little of all the
very wise and sound sayings that Daniel produces from what is after
all a somewhat limited and protected experience) but rather that we
object to an absence of personality'. 'The question of personality in
literature', she adds, 'is not an easy one, but I think it depends on an
impression of vital responsiveness in characters who change according to the company they keep' (*Daniel Deronda*, ed. Hardy, p. 19).

As we have seen, the personalities and types of women portrayed
in literature traditionally tend to be defined as well as judged – for
better or for worse – in terms of their primary sexual or romantic
relationship to the male protagonist (mother to Coriolanus, daughter
to Prospero, wife to Macbeth) and/or split into dialectically opposite
characters – virgin, whore; wife, mistress; prima-donna, *ingénue*;
virtuous, wicked; bimbo, career-bitch; victim, villainess. Yet if, as

Shakespeare noted, each man in his time plays many parts on the stage of the world, so does every woman. None the less, given the historical predominance of male protagonists and male authors it is hardly surprising that the most fully realised depictions of female characters both in 'high literature' and in popular genres who most conspicuously depart from the either/or, the one/the other, formulas tend (there are, of course, exceptions) to be the heroines of novels by women writers.

For instance, in George Eliot's *Daniel Deronda* and Margaret Mitchell's *Gone With the Wind*, Gwendolen Harleth and Scarlett O'Hara are portrayed in various contexts: as favourite daughters; as pampered young belles; as desperately trying to support dependent relatives; as having to make choices between comparably intolerable personal and moral alternatives; as wives to men they do not love, in love with men they cannot have; as making mistakes as well as learning things about themselves and about the world. Eliot and Mitchell also describe their heroines from altogether different angles, as they appear to various other characters with differing points of view – supportive and pejorative, admiring and condemnatory, sympathetic and critical, understanding and satirical. Scarlett, for instance, is idealised and shielded by Melanie; she is seen through, supported and condemned as well as loved by Mammy; and she is viewed with ironic amusement as well as with bitter love and admiration by Rhett, and so on. Moreover, markedly unlike most female characters in novels written by men, and for that matter in most romantic novels by women, Scarlett is by no means defined solely in terms of her sexual and romantic relationships. She is also defined at Tara and then in Atlanta by the work she does, like a man. Like most women in real life, she is also defined in terms of whole networks of differing social and familial obligations and relationships: with her adored mother Ellen, and with her earthy, immigrant father Gerald; with her two sisters Suellen and Carreen; with her three children Wade, Ella and Bonnie; with female friends and rivals such as Melanie Hamilton, Cathleen Calvert and Honey and India Wilkes; with the blacks at Tara and in Atlanta, Mammy, Dilcey, Prissy, Pork and Uncle Peter; with the ex-convict Archie; with Grandma Fontaine and Will Benteen; with Aunt Pittypat, Aunt Eulalie and Aunt Pauline; and not least with the first triumvirate of Atlanta matrons, Mrs Merriwether, Mrs Elsing and Mrs Meade.

Both *Daniel Deronda* and *Gone With the Wind* treat what happens to pretty and charming women who would seem to have been ideally fitted by nature and by art to play the traditional feminine roles ('in youth an adored darling' and so on) when their worlds turn upside down, the firm fails, the family money is lost, the army loses and their only real choice seems to be between the Darwinian alternatives, adapt or perish.

> 'Mercy me, all our field hands are gone and there's nobody to pick [the cotton]!' mimicked Grandma Fontaine and bent a satiric glance at Scarlett. 'What's wrong with your own pretty paws, Miss, and those of your sisters?'
> 'Me? Pick cotton?' cried Scarlett aghast, as if Grandma had been suggesting some repulsive crime. 'Like a field hand? Like white trash? Like the Slattery women?'
> 'White trash indeed! Well isn't this generation soft and ladylike! Let me tell you, Miss, when I was a girl my father lost all his money and I wasn't above doing honest work with my hands and in the fields too, till Pa got enough money to buy more darkies. I've hoed my row and I've picked my cotton and I can do it again if I have to. And it looks like I'll have to. White trash indeed! (p. 448)

Both heroines face economic disaster and the need to support their own dependent relatives, with the manifest handicap of a lack of any professional training and any professional skills:

> Nothing her mother had taught her was of any value whatsoever now and Scarlett's heart was sore and puzzled. . . . 'Nothing, no nothing, she taught me is of any help to me! . . . . Better I had learned to plow or chop cotton like a darky. Oh, Mother, you were wrong!' (p. 434)

Indeed, the only work-options open to young gentlewomen in distress in both these novels are much the same ones that have traditionally been open to their black sisters – domestic service, if not grinding work as a farm labourer, prostitution and at the very best some form of show business. Initially, Eliot's Gwendolen hopes that, because she is so pretty and graceful and has such a nice voice and ladylike bearing, she may soon support herself and her family by performing on the London stage: 'I suppose I have no particular talent, but I *must* think it is an advantage, even on the stage, to be a lady and not a perfect fright' (p. 302). But the dedicated artist, Klesmer, to whom she turns for advice, effectively dispels her illusions: 'A mountebank's child who helps her father to earn shillings when she is six years old – a child that inherits a singing throat from a long line of choristers and learns to sing as it learns to talk, has a likelier beginning.'

The truth is, he tells her, after 'your education in doing things slackly for one-and-twenty years . . . you would find mortifications in the treatment you would get when you presented yourself on the footing of skill.'

> You would be subjected to tests; people would no longer feign not
> to see your blunders. You would at first only be accepted on trial.
> You would have to bear what I may call a glaring insignificance: any
> success must be won by the utmost patience. . . . You have asked
> my judgment on your chances of winning. I don't pretend to speak
> absolutely; but measuring probabilities, my judgment is: - you will
> hardly achieve more than mediocrity.

She just might, Klesmer tells Gwendolen, get by on her beauty alone:
'Not without some drilling, however: as I have said before,
technicalities have in any case to be mastered.' But of course the kind
of woman who expects to get by that way has far more in common
with a professional prostitute than a genuine artist:

> She is usually one who thinks of entering on a luxurious life by a
> short and easy road – perhaps by marriage – that is her most brilliant
> chance, and the rarest [i.e. she's more likely to end up a kept woman
> or worse]. Still, her career will not be luxurious to begin with: she
> can hardly earn her own poor bread independently at once, and the
> indignities she will be liable to are such as I will not speak of. (pp.
> 303–4)

If only to support her dependent relatives financially (apart from
being a miserable job, the pay offered to her as governess of the
bishop's children was minimal),[7] Gwendolen has to marry
Grandcourt, because the only real training she has *is* training for
economic dependency, to be ornamental: 'In sum, you have not been
called upon to be anything but a charming young lady, whom it is an
impoliteness to find fault with' (p. 297). Likewise, Scarlett has to
offer herself, exactly like a prostitute, to Rhett; and when he can't
give her the money she needs to support herself and her dependants
she has to marry Frank Kennedy. In other words (p. 724) she was
forced by economic necessity to 'sell' herself to a man she 'didn't love
– and bear his child'. She also has to learn to run a sawmill, and
discovers in the process that she is good at business:

> 'Just imagine Frank trying to operate a sawmill! God's nightgown!
> If he runs this store like a charitable institution, how could he expect
> to make money on a mill? The sheriff would have it in a month.
> Why, I could run this store better then he does! And I could run a
> mill better than he could, even if I don't know anything about the
> lumber business!'
> A startling thought, this, that a woman could handle business
> matters as well or better than a man, a revolutionary thought to
> Scarlett. . . . She sat quite still, with the heavy book across her lap,
> her mouth a little open with surprise, thinking that during the lean
> months at Tara she had done a man's work and done it well. She had
> been brought up to believe that a woman alone could accomplish
> nothing, yet she had managed the plantation without men to help her
> until Will came. Why, why, her mind stuttered, I believe women

could manage everything in the world without men's help – except
having babies, and God knows, no woman in her right mind would
have babies if she could help it.
    With the idea that she was as capable as a man came a sudden rush
of pride and a violent longing to prove it, to make money for herself
as men made money. Money which would be her own, which she
would neither have to ask for nor account for to any man. (pp. 619–
20)

Subsequently, as her horrified husband observes, she ceases to be the
adorably soft, sweet, feminine person he had taken to wife. In the
brief period of their courtship, Frank thought he had never known a
woman more attractively feminine in her reactions to life, ignorant,
timid and helpless. Now her reactions were 'all masculine'. Despite
her pink cheeks and dimples and pretty smiles, she 'talked and acted
like a man'. Her voice was brisk and decisive and she made up her
mind instantly and with no girlish shilly-shallying. 'She knew what
she wanted and she went after it by the shortest route, like a man, not
by the hidden and circuitous routes peculiar to women' (pp. 639–40).
For instance, she told a prospective customer that her lumber was
cheaper and better than her competitors' and ran up a long column of
figures in her head and gave him an estimate then and there to prove
it. To her mortified husband, it was bad enough that she intruded
herself among strange rough workmen, but it was 'still worse for a
woman to show publicly that she could do mathematics like that'.
Everyone in Atlanta was blaming him for allowing his wife to unsex
herself. 'On top of everything else, she was actually making money
out of the mill, and no man could feel right about a woman who
succeeded in so unwomanly an activity' (p. 638).[8]
    Of course the sweet, adorable, helpless feminine persona was what
was always an act. For Scarlett, 'child of Gerald', had found the road
to ladyhood hard. As a child, her preferred playmates were not her
demure sisters or the well-brought-up Wilkes girls but the negro
children on the plantation and the boys of the neighbourhood, and
she could climb a tree or throw a rock as well as any of them (p. 58).[9]
As Scarlett grew older, she learned from her mother and her Mammy
the arts and graces of being attractive to men: 'It was Gerald's
headstrong and impetuous nature in her that gave them concern, and
they sometimes feared they would not be able to conceal her
damaging qualities until she had made a good match.' But Scarlett
intended to marry, and marry Ashley, 'and she was willing to appear
demure, pliant and scatterbrained if those were the qualities that
attracted men'.

Just why men should be this way, she did not know. She only knew
that such methods worked. . . . She only knew that if she did or said

thus-and-so, men would unerringly respond with the complimen-
tary thus-and-so. It was like a mathematical formula and no more
difficult, for mathematics was the one subject that had come easy to
Scarlett in her schooldays.

And thus the young actress prepares: by the time she was sixteen, she
had learned 'how to walk pigeon-toed so that her wide hoop skirts
swayed entrancingly, how to look up into a man's face and then drop
her eyes and bat the lids rapidly so that she seemed a-tremble with
gentle emotion'. 'Most of all she learned how to conceal from men a
sharp intelligence beneath a face as sweet and bland as a baby's':

> 'You must be more gentle, dear, more sedate,' Ellen told her
> daughter. 'You must not interrupt gentlemen when they are speak-
> ing, even if you do think you know more about matters than they
> do. Gentlemen do not like forward girls.' (pp. 59-60)

The sole point of all this artifice is to assure a good match. 'I wish to
Heaven I was married,' the sixteen-year-old Scarlett had bitterly
confided to Mammy while dressing for the barbecue:

> 'I'm tired of everlastingly being unnatural and never doing
> anything I want to do.' 'I'm tired of acting like I don't eat more than
> a bird, and walking when I want to run and saying I feel faint after a
> waltz, when I could dance for two days and never get tired. I'm tired
> of saying, "How wonderful you are!" to fool men who haven't got
> one-half the sense I've got, and I'm tired of pretending I don't know
> anything, so men can tell me things and feel important while they are
> doing it. . . . Why is it a girl has to be so silly to catch a husband?'
> 'Ah specs it's kase gempmums doan know whut dey wants. Dey
> jes' knows whut dey thinks dey wants. An' givin' dem whut dey
> thinks dey wants saves a pile of mizry an' bein' a ole maid. An' dey
> thinks dey wants mousy lil gals wid bird's tastes an' no sense at all. It
> doan make a gempmum feel lak mahyin' a lady ef he suspicious she
> got mo sense dan he has.'
> 'Don't you suppose men get surprised after they're married to find
> that their wives do have sense?'
> 'Well, it's too late den. Dey's already mahied. 'Sides, gempmums
> specs dey wives ter have sense.' (p. 79)

Whether or not they personally like, or dislike, or would or would
not like to be like Margaret Mitchell's heroine, most women (yellow,
red, black, white, British, American, Japanese, Catholic, Jewish,
Islamic) will almost inevitably recognise or remember experiencing –
albeit in terms of the more or less restrictive customs and contexts of
their own times and cultures – certain comparably artificial and
stifling processes of feminisation. Some of the requisitely artificial
behaviour, along with the crushing burden of negatives and prohibi-
tion of any natural reactions of resentment or defiance, is very much
the same obligingly servile demeanour traditionally demanded of a

geisha. Or a slave. As Mammy warns Scarlett, 'Young misses what frowns an' pushes out dey chins an' says "Ah will" an' "Ah woan" mos' gener'ly doan ketch husbands.' 'Young misses should cas' down dey eyes an' say, "Well, suh, Ah mout" an' "Jes as you say, suh" ' (p. 9). Margaret Mitchell may have idealised the Old South in some ways, but not in this one. In 1835, a Mississippi governess, Margaret Wilson, described woman's slavelike status, unable 'to avert or repel' her doom, forced to rely 'on beings' over whom 'she had no control excepting the mockery submission of the hour when she is marked out by her tyrant for a still deeper slavery', yet must go on 'smiling, cheering' her tormentor. Recalling how she was obliged to submit without protest to her father's authority, another Southern woman longed to inform him that 'there is a word sweeter than "mother, home, or heaven", and that word is "liberty" ' (Wyatt-Brown (1982), pp. 229-30). For that matter, historically speaking, the same equation, woman=slave, that John Stuart Mill made in the nineteenth century and Freud objected to (see above, p. 88) was made time after time by women in real life as well as in previous and subsequent works of art.

For instance, in a novel published in 1724, Daniel Defoe's Roxana quoted the lines 'O! 'tis pleasant to be free,/The sweetest Miss is Liberty' and thus refused a marriage proposal on the grounds that she had differing notions of matrimony from what 'receiv'd Custom had given us of it':

> I thought a Woman was a free Agent, as well as a Man, and was born free, and cou'd she manage herself suitably, might enjoy that Liberty to as much Purpose as the Men do; [but] that the Laws of Matrimony were indeed, otherwise. . . . That the very Nature of the Marriage Contract was, in short, nothing but giving up Liberty, Estate, Authority, and every-thing, to the Man, and the Woman was indeed, a meer Woman ever after, that is to say, a Slave. . . . I added, that whoever the Woman was, that had an Estate, and would give it up to be the Slave of *a Great Man*, that Woman was a Fool [and that] a Woman was as fit to govern and enjoy her own Estate, without a Man, as a Man was, without a Woman; and that, if she had a mind to gratifie herself as to Sexes, she might entertain a Man, as a Man does a Mistress.
>
> (*Roxana or the Fortunate Mistress*, pp. 147-9)

Nothing her suitor said could logically answer 'the Force of this, as to Argument': the fact of socially, sexually, economically and institutionally enforced inequality was undeniable. He could only plead 'custom and practice', arguing that 'the other Way was the ordinary Method that the World was guided by' and that he was of the opinion 'that a sincere Affection between a Man and his Wife' answered all objections about 'the being a Slave, a Servant *and the like*'. 'Aye', said Roxana, '*that is the thing I complain of*: the Pretence of Affection takes from a Woman every thing that can be call'd *herself*; she is to have no Interest; no Aim, no View; but all is the Interest, Aim, and View, of the Husband; she is to be the passive Creature you spoke of . . . she is to lead a life of perfect Indolence.' Yet a marriage contract, Roxana observes, may prove by far the most expensive way for a woman to purchase her ease, 'for very often when the Trouble was taken off of their Hands, so was their Money too'. She therefore concluded that 'it was far safer for the Sex not to be afraid of the Trouble', but to be really afraid for their money and learn to look after it themselves, for 'the Staff in their own Hands, was the best Security in the World' (pp. 149, 153).

In a letter about *An Enemy of the People*, Henrik Ibsen noted that he had given certain characteristics to the protagonist, Dr Stockmann, 'which will permit people to tolerate various things from his lips which they might not accept so readily if they had issued from mine' (Ibsen, transl. Meyer (1980), p. 110). And down through the centuries other authors have, as it were paradoxically, managed to get away with saying the unsayable – saying things that audiences would not have tolerated having said to them directly – in 'high' literature and popular novels alike by putting the taboo statement in the mouth of a manifestly 'wicked' character ('I count religion but a childish toy/And hold there is no sin but ignorance' says Marlowe's 'Machiavell'). Or by giving their most radical arguments to an erring or misguided character who subsequently retracts the heresy, even as Defoe's Roxana later repents and recants. Yet valid arguments and statements of fact cannot be logically invalidated simply by impugning the integrity of the witness. They will reverberate in the memory. This is the reason why lawyers deliberately introduce technically 'inadmissible' evidence with the certain knowledge that the judge will immediately instruct the jury to disregard it: it is no more possible in fact or in fiction to disregard impressive arguments you have just heard, or evidence you have just seen, than it is to obey the classic commandment, 'Try to count to ten *without* thinking of a rabbit'. Whatever character posits them, and however disreputable or discredited that character may be, whenever radical arguments are made in fiction it is highly probable that comparable arguments historically have been, or will subsequently be, posited in fact. As were Roxana's logical arguments equating the legal and economic status of a married women with the status of a slave. 'I must recollect', wrote yet another white Southern woman in 1850, 'that I belong to that degraded race called woman – who whether her lot be cast among Jew, or Turk, heathen or Christian is yet a *Slave*' (see this 'common matronly reaction' in a letter from Frances Peters quoted in Wyatt-Brown (1982), p. 224).

Although there are obvious differences, certain trans-temporal, trans-racial, trans-religious and trans-national processes of culturally programming young girls to project the slave-like image of ideal 'femininity' seem strikingly similar. Compare, for instance, the processes of feminisation that Scarlett went through in *Gone With the Wind* and that Catherine Earnshaw goes through in *Wuthering Heights* (see below), with the ones described by Karen Blixen in *Out of Africa*.

Karen Blixen's servant, Farah, had adopted into his household a little motherless girl of the Somali tribe, whom he took on, 'not, I think, without an eye to a likely profit when her time to marry should come, after the pattern of Mordecai and Esther':

> This little girl was an exceedingly bright and vivacious child. . . . When she first came to live with us she was eleven years old, and was ever breaking away from the domain of the family to follow me about. She rode my pony and carried my gun, or she would run with the Kikuyu Totos to the fishing pond, tucking up her skirts and galloping barefooted round the rushy bank with a landing-net. . . . But with time, and under the influence of the grown-up girls, she was transformed, and was herself fascinated and possessed by the process of her transformation. Exactly as if a heavy weight had been tied on to her legs, she took to walking slowly, slowly; she held her eyes cast down after the best pattern, and made it a point of honour to disappear at the arrival of a stranger. Her hair was cut no more, and when the day came that it was long enough, it was, by the other girls, parted and plaited into a number of little pigtails. The Novice gave herself up gravely and proudly to all the hardships of the rite.

'It was', Blixen concludes, 'a curious thing to see how, as she grew up, the maidens took her in hand, and scrupulously formed her into a young virgin *comme il faut*' (*Out of Africa*, pp. 188–9). As in the case of Chinese foot-binding, in the cultural production of 'femininity' – to quote a line from *Hamlet* (III, iv, 168) completely out of context – 'Use' (practice, custom, habit) 'almost can change the stamp of nature'.

In a remarkably perceptive essay on *Wuthering Heights*, Andrea Dworkin shows how the feminisation of Catherine Earnshaw destroys her authenticity, honour and wholeness just as, in the case of her soul-mate, Heathcliff, sadism is culturally produced in men through physical and psychological abuse and humiliation by other men. As children, the boy, the dark, ragged, black-haired child, the 'gypsy brat', Heathcliff and the girl Cathy are alike, as one. 'They are the same, they have one soul, one nature.' Each knows the other because each is the other: 'Whatever our souls are made of, his and mine are the same', says Cathy. They are wild together, roaming the moors outside the bounds of polite society, vagabonds, lawless. They sleep as children in the same cradled bed. The social distinctions between them mean nothing to them. Theirs is a love based on sameness, not difference: 'It is a love outside the conventions or convictions of gender altogether' (Dworkin, pp. 69-70).

In subsequently destroying the sameness, society destroys the two young people. Persecuted by Cathy's brother, Hindley, because he is so dark and dirty and gypsy-like, Heathcliff is the victim of a 'virtually racial' exclusion, of systematic intellectual deprivation and physical brutalisation. After visiting in the genteel Linton household, Cathy in turn 'finds Heathcliff's attitude and expression "black and cross" '; 'she laughs at him because he is dirty, and for herself she takes on the manners of a lady – "pulling off her gloves and displaying fingers wonderfully whitened with doing nothing and staying indoors" ' (Dworkin, p. 71). Heathcliff tries to maintain an intellectual equality with Cathy but hard labour and domestic eviction make that equality impossible. At the same time his 'wild, sweet Cathy'[10] is spoiled, flattered, domesticated, petted, housebound, gentrified, Heathcliff is forced out of the house into hard labour, 'treated like an animal because he is presumed to have an animal nature, savage and dark'. 'The social conditions create the nature.' Heathcliff is a culturally created werewolf, preying on the domesticated species that outlawed him. Determined for revenge, Heathcliff becomes monstrously sadistic, while Catherine becomes a shadow of herself: 'In betraying Heathcliff, she betrays herself, her own nature, her integrity; this betrayal is precisely congruent with becoming feminine, each tiny step toward white, fair, rich, a step away from self and honour, a slow, lazy, spoiled abandonment of self, a failure of honour and faith.' Heathcliff's sadism has a different genesis: he is patriarchy's scapegoat until he becomes its male prototype, 'taught, through emotional and physical torture, to snuff out empathy' (Dworkin, pp. 73-4).

What is interesting is that whereas male authors generally (some of the very greatest ones are obvious exceptions) tend to define woman as the Other – as better, or worse, but in any case altogether different from men – women writers often put a positive emphasis on sameness, on the dramatic denial of essential difference: Heathcliff is 'more myself than I am', says Cathy in a cry of complete, absolute, ultimate identification. 'My great miseries in this world have been from Heathcliff's miseries, and I watched and felt each from the beginning; my great thought in living is himself . . . Nelly, I *am* Heathcliff – he's always, always in my mind – not a pleasure, any more than I am always a pleasure to myself – but as my own being' (*Wuthering Heights*, p. 82).

This emphasis occurs in high literature and popular genres alike. Even as George Eliot stressed certain ways in which the Alcharisi was more like her formidable father than the gentle Mirah, throughout *Gone With the Wind* Mitchell stresses ways in which Scarlett is more like her father than her sisters, and ultimately most of all like Rhett. 'Yes, I'm sorry for you – ' Rhett tells her bitterly, 'sorry to see you throwing away happiness with both hands and reaching out for something that would never make you happy' (compare Heathcliff's litany to Cathy: '*Why* did you despise me? . . . for the poor fancy you felt for Linton', p. 161).

> If I were dead, if Miss Melly were dead and you had your precious honorable lover, do you think you'd be happy with him? Hell, no! You would never know him, never know what he was thinking about, never understand him. . . . Whereas, we, dear wife of my bosom, could have been perfectly happy if you had ever given us half a chance, for we are so much alike. We are both scoundrels, Scarlett, and nothing is beyond us when we want something. We could have been happy, for I loved you and I know you, Scarlett, down to your bones, in a way that Ashley could never know you. And he would despise you if he did know. (p. 939)

'It was so obvious', he tells her yet again at the end, 'that we were meant for each other':

> 'So obvious that I was the only man of your acquaintance who could love you after knowing you as you really are   hard and greedy and unscrupulous, like me.' (p. 1030)
>
>   Suddenly, she was sorry for him, sorry with a completeness that wiped out her own grief and her fear of what his words might mean. It was the first time in her life she had ever been sorry for anyone without feeling contemptuous as well, because it was the first time she had ever approached understanding any other human being. And she could understand his shrewd caginess, so like her own, his obstinate pride that kept him from admitting his love for fear of a rebuff. (p. 1031)

One male author who puts a stress on likenesses comparable to the ones that Mitchell and Brontë placed on fundamental similarities as opposed to superficial differences between individual men and women is Shakespeare. Indeed in a mismatch, a sell-out of a soulmate, a mating of a wild animal to a domestic animal comparable to Catherine Earnshaw's marriage to the genteel Edgar Linton, and Scarlett's rejection of Rhett for the 'honourable' Ashley Wilkes,

Shakespeare's Antony betrays himself as well as his dark lady, Cleopatra, by entering into a political marriage with the fair and virtuous Octavia. Looked at from the orthodox perspective of a course in 'Mate Selection' based on similarities in skin colour, nationality and social station, the ideally virtuous and ladylike Octavia is the perfect match for a Roman general, just as Cathy described Edgar Linton as an ideally rich, young, pleasant and respectable husband. But in true affinities, Antony is to his tawny 'gypsy' Cleopatra (I, i, 10) as Cathy is to her 'gypsy', Heathcliff:[11]

> ENOBARBUS. Octavia is of a holy, cold, and still conversation.
> MENAS.   Who would not have his wife so?
> ENOBARBUS. Not he that is himself not so; which is Mark Antony.
> (*Antony and Cleopatra*, II, vi, 119–21)

Andrea Dworkin is certainly right to observe that there are racial undercurrents in Emily Brontë's portrayal of the dark, gypsy-like Heathcliff; and the comparable affinities between the dark 'gypsy' Cleopatra and her Antony are obviously Shakespearian equivalents to (if not the most dramatic sources for) the ultimate affinities Brontë establishes between Heathcliff and Cathy that transcend all racial, national and social differences as well as differences in gender.[12] Both couples are life-mates as well as soul-mates. Where Cathy and Heathcliff (he is constantly described as her 'friend') roamed the moors outside the bounds of polite society, Antony and Cleopatra roam the streets of Alexandria in disguise. Primarily defined, as well as described, by Shakespeare as a 'mutual pair', Cleopatra goes fishing with Antony, wears his armour, laughs him out of humour and drinks him to his bed.

Past and present critical and ideological preoccupations with sexual differences have caused past and present commentators alike to ignore these and other ways in which individual men and women in certain works of literature, as in life, very often have at least as much, if not far more in common with each other than they do with other members of their own sex. For instance, in *Wuthering Heights* Heathcliff and Cathy are likewise associated with the outdoors, with outlaws, with demons, darkness, with wild animals, rocks and thorns and oak-trees, in contrast to Edgar and Isabella Linton, who are associated with angels, with light, with honeysuckle, with elegant houses, with social life indoors, with soft, pampered house-pets. Whereas other writers often define comparable differences as sexually linked (the forces associated with Cathy and Heathcliff are often portrayed as masculine, and the forces associated with the Lintons as feminine) the fundamental difference here defines differing species (of the same genus) that obviously include both sexes. To marry Isabella to Heathcliff is like putting a house-cat into a cage with a wildcat. Likewise, the efforts to turn a wildcat like Cathy into a house-pet cause her to pine away. This is why, when warning Isabella to stay away from Heathcliff, Nelly describes him as a bird of bad omen; 'no mate for you', while Cathy describes him as a 'pitiless, wolvish man': 'he'd crush you, Isabella, like a sparrow's egg'. Neither Cathy, nor Isabella (nor Heathcliff nor Edgar) is, or can be, complete or happy in the element of the other. Thus, in a dramatic inversion of a dream so heavenly that when you wake you cry to dream again, Cathy once dreamed she went to heaven but was miserably sick for home, for Heathcliff, there:

> Heaven did not seem to be my home; and I broke my heart with weeping to come back to earth; and the angels were so angry that they flung me out into the middle of the heath on the top of Wuthering Heights; where I woke sobbing for joy. . . . I've no more business to marry Edgar Linton than I have to be in heaven. (p. 80)

Heathcliff likewise cries when Cathy dies – 'Where is she? Not *there* – not in heaven, not perished – where? . . . Be with me always – take any form – drive me mad! only *do* not leave me in this abyss, where I cannot find you! Oh, God! it is unutterable! I *cannot* live without my life! I *cannot* live without my soul' (p. 167).

Shakespeare's Cleopatra, of course, expressed comparable feelings about Antony when he died:

> Noblest of men, woo't die?
> Hast thou no care of me? Shall I abide
> In this dull world, which in thy absence is
> No better than a sty? O, see, my women,
> The crown o'th' earth doth melt. . . . Young boys and girls
> Are level now with men. The odds is gone,
> And there is nothing left remarkable
> Beneath the visiting moon.
>
> (IV, xv, 59–68)

and compare, also, the classic couplet addressed to 'C.M.B.' in *Sparrow* (1981), p. 13:

> Heaven, without you, would be too dull to bear,
> And Hell will not be Hell if you are there.

There is also a sense of losing one's own soul, denying one's own identity when losing or denying the other in these works. When in the end of *Gone With the Wind* Scarlett finally tells Rhett how old she is he notes that twenty-eight is 'a young age to have gained the whole world and lost your own soul, isn't it?'

> 'Don't look frightened. I'm not referring to hell fire to come for your affair with Ashley. I'm merely speaking metaphorically. Ever

since I've known you, you've wanted two things. Ashley and to be rich enough to tell the world to go to hell. Well, you are rich enough and you've spoken sharply to the world and you've got Ashley, if you want him. But all that doesn't seem to be enough now.'

She was frightened but not at the thought of hell fire. She was thinking: 'But Rhett is my soul and I'm losing him. And if I lose him, nothing else matters! No, not friends or money or – or anything. If only I had him I wouldn't even mind being poor again. No, I wouldn't mind being cold again or even hungry. . . .' (p. 1023)

And in one of the most intense statements in literature, Brontë's Cathy insists to Nelly that 'surely you and every body have a notion that there is, or should be, an existence of yours beyond you'. For what, she asks 'were the use of my creation if I were entirely contained here'. She then compares her love for Heathcliff to 'the eternal rocks':

If all else perished, and *he* remained, I should still continue to be; and if all else remained, and he were annihilated, the Universe would turn to a mighty stranger. I should not seem a part of it. (p. 82)

This isn't just another instance of woman's love being her whole existence, while man's love is of himself a thing apart, since Heathcliff felt exactly the same way about Cathy, 'his counterpart'.

The crucial point is the dramatic emphasis on sameness, as opposed to differences between individual men and women in the various works discussed here. Just as Edgar Linton and his sister Isabella have more in common with each other than either has in common with Heathcliff and Cathy (who are like brother and sister, species-mates as well as soul-mates), Shakespeare's Octavia and Octavius have more in common with each other than either has with Cleopatra or her Antony (even as, in *King Lear*, Cordelia has more in common with the comparably loyal and truthful Kent, and with Gloucester's unjustly rejected son, Edgar, than she does with her own sisters, Goneril and Regan) and so on and on: in temperament and dominance, the Alcharisi has more in common with her father than with Mirah in *Daniel Deronda*; and Scarlett has more in common with her father and with Rhett than with her mother and her sisters in *Gone With the Wind*. If for no other reason, literature would be worth recommending to students just to challenge, dramatically, the very theories and stereotypes about gender it has officially been alleged to uphold. Time after time, in literature, men and women placed in comparable contexts respond in identical ways. Indeed certain works stress the way outside forces – circumstances, social pressures, and individual influences – may alter if not entirely determine the identities of men and women alike.

THE CONSTRUCTION OF IDENTITY:
PRINCESSES, PAUPERS, TRADING PLACES AND
ALTERED STATES

> You see, really and truly, apart from the things anyone can pick up (the dressing and the proper way of speaking, and so on), the difference between a lady and a flower girl is not how she behaves, but how she's treated.
>
> Eliza Doolittle in George Bernard Shaw's *Pygmalion*

> She haunted many a low resort
> Near the grimy road of Tottenham Court,
> She fleeted about the no man's land
> From 'The Rising Sun' to 'The Friend at Hand' . . .
> And who would ever suppose that that
> Was Grizabella, the Glamour Cat.
>
> T. S. Eliot, 'Grizabella'

> I will preserve myself; and am bethought
> To take the basest and most poorest shape
> That ever penury in contempt of man
> Brought near to beast . . . . . .
> . . . . . . and with presented nakedness outface
> The winds and persecutions of the sky. . . .
> Poor Turlygood, poor Tom! That's something yet.
> Edgar I nothing am.
>
> Edgar in Shakespeare's *King Lear*

* * * *

From works of 'high literature', such as Shakespeare's *King Lear* and Emily Brontë's *Wuthering Heights* on through Mark Twain's *The Prince and the Pauper*, Eddie Murphy's *Trading Places* and Tom Wolfe's *The Bonfire of the Vanities*, readers and audiences have observed, with horrified fascination, what happens to characters in literature whose high social rank and secure status is taken away and they have to fend for themselves. From medieval '*de casibus*' tragedies of the 'falls of princes' to the present time, various works serve as case-studies of the ways that an individual's behaviour and perceptions (the differing ways a character is perceived and treated by others and consequently defines himself or herself) may be altered by circumstances. For instance, recalling the days before war and poverty had irrevocably altered her, Scarlett O'Hara perceives her past self in the same way she remembers departed friends and relatives, like the ghost of a person who had long since ceased to exist: 'There rose up in her mind the memory of Scarlett O'Hara who loved beaux and pretty dresses and who intended, some day, when she had the time, to be a great lady like Ellen' and her heart was suddenly 'dull with pain, with weariness, as she thought of the long road she had come since those days' (p. 926):

> She had set her feet upon that road a spoiled, selfish and untried girl, full of youth, warm of emotion, easily bewildered by life. Now at the end of the road, there was nothing left of that girl. Hunger and hard labor, fear and constant strain, the terrors of war and the terrors of Reconstruction had taken away all warmth and youth and softness. . . . She had become what Grandma Fontaine had counseled against, a woman who had seen the worst and so had nothing to fear. Not life nor Mother nor loss of love nor public opinion. Only hunger and her nightmare dream of hunger could make her afraid. A curious sense of lightness, of freedom, pervaded her now that she had finally hardened her heart against all that bound her to the old days and the old Scarlett. (pp. 542–3)

A comparably curious sense of release is experienced by the protagonist in *The Bonfire of the Vanities* when he realises that the privileged character, 'the Master of the Universe' who he once thought that *he* was, has ceased to exist:

> I'm not Sherman McCoy any more. I'm somebody else without a proper name. I've been that other person ever since the day I was arrested. . . . At first I thought I was still Sherman McCoy, and Sherman McCoy was going through a period of very bad luck. Over the last couple of days, though, I've begun to face up to the truth. I'm somebody else. I have nothing to do with Wall Street or Park Avenue or Yale or St. Paul's or Buckley. . . . I'm not the person my wife married or the father my daughter knows. I'm a different human being. I exist *down here* now . . . Reade Street and 161st Street and the pens. . . .
> 'Ayyyyy, wait a minute,' said Killian. 'It ain't that bad yet.'
> 'It's that bad,' said Sherman. 'But I swear to you, I feel better about it now. You know the way they can take a dog, a house pet, like a police dog that's been fed and pampered all its life, and train it to be a vicious watchdog?' . . .
> 'I've seen it done,' said Quigley, 'I saw it done when I was on the force.'
> 'Well, then you know the principle,' said Sherman. 'They don't alter that dog's personality with dog biscuits or pills. They chain it up, and they beat it, and they bait it, and they taunt it, and they beat it some more, until it turns and bares its fangs and is ready for the final fight every time it hears a sound.'
> 'That's true,' said Quigley.
> 'Well, in that situation dogs are smarter than humans,' said Sherman. 'The dog doesn't cling to the notion that he's a fabulous

house pet in some terrific dog show, the way a man does. The dog
gets the idea. The dog knows when it's time to turn into an animal
and fight.' (p. 626)

It's not just hazards of fortune or altered circumstances that can alter
personality. The same processes Sherman described with reference to
the deliberate production of a vicious dog occur in the systematic
brutalisation of human beings as portrayed by Shakespeare and by
Emily Brontë alike. 'Thou calld'st me dog before thou hadst a cause',
says the pariah, Shylock, thus turning and baring his fangs for his
final fight with the Venetians who had taunted him and baited him
and spat on him, 'But, since I am a dog, beware my fangs' (*The
Merchant of Venice*, III, iii, 6-7).

As Andrea Dworkin has observed, although writers such as Emily
Brontë and Shakespeare have been canonised and ikonised, 'what
they know about life is ignored'. For instance, in her portrayal of the
systematic degradation and brutalisation of the boy Heathcliff by
Hindley Earnshaw, Brontë also showed 'the ineluctable logic of what
has become a contemporary sociological cliché: child abusers have
often been abused as children'. 'We might have short-circuited a
century of pain had we bothered to learn from her' (Dworkin (1988),
p. 75). In *Wuthering Heights* the vengeful sadism of the adult
Heathcliff has in it the more horrible patience of the abused child, as
in a 'parable of race oppression' he turns on and destroys the class that
oppressed him, likewise 'destroying in himself finally and forever
anything fragile or sensitive that might have survived his own
training in pain' (pp. 75-6). As the superior servant, Nelly (who later
was ashamed of treating Heathcliff so unjustly) remembers,

> He seemed a sullen, patient child; hardened, perhaps, to ill-treatment:
> he would stand Hindley's blows without a wink or shedding a tear,
> and my pinches moved him only to draw in a breath and open his
> eyes, as if he had hurt himself by accident and nobody was to blame.
> (*Wuthering Heights*, p. 36)

Later, however, when Nelly finds the boy 'wrapt in dumb medi-
tation' and inquires the subject of Heathcliff's thoughts, he answered
gravely:

> 'I'm trying to settle how I shall pay Hindley back. I don't care
> how long I wait, if I can only do it, at last. I hope he will not die
> before I do!'
> 'For shame, Heathcliff!' said I. 'It is for God to punish wicked
> people; we should learn to forgive.'
> 'No, God won't have the satisfaction that I shall,' he returned. 'I
> only wish I knew the best way! Let me alone, and I'll plan it out,
> while I'm thinking of that, I don't feel pain.' (pp. 59-60)

Heathcliff ultimately takes pleasure in brutalising Hareton Earnshaw in the same way Hareton's father had brutalised him, likewise denying him an education so that Hareton comes to despise and hate the books he cannot read: 'I've got him faster than his scoundrel of a father secured me, and lower; for he takes a pride in his brutishness. I've taught him to scorn everything extra-animal as silly and weak' (p. 219). And so the sins of the fathers are visited upon the children, even unto the next generation.

Writing in the *Westminster Review* in 1898, an admirer of Emily Brontë's, Angus Mackay, observed that 'if we look only to the *quality* of imagination in *Wuthering Heights* – its power, its intensity, its absolute originality – it is scarcely too much to say of Emily that she might have been Shakespeare's younger sister' (Allott (1970), pp. 102). Heathcliff, for instance, 'fascinates the imagination, and in some scenes almost paralyses us with horror, and yet that subtle human touch is added which wrings from us pity and almost respect'. In this, Mackay concludes, he reminds us of Shakespeare's Shylock. As we shall see, Heathcliff resembles Shylock in other ways as well, even as the identical warnings that Brontë transmits through the case-history of Heathcliff are also transmitted throughout Shakespearian drama, most notably through the case-histories of Shylock and Caliban.

In the instances of Shylock and Heathcliff, Shakespeare and Emily Brontë give us very practical, as well as obvious moral reasons, for never doing unto others anything that we would not want done to us, or done to our progeny. For (in the words of *Macbeth*, I, vii, 8–12) in such cases,

> we but teach
> Bloody instructions, which being taught return
> To plague the inventor. This even-handed justice
> Commends th' ingredience of our poisoned chalice
> To our own lips.

We cannot fail to see Shylock's, or Heathcliff's, horrific vindictiveness as the inevitable product of systematic vilification and injustice and thus they are the creations of their oppressors: 'You call me misbeliever, cut-throat dog,/And spit upon my Jewish gaberdine' (I, iii, 106–7) cries Shylock to Antonio, who insists he is just as like to do so again, 'To spit on thee again' and 'spurn thee' as 'a stranger cur' again, and so we watch Antonio and Shylock in turn 'feed fat' their ancient tribal grudge to the point where it seems that somebody is inevitably going to bleed. After all, as Shylock himself asks us in the most famous series of rhetorical questions in Shakespearian drama, since Jews and Gentiles (like men and women, blacks and whites, colonised and colonisers, conquered and conquerers) are so obviously alike in so many other ways, are they not equally likely to behave towards other people in very much the same way other people have behaved towards them?

> Hath not a Jew eyes? Hath not a Jew hands, organs, dimensions, senses, affections, passions, fed with the same food, hurt with the same weapons, subject to the same diseases, healed by the same means, warmed and cooled by the same winter and summer, as a Christian is? If you prick us, do we not bleed? If you tickle us, do we not laugh? If you poison us, do we not die? And if you wrong us, shall we not revenge? If we are like you in the rest, we will resemble you in that. If a Jew wrong a Christian what is his humility? Revenge. If a Christian wrong a Jew, what should his sufferance be by Christian example? Why, revenge. *The villainy you teach me I will execute; and it shall go hard but I will better the instruction.*
>
> (*The Merchant of Venice*, III, i, 50–62, [my italics])

In his essay on 'Literature as an equipment for living' (also quoted above p. 94) Kenneth Burke has observed that readers and audiences generally turn to literature in order to satisfy a host of differing emotional and psychological needs, and thus expect it to serve any number of differing purposes. Burke's general categories of needs and purposes are 'consolation, vengeance, admonition, exhortation, and foretelling'. And of all the lines in Shakespeare, Shylock's great speech about revenge could be said to serve simultaneously to fulfil all of these purposes except one. There is, alas, absolutely no consolation to be found anywhere in it. But you can read it as an admonition, a warning, an exhortation and a prophecy in so far as individuals (such as Shylock or Heathcliff) or groups of people who have been laughed at, mocked at, threatened, disgruntled, humiliated and hindered on account of their social or racial or religious origins are likely, when given the opportunity, to demand the pound of flesh they have coming to them from their oppressors. For regardless of whether the words 'we' and 'us' are used with references to Jews or Christians or Blacks or Palestinian Arabs or Shiite Muslims, the answer to Shylock's question, 'If you wrong us, shall we not revenge?' is – in desire if not in fact – far more likely to be 'yes' than 'no'.

And as Shakespeare and Emily Brontë likewise remind us, the same holds true for women. In *Othello* the put-upon wife, Emilia, expresses the identical sentiments that the put-upon Jew, Shylock, expressed in *The Merchant of Venice*: turn about is fair play. 'I do think', says Emilia to Desdemona, 'it is their husbands faults/If wives do fall'.

> Say that they slack their duties,
> And pour our treasures into foreign laps;
> Or else break out in peevish jealousies,

Throwing restraint upon us; or say they strike us,
Or scant our former having in despite;
Why, we have galls; and though we have some grace,
Yet have we some revenge. *Let husbands know*
Their wives have sense like them; they see and smell,
And have their palates both for sweet and sour
As husbands have. What is it that they do
When they change us for others? Is it sport?
I think it is. And doth affection breed it?
I think it doth. Is't frailty that thus errs?
It is so too. And have we not affections,
Desires for sport, and frailty, as men have?
Then let them use us well; else let them know
The ills we do their ills instruct us so.

(*Othello*, IV, iii, 84–101, [my italics])

What's especially interesting here is that the words Shakespeare puts into the mouths of Emilia and Shylock are virtually interchangeable. Their reaction to ill-use is the same independently of biological gender, race, or creed: the ills we do your ills instruct us so. The villainy you teach us we will execute, and it will go hard with you, for if we possibly can we will better your instruction.

Emily Brontë shows the same process occurring independently of breeding or gender in *Wuthering Heights*. Treated as cruelly and brutally and unjustly by Heathcliff as he was treated by Hareton, the gently bred Isabella Linton responds in exactly the same way, finding real or imagined satisfaction only in revenge. When Heathcliff is desolated by the death of his Cathy, Isabella positively delights in the contemplation of his agony:

> Had it been another, I would have covered my face in the presence of such grief. In *his* case, I was gratified: and ignoble as it seems to insult a fallen enemy, I couldn't miss this chance of sticking in a dart; his weakness was the only time when I could taste the delight of paying wrong for wrong.

'Fie, fie, Miss!' cries Nelly, making exactly the same appeal to the scriptures that she had earlier made to Heathcliff: 'One might suppose you have never opened a Bible in your life. If God afflict your enemies, surely that ought to suffice you. It is both mean and presumptuous to add your torture to his!' And as it were in a deliberately parallel speech, Isabella in turn expresses the same sentiments about God's vengeance that Heathcliff did – she'd rather have the satisfaction of revenging herself:

> But what misery laid on Heathcliff could content me, unless I have a hand in it? I'd rather he suffered *less*, if I might cause his sufferings, and he might *know* that I was the cause. Oh, I owe him so much. On only one condition can I hope to forgive him. It is, if I may take an

eye for an eye, a tooth for a tooth, for every wrench of agony return a wrench, reduce him to my level. As he was the first to injure, make him the first to implore pardon; and then – why then, Ellen, I might show you some generosity. But it is utterly impossible I can ever be revenged, and therefore I cannot forgive him. (p. 179)

It is easy to argue that other people or dramatic characters ought to leave vengeance to God, until someone has grievously wronged us, or ours, in which case it is not altogether inconceivable that we – or any individual or nation or group, will subsequently respond with a vindictive ferocity comparable to Shylock's or Heathcliff's. Or to Isabella's. That is, if we can.

For as Isabella reminds us, women often lack the material – the social, economic and political weaponry – to defend themselves against injustice, much less avenge themselves against any man without the aid of some other man. For instance, Shakespeare's Beatrice has to ask Benedick to 'kill Claudio' and so avenge the injustice done to her friend (*Much Ado About Nothing*, IV, i, 287, 302, 312–13). Likewise, Mattie Ross, the heroine of *True Grit*, had to hire Rooster Cogburn to go into the territory with her to get the man who killed her father, and even this achievement is exceptional. For the most part, a woman's desire for revenge/justice (again like Isabella's desire to have Heathcliff at her mercy) takes the form of impossible dreams, of wish-fulfilment fantasies such as the ones expressed by Eliza Doolittle in her immortal aria, 'Just You Wait, Professor Higgins', in *My Fair Lady*:

> Just you wait.
> You'll be sorry, but your tears will be too late.
> As they lift their guns up higher,
> I'll shout, 'Ready! *Aim! FIRE!*'
> Oh ho ho, Professor Higgins,
> Just you wait.

In Shaw's original *Pygmalion* as in the musical based on it, Eliza Doolittle is, in more than one way, a creation of her Svengali, Henry Higgins. She can't go back to the person she was before she met him and defines herself with reference to him even as she turns against him. The same thing happens to a woman portrayed as a product of the man who rejected her in a bitterly ironic and paradoxical treatment of these various themes by Doris Lessing. See *The Golden Notebook*, p. 448:

> Ella finds this story inside herself: A woman [is loved and then rejected] by a man who criticises her throughout their long relationship for being unfaithful to him and for longing for the social life which his jealousy bars her from and for being 'a career woman'.

This woman who, throughout the five years of their affair in fact never looks at another man, never goes out, and neglects her career becomes everything he has criticised her for being at the moment when he drops her. She becomes promiscuous, lives only for parties and is ruthless about her career, sacrificing her men and her friends for it. The point of the story is that this new personality has been created by him; and that everything she does – sexual acts, acts of betrayal for the sake of her career, etc., are with the revengeful thought: There, that's what you wanted, that's what you wanted me to be. And, meeting this man again after an interval, when her new personality is firmly established, he falls in love with her again. This is what he always wanted her to be; and the reason why he left her was in fact because she was quiet, compliant and faithful. But now, when he falls in love with her again, she rejects him and in bitter contempt: what she is now is not what she 'really' is. He has rejected her 'real' self. He has betrayed a real love and now loves a counterfeit. When she rejects him she is preserving her real self, whom he has betrayed and rejected.

Sometimes the 'real' self seems irrevocably warped by external pressures. Yet sometimes resistance to oppression can take positive forms of self-affirmation as well as self-defence. As Catherine Belsey observes, the dramatisation of political tyranny in certain Renaissance plays (such as *The Duchess of Malfi*) gave birth 'however tentatively' to the concept of the autonomous subject; thus absolutism, the plays imply, produces precisely the resistance it sets out to exclude (Belsey (1985), p. 109). And it could be that the idea of an autonomous self that should not be violated and cannot finally be annihilated may be a necessary prerequisite for resistance, just as literary works and philosophies such as stoicism and existentialism that stress inviolable integrity tend, historically, to serve as forms of resistance to tyranny (for classic modern examples see Solzhenitsyn's *The First Circle* and Camus's *The Plague*). For that matter, the Senecan affirmation, '*Medea superest*', and the seventeenth century affirmation, 'I am Duchess of Malfi still', have their modern counterparts in literature and films likewise concerned with an individual's psychological resistance to the oppressor's wrong, the proud man's contumely. See, for instance, the ultimate self-affirmation that finally occurs in the dialogue which marks the end of Celie's submission to oppression in Alice Walker's *The Color Purple* (p. 176):

> I curse you, I say.
> What that mean? he say.
> I say, Until you do right by me, everything you touch will crumble.
> He laugh. Who you think you is? he say. You can't curse nobody. Look at you. You black, you pore, you ugly, you a woman. Goddam, he say, you nothing at all.

> Until you do right by me, I say, everything you even dream about will fail. I give it to him straight, just like it come to me. And it seem to come to me from the trees. . . . I'm pore, I'm black, I may be ugly . . . a voice say to everything listening. But I'm here.[13]

What we have here, and also have at the moment when Isabella Linton contemplates the power Hindley's gun would give her over Heathcliff (Dworkin, p. 34), 'is not so much a matter of revenge, as a single lucid perception of the right to self defence'. If there is a genetic 'self' that is biologically programmed to resist invasion from microbes, there may be a psychological sense of integrity that has likewise evolved to defend us against moral and psychological assaults. Certainly a sense of personal identity that transcends its origins and context has been perceived and experienced *as if* it were a reality by living human beings, as well as by fictional characters such as Celie. For instance, there is in many of us a sense that although we may play many different roles on the stage of the world, it is our own self that is playing them. And certainly most of us have a sense of a self (or of a whole complex of memories and values and inherited characteristics constituting our myriad selves) that can be outraged, warped or violated, even as most people feel that they have minds, if not immortal souls that can be lost.

As we have seen, the idea that hearts, souls and minds can be warped by systematic persecution and vilification is what lies behind the dramatic portrayal of characters such as Heathcliff and Shylock in ways that evoke pity for their suffering as well as horror at their cruelty. Paradoxically, therefore, we in the audience are encouraged to grant these characters the mercy they themselves refused to extend to others. By now, this kind of appeal to the mercy of the audience – or the jury – has become so familiar that the delinquents' plea to Officer Krupke in *West Side Story*, 'We're depraved because we're deprived' evokes laughter at the banality of the cliché as well as a rueful recognition that there is some truth in it.[14] Yet one could argue that the plea for, as well as the quality of mercy pleaded for in *West Side Story* is a legacy passed on to us by some of the greatest artists in Western Europe: the adjective 'great' can here be legitimately applied to this tradition in opposition to the trashiest genres, such as pornography and propaganda of the *Der Stürmer* ilk, that are explicitly designed to snuff out *any* empathy or mercy for 'the Other'.

For instance, Ben Jonson once observed that the goal of the dramatic poet is 'To make the spectators understanders'. And in drama if not in real life, to understand all is to come very close to forgiving all, since we know how much a character has suffered. Various processes of dramatic identification, of imaginatively envisaging oneself in the place of another just as the second wife of Max de Winter felt temporarily transformed into Rebecca, are of course common both to the actors in and the audience at any engrossing play or film.[15] But in certain works actors and audiences alike are encouraged to identify to a greater or lesser degree with characters quite alien to themselves and temporarily at least, we are thus encouraged to look at what we most despise or fear with a measure of compassion and understanding. A quick look at the processes of alienation and empathy that interact in *The Tempest* can serve to illustrate these points.

It should first be noted, though by now it should be too obvious to need saying, that in so far as they evoke pity, mercy, empathy, most of the works surveyed here have likewise identified themselves with values and virtues traditionally associated with the 'feminine' principle. That is, with those characteristics (soft, tender, merciful, gentle, 'bleeding hearts') that on the one hand have been extolled as attributes of the Mother of God, and on the other hand have been denigrated and despised as effeminate, but in either case are traditionally associated with female characters in literature: 'O, I have suffered/With those I saw suffer' says the sympathetic Miranda in *The Tempest*: 'I think the monster just needed love' said lovely Marilyn of the Creature from the Black Lagoon, a fish-like monster directly descended from Shakespeare's Caliban. Looked at from a political angle, the sympathies evoked by the Alien Other, Caliban, are also worth further consideration. As Andrea Dworkin has shown, the systematic brutalisation of the dark gypsy brat Heathcliff can be seen as a kind of allegory of race oppression, just as *The Merchant of Venice* may be symbolically interpreted as a minatory account of the way that ancient tribal grudges tend to feed on and finally bleed each other to death. And as has long been noted, *The Tempest* can be read as an allegory of colonialism that, in effect, contains its own condemnation of the processes it portrays.

ENEMY ALIENS AND DRAMATIC EMPATHIES

> Grandcourt held that the Jamaican negro was a beastly sort of baptist Caliban; Deronda said he had always felt a little with Caliban, who naturally had his own point of view . . . Mrs. Torrington was sure she should never sleep in her bed if she lived among blacks; her husband corrected her by saying that the blacks would be manageable enough if it were not for the half-breeds; and Deronda remarked that the whites had to thank themselves for the half-breeds.
>
> George Eliot, *Daniel Deronda*

This thing of darkness I acknowledge mine.

Prospero in *The Tempest*

*   *   *   *

Although the action takes place on an enchanted island somewhere between Tunis and Naples, references to the Bermudas place *The Tempest* in the context of the colonisation of the New World. It was performed at the court of King James in 1611, only two years after ships on the way to Jamestown were wrecked on Bermuda and the survivors wrote back about their providential landing there. And when it is looked back at from this historical distance, the way the native inhabitant of the island, Caliban, is treated by the Europeans in *The Tempest* seems a dire prophecy of the fate of the American Indian. He first escorted the new arrivals around the island, taught them its lore and showed them how to find water and food. He is later treated like a slave, taught only enough of the settlers' language to learn how to curse, confined to a cell, made to do hard labour and tormented if he does not do so obediently. The excuse for his ill treatment and enslavement is, of course, that he tried to rape a white woman. Later arrivals ply Caliban with liquor, plan to exhibit him as a freak, make fun of him, and so on. Looked at historically all of these seem sadly familiar ways of defining an enemy so as to justify the confinement and oppression of some naturally inferior, brutish, god-forsaken, vile, slave-like race of potential terrorists who are also associated with the demonic.

What is as historically striking as it is depressing is to note how much the adjectives used almost four hundred years ago to describe Caliban (and to denigrate his mother, Sycorax), resemble the adjectives used a thousand years ago, in *Beowulf* to describe the tribal enemy Grendel (and to denigrate his mother), as well as the adjectives Americans used to describe the Japanese in Treasury Department polls taken in the nineteen forties: 'ungodly, subhuman, beastly, sneaky and treacherous' (Sheehan (1989), p. 154). There just isn't any significant difference in these descriptions of the enemy. Caliban is described as a ungodly monster, the son of a witch, brutish, subhuman, treacherous. In the ancient epic, *Beowulf*, Caliban's counterpart is the tribal enemy Grendel, the subhuman creature who inhabits the fens and marshes and sneaks up on the mead hall at night. Grendel is an ungodly monster, an evil spirit, an outcast who is directly descended from Cain (compare the way blacks have been anathematised as descendants of Ham).

What's equally depressing is that the other major way of defining a tribal adversary that has recurred throughout the twentieth century – that is, as a superhuman, supernaturally powerful Dragon – also occurs in *Beowulf*. In subsequent epics (see Book I of Spenser's *Faerie Queene*) the kind of Dragon – the mighty 'wyrm' – that Beowulf went down fighting was associated with the Great Satan, the 'wyrm'-as-serpent, the anti-Christ. Sometimes all these stereotypes are combined. In the Third Reich, for instance, Jews were Grendelised in propaganda films portraying them as physically and morally subhuman monsters, and Calibanised as out to ravish beautiful Aryan virgins, and *simultaneously* Dragonised (the all-powerful International Jewish Conspiracy threatened to take over the world). At the height of the Cold War, America Dragonised Communism: the International Communist Movement was its Great Satan, and Russia was the Evil Empire behind all the woes of the West, while the Chinese and Korean soldiers were Grendelised. These ways of defining the national enemy remain so constant that they almost seem extensions of the ways one thinks of individual enemies: as inferior or as terrifyingly invincible, as born slaves, eternal victims, or eternal threats, but in any case *not* persons like ourselves to be negotiated with as equals, but subhuman beings or demonic monsters that must be wiped off the face of the earth (the only good Indian is a dead Indian, the only solution to the Jewish problem is a Total Solution). The same Dragon/Grendel/Caliban clichés are presently being parroted all over the world at the peril of those who do the defining as well as those who are so defined. For, of course, defining someone or some group in a given way is, sometimes at least, to transform them into the projected type of enemy. Or worse. Heathcliff was Grendelised to the point where he turned into a Dragon.

To return to *The Tempest*, the political allegory contains its own criticisms of the colonialist mentality in so far as the treatment of Caliban evokes the audience's sympathy for him. Not one individual I know personally who has read or seen this play has not felt sorry for Caliban; many people like him better than any other character in the play. The least popular characters in *The Tempest* are the courtiers who pretend to civility but are more treacherous and ultimately contemptible than Caliban. At least his brutish physical desire for Miranda does not seem unnatural in the same way that a determination to kill your own brother seems unnatural. Throughout the action, Caliban is treated sympathetically and indeed affectionately by the author (who gives him some of the best lines in the show) in a way the heartless courtiers never are. They are cool, they are witty but they evoke no feeling, whereas 'Deronda said he always felt a little for Caliban, who naturally had his own point of view'. He certainly does: since Shakespeare gives him a just claim to the island, he is as entitled to feel that Prospero is a usurper as Prospero is entitled to see Antonio as one. Perhaps significantly, in *The Forbidden Planet*, a classic science fiction film based on *The Tempest*, the Caliban figure is seen as a psychic component of the Prospero figure, like the Freudian id in opposition to the superego. This interpretation may be derived from Shakespeare's original script. 'This thing of darkness I acknowledge mine', says Prospero, who here as elsewhere seems to be speaking as, if not for, the playwright himself (for whose are Shakespeare's things of darkness if *not* his?). You can thus see *The Tempest* as one of those works wherein the conflicting characters are designed to correspond with the forces that contend on the psychological level of action so that Caliban is associated internally as well as externally with brute, physical nature (that can't be done without but must be controlled); Ariel with fancy, imagination, art; Miranda with innocence; Antonio with cynicism and with evil; Prospero with experience, and/or with an artist trying to control all these forces at once.

And in an odd way the highest achievement of Prospero's art is empathy. Through a series of identifications he ultimately acknowledges everything – good or evil – in this play as his own: my daughter, my brother, this thing of darkness, my brave spirit. When he is ready to inflict revenge on those who exiled him he is informed by his delicate spirit, Ariel, how his enemies are so full of sorrow and dismay that if he 'now beheld them' his affections 'would become tender'. 'Dost thou think so?' Prospero asks.

ARIEL. Mine would, sir, were I human.

And so, Prospero concludes, 'mine shall' (V, i, 18–20). In this play, it's as if 'tender affections', imaginative apprehension and 'kindly' sympathy for the suffering of others are what constitute humanity:

Hast thou which art but air, a touch, a feeling
Of their afflictions, and shall not myself,
One of their kind, that relish all as sharply,
Passion as they, be kindlier mov'd than thou art?
Though with their high wrongs I am struck to th' quick
Yet with my nobler reason 'gainst my fury
Do I take part; the rarer action is
In virtue than in vengeance; they being penitent,
The sole drift of my purpose doth extend
Not a frown further.
                (V, i, 21–30)[16]

Defending poetry and poets in lines that concur with Prospero's, the radical Romantic poet, Shelley, concluded that 'The great secret of morals is love – or a going out of our own nature.' To 'be greatly good', we 'must imagine intensely and comprehensively'; we must put ourselves 'in the place of another, and of many others'; we must experience 'the pains and pleasures of our species' as our own (Shelley's *Works*, vii. 101, 118). Shelley's manifesto is, of course, characteristic of an old-fashioned and currently devalued 'liberal humanism', but the universalist sympathies it encouraged may now need reaffirmation as a matter of urgent historical necessity. As Christopher Hitchens has concluded, by now it seems all too painfully true that 'We still live in the prehistory of the human race, where no tribalism can be much better than another, and where humanism and internationalism, so much derided and betrayed, need an unsentimental and decisive restatement' (Hitchens (1989), p. 357). There is therefore something profoundly positive to be said for the appeals made to sameness and to mercy and to internationalism in art.

Looked at historically, ever since Aeschylus wrote the *Persians*, to treat 'the Other' sympathetically, and so to challenge prejudice, would seem to have posed an irresistible challenge to major artists. For instance (Fitz (1977), pp. 313–14), in his later tragedies Shakespeare goes out of his way to elicit the audience's sympathy for such 'inherently unsympathetic' figures as 'a stubborn and mentally infirm octogenarian, a murderer, a mama's boy, and (most difficult of all) a disreputable woman'. He thus 'makes extreme demands on the tolerance (or perhaps on the Christian charity, in the most radical sense) of his audience'. 'We are not expected to agree, in every case, that the protagonist is more sinned against than sinning'; but we are expected, 'on the basis of common humanity with the offending character', to offer sympathy unqualified by the necessity for moral exoneration. What Shakespeare's personal intent was we will never know. As D. M. Cohen has argued, Shakespeare may have humanised Shylock simply to 'enrich his drama', and not in order to plead for racial or religious tolerance (Cohen (1980), pp. 53–63). For that matter, the dramatic impact of sympathetic portrayals of, say, individual Jews, monsters, whores, homosexuals or interracial lovers necessarily depends on the continuing strength of the taboos against treating such types sympathetically. If there were no such thing as racial prejudice there would be no dramatic impact one way or the other in presenting a Negro–White marriage as a complete and glorious success resulting in lots of children and grandchildren. But be that as it may. In marked contrast to major artists, minor artists generally seem afraid to challenge racial and sexual prejudices, while truly trashy genres go out of their way to reinforce them. Looked at politically, the literary tradition at its greatest is often far ahead of the critical tradition on *account* of the empathies it evokes. For that matter, emotional responses critically derided as 'sentimentalist' such as the romantic, passionately sympathetic responses to the characters in plays such as *Othello* or *Antony and Cleopatra*, are by all odds the most politically radical (racially, sexually, socially) ways of responding to them.

Of course you can, at one stroke, snuff out empathy and deny the humane internationalism and radical sympathies (for interracial lovers, disreputable women, and so on) encouraged in art by positing critical arguments that *any* given work is ultimately devised to uphold whatever tribal or sexual or social taboos or traditions its erring characters violate. Allan Bloom thus manages to reduce *Othello* and *The Merchant of Venice* to case-histories demonstrating the inevitably disastrous consequences of mixed marriages by turning Desdemona and Jessica into 'the real villains of the Venetian plays' (Hovey (1988), pp. 42–3): 'Rebelling against their fathers, who [realistically and sensibly reject intermarriage with a member of a different race or religion] they seek to join black and white, Christian and Jew, but only succeed in bringing degradation to themselves and tragedy to Brabantio and Shylock'. Thus Desdemona, Bloom concludes, got pretty much what she had coming to her (Bloom (1981), p. 62). By contrast, Bloom complains that Shakespeare so grievously failed to punish Jessica with comparable severity. Jessica, he asserts, 'is one of the very few figures in Shakespeare who do not pay the penalty for their crimes; and disobedience to one's parents, be they good or bad, is a crime for Shakespeare' (Bloom, p. 30). Both of these assertions are, however, contrary to fact. For the truth is that in numerous other plays by Shakespeare the 'crime' of disobedience to a parent likewise goes unpunished. Hermia, Celia and Anne Page disobey their fathers, Florizel elopes with Perdita and all of them get off scot free of any penalty for their crimes and, presumably, live happily ever after with their chosen mates. Indeed, 'father prohibits girl from marrying boy she loves; girl elopes with boy; true love triumphs and all ends happily' would seem the formulaic outline of innumerable romantic comedies that Shakespeare uses as a point of departure in creating the tragic actions of *Romeo and Juliet* and *Othello*. What's disturbing about the portrayal of Jessica in *The Merchant of Venice* (which is in outline a romantic comedy) is not that her disobedience goes unpunished, but that she feels less guilty towards and/or less sympathy for Shylock than we feel she ought to. Or than we do. We, after all, are the ones who are haunted by Shylock's lines lamenting the loss of the ring she so heedlessly exchanged for a monkey: 'I had it of Leah when I was a bachelor; I would not have given it for a wilderness of monkeys' (III, i, 105–6). Like Caliban, Shylock is given his own point of view.

Shelley is certainly right in arguing that the best works of art encourage us, as virtually no other form of discourse does, to put ourselves in the place of the other and of many others, or like an actor, to emotionally project ourselves into their situation. 'There but for the Grace of God go I' is well-nigh inevitably our emotional response to the portrayals of characters brought down from high place to low by circumstances or oppression, or by their own errors, in 'high' literature and popular genres alike. To feel smugly superior to such figures from King Lear to Grizabella the Glamour Cat won't do. Shuddering at the sight of Cathleen Calvert, who was once a dashing belle, but now 'looked poor white, shiftless, slovenly, trifling' (*Gone With the Wind*, p. 707), Scarlett realised 'how narrow was the chasm between quality folk and poor whites'. Priding herself on not having fallen so low – 'There but for a lot of gumption am I' she thought, 'lifting her chin and smiling' – she is shamed by a reproving look from another character. And so is any reader who might feel that, so placed, *they'd* never have fallen so low as Cathleen. The terrifying narrowness of the chasm between where we are and where we can fall to is likewise stressed when Tom Wolfe's Sherman stops identifying himself with the ruling class, with the aristocracy, and sees himself as no different from any other client of the criminal lawyers, Dershkin, Bellavita, Fishbein & Schlossel (p. 625): 'I'm standard issue. Every creature has its habitat, and I'm in mine right now . . . if I think I'm above it, I'm only kidding myself, and I've stopped kidding myself.' And of course an ultimate alternation and alteration occurs when King Lear himself identifies with the poorest of the poor:

> Poor naked wretches, whereso'er you are,
> That bide the pelting of this pitless storm,
> How shall your houseless heads and unfed sides,
> Your loop'd and window'd raggedness, defend you
> From seasons such as these? O, I have ta'en
> Too little care of this! Take physic, pomp;
> Expose thyself to feel what wretches feel,
> That thou mayst shake the superflux to them,
> And show the heavens more just.
>
> (*King Lear*, III, iv, 28–36)

It could be that Shelley was right in arguing that it is in its extensions of imaginative sympathies from the One to the Other and to many others – including types generally regarded as inessential others as well as the types we most fear and despise – that the true moral value of the literary tradition resides.

But be that as it may. As Caliban and the Marquise de Merteuil alike concluded, literature can be seen as a source of power, of know-how – to say nothing of sheer pleasure – quite independently of its moral function. 'Remember first to possess [Prospero's] books', Caliban tells his co-conspirators, 'for without them/He's but a sot, as I am' (III, ii, 87–9). It is because the knowledge contained in books gives one group power over the other that it was long forbidden to teach blacks and Indians to read in certain American states. Compare Heathcliff's systematic efforts to turn Hindley's bright son, Hareton, into a kind of Caliban and keep him one by teaching him to scorn everything 'extra-animal' as silly and weak, to despise the books he could not read, and so take pride in his brutish ignorance (*Wuthering Heights*, p. 219). There could be no more efficient way to keep persons or races down where you want them.

After all, as the Marquise de Merteuil clearly realised, books are useful precisely because you need not necessarily derive from them the message your rulers want you to. On the contrary. You can choose your own role models from wicked characters as well as from virtuous types. You can emulate the Alcharisi, and refuse to do what orthodoxy says you ought to do and do what it says you ought not to do. Like the Marquise herself, you can learn a lot from what is said between the lines and from what certain authors do not say or dare not say. You can learn models of behaviour traditionally deemed attractive and admirable, and, if you will, use them as cover-ups to do as you wish. Or reverse them so as to identify yourself as a rebel. And so on. These truisms tend to be ignored in arguments about the academic study of high literature and popular genres alike.

So does the obvious fact that in nothing else studied can more delight be experienced while in the pursuit of knowledge. Where can our hearts and brains and courage be more enriched than on the yellow brick road to the Emerald City of Oz?

Notes

CHAPTER ONE

1. Here as elsewhere, intertextuality, direct and indirect allusions, cross-references and tributes to other works enrich the enjoyment of readers who recognise the sources, although Wolfe's novel would be perfectly comprehensible regardless of whether you know 'who Christopher Marlowe was'. Compare, for instance, Shakespeare's allusion to Marlowe as 'the dead shepherd' ('now I find thy saw of might'), when he quotes the line, 'Who ever loved that loved not at first sight?' from Marlowe's 'Hero and Leander' in *As You Like It* (III, v, 80-1). For that matter, this kind of artistic insider-trading is by no means limited to ancient or modern works of 'high' literature, such as Eliot's 'The Waste Land' and Joyce's *Ulysses*: it is characteristic of virtually every genre. The country and western lament, 'I Didn't Know God Made Honky-Tonk Angels' inspired the echoing song, 'It Wasn't God Who Made Honky-Tonk Angels' ('Too many married men still think that they are single,/And cause many a young girl to go wrong') in exactly the same way that Christopher Marlowe's poem, 'A Passionate Shepherd to His Love' inspired Sir Walter Ralegh's answer, 'The Nymph's Reply to the Shepherd'; and an enjoyment of the one is, likewise, enhanced by familiarity with the other.

2. In this regard, as elsewhere, the legend of Faustus also has obvious affinities with the story of Frankenstein, to which innumerable films are likewise indebted. For a detailed discussion of the Frankenstein paradigm, see Chris Baldick (1987), *In Frankenstein's Shadow: Myth, Monstrosity, and Nineteenth Century Writing*, Oxford.

3. Russian males have proved the hardest of all enemies for Hollywood to stereotype. They don't look or act like sissies. They fought too heroically in the Second World War to be put down as sneaky cowards. They sent the first man into space, so they can't be stereotyped as subhuman morons. And they are as anti-aristocratic as Americans. The only stereotype that emerges from all this, rather like Yuri Gagarin, is far too comparable to the ideal American he-man to be much of a villain. Oscar Homolka made a career out of playing older Russian characters, but he himself is hard to stereotype as a bad guy.

4. As Tom Wolfe observes in his essay on Cary Grant, the new breed of hero is no more realistic than the matinee idols of yesteryear. No fewer men, nowadays, wear coats and ties than they did in the forties and fifties and early sixties, but far fewer heroes wear them on screen. There is,

undoubtedly, a great box-office appeal 'in the rawness, the lubricity, the implicit sadism' of the macho hero as portrayed in combination with 'what Hollywood imagines to be the sexual verve of the lower classes', especially as embodied in the magnificent form of the young Marlon Brando. Yet it is probably true that the embarrassingly small number of American men who actually look and act like Brando, or the young Clint Eastwood, or Sylvester Stallone is roughly equivalent to the number of American women who 'really wish to see Mister Right advancing toward them in a torn strap-style undershirt with his latissimae dorsae flexed' (pp. 137–8). For that matter, as Cary Grant himself observed, acting styles obviously go in fads:

> It's like girls at a dance. One night a fellow walks in wearing a motorcycle jacket and blue jeans and he takes the first girl he sees and embraces her and crushes her rib cage. 'What a man!' all the girls say, and pretty soon all the boys are coming to the dances in motorcycle jackets and blue jeans and taking direct action. That goes on for a while, and then one night in comes a fellow in a blue suit who can wear a necktie without strangling . . . the girls say 'What a charmer!' and they're off on another cycle. . . . Well, as for me, I just keep going along the same old way.

And, indeed, the legendary drawing power of Cary Grant's films may have resulted from the fact that he so consistently treated the heroine 'not merely as an attractive woman' but as 'a witty and intelligent woman' (Wolfe (1981), pp. 137–40). It is also perhaps significant that the most enduring ikon of the motorcycle jacket type is James Dean whose film persona, in contrast to macho types today, also displayed a remarkably sensitive soul.

5. Infected by war fever, young men never heed the voice of past experience either. Compare, for instance, Rubens's description of his painting about the 'Horrors of War' with the anti-war arguments made by the 'old wise man' in Chaucer's *The Tale of Melibee* (ll. 1035 ff):

> 'Up stirten thanne the younge folk atones, and the mooste partie of that compaignye han scorned this old wise man, and bigonnen to make noyse, and seyden that/right so as, wyhil that iren is hoot, men sholden smyte, right so men sholde wreken hir wronges whil that they been fresshe and newe; and with loud voys they criden 'Werre! werre!'/ Up roos tho oon of thise olde wise, and with his hand made contenaunce that men sholde holden hem stille and yeven hym audience./ 'Lordynges,' quod he, 'ther is ful many a man that crieth 'Werre! werre!' that woot ful litel what werre amounteth./ Werre at his bigynnyng hath so greet an entryng and so large, that every wight may entre when hym liketh, and lightly fynde werre;/ but certes what end that shal therof bifalle, it is nat light to knowe./ For soothly, whan that werre is ones bigonne, ther is ful many a child unborn of his mooder that shal sterve yong by the cause of thilke werre, or elles lyve in sorwe and dye in wrecchednesse.'

And then see 'old man MacRae's' virtually identical warnings to the young Georgia hotheads in *Gone With the Wind:*

> 'What's it all about? What are they saying?'
> 'War!' shouted India, cupping her hand to his ear.
> 'They want to fight the Yankees!'
> 'War, is it?' he cried, fumbling about him for his cane and heaving himself out of the chair with more energy than he had shown in years. 'I'll tell 'um about war. I've been there'. . . . He stumped rapidly to the group, waving his cane and shouting and because he could not hear the voices around him, he soon had undisputed possession of the field.

'You fire-eating young bucks, listen to me. You don't want to fight. I fought and I know. Went out in the Seminole War and was a big enough fool to go to the Mexican War, too. You all don't know what war is. . . . It's going hungry, and getting the measles and pneumonia from sleeping in the wet. And if it ain't measles and pneumonia, it's your bowels. Yes sir, what war does to a man's bowels — dysentery and things like that ' (p. 109).

6. Karen Blixen's lover, Denys Finch-Hatton, appears to have been a rare, if not unique, example of a woman's ideal man who crossed the borderline between life and art. He was not only a big-game hunter and aviator, he was a classically educated aristocrat. Blixen's husband, Bror, was much closer to the he-man paradigm and is said to have been a real-life model for the big-game hunter in Hemingway's story, 'The Short, Happy Life of Francis Macomber'. By contrast, Denys Finch-Hatton taught the young Karen Blixen to read the Bible and Shakespeare and appears to have combined aristocratic *sprezzatura*, brilliance and sophistication with flying airplanes, going on safaris, shooting lions and so on. Rather like Sir Percy Blakeney, the 'damned elusive Pimpernel' in Baroness Orczy's novel, Finch-Hatton thus fused the noble, 'British aristocrat' persona with that of a dashing man of action, rather in the manner of successive, romantic heroes portrayed by Leslie Howard (as Sir Percy), David Farrar and Stewart Granger, in movies such as *King Solomon's Mines*. This is why to so many admirers of Blixen's memoirs, the comparatively boyish looking, quintessentially American 'Sundance Kid', Robert Redford, seemed utterly miscast as Finch-Hatton in the film. The reasons given for the casting of Redford opposite Meryl Streep in *Out of Africa* all had to do with the American box office. But the *non-boyish* British gentleman type which was once so popular with women currently appears to be extinct on both sides of the Atlantic.

7. It should be noted that 'there's no place [for a woman] like home' is *not* the ultimate message communicated by Baum's whole series of books about Oz. On these points, see Gore Vidal's essay on 'The Oz Books', in *Pink Triangle and Yellow Star* (1983), pp. 89, 100. Apart from allaying the worries of her Auntie Em and Uncle Henry, precisely *why* Dorothy really wanted to go back to Kansas was never any clearer to Vidal than it was to me: 'Or, finally, to Baum.' Eventually, he moves Dorothy (with aunt and uncle) to Oz. A banker is about to foreclose the mortgage on Uncle Henry's farm and Dorothy will have to go to work, says Aunt Em, stricken. 'You might do housework for someone, dear, you are so handy; or perhaps you could be a nursemaid to little children.' Dorothy smiled. 'Wouldn't it be funny', she said, 'for me to do housework in Kansas, when I'm a Princess in the Land of Oz?' It is decided that she will signal Ozma and depart for the Emerald City where Uncle Henry and Aunt Em are subsequently granted asylum. And so, here as elsewhere in the Oz books, 'the child's situation *vis-a-vis* the adult' is most effectively reversed.

> 'Don't be afraid,' she said to them. 'You are now in the Land of Oz, where you are to live always, and be comfer'ble an' happy. You'll never have to worry over anything again, 'cause there won't be anything to worry about. And you owe it all to the kindness of my friend Princess Ozma.

'And never forget it, one hears for mutter.' (p. 101). Vidal also makes perhaps the single most important point about the Oz books: 'Essentially Baum's human protagonists are neither male nor female but children, a separate category in his view if not in that of our latter-day sexists'. Indeed the lost Princess of Oz first appears as a boy named Tip, into which form she was changed by the witch Mombi, and is subsequently transformed back into the beautiful Ozma by Glinda the Good Sorceress – without undue trauma either for him/her or for the children reading about the transformation.

CHAPTER TWO

1. In Hebrew mythology, Lilith was Adam's first wife, who, having refused to subordinate herself to him, flew away and became a demon. See Robert Graves and Raphael Patai (1983), *Hebrew Myths: The Book of Genesis,* Greenwich House, p. 65:

> Adam and Lilith never found peace together; for when he wished to lie with her, she took offence at the recumbent posture he demanded. 'Why must I lie beneath you?' she asked. 'I also was made from dust and am therefore your equal.' Because Adam tried to compel her obedience by force, Lilith, in a rage, uttered the magic name of God, rose into the air and left him.

Subsequently, after the Fall woman's (Eve's) subordination to man (Adam) was decreed, as if engraved on tablets of stone for all eternity, by the Judaeo-Christian deity Himself: 'Thy desire shall be to thy husband and he shall rule over thee' (*Genesis* 3: 16).

On religion as the major historical agent of sexism, see Rosalind Miles (1988), *The Women's History of the World*, pp. 57–95, and Karen Armstrong, *The Gospel According to Woman: Christianity's Creation of the Sex War in the West*. And see also Christopher Hill's conclusions in 'History and the Present' (South Place Ethical Society, 1989), p. 13:

> One of the things I am most ashamed of is that for decades I proudly illustrated the spread of democratic ideas in 17th century England by quoting the ringing Leveller declarations, 'The Poorest he that is in England hath a life to live as the greatest he', 'every man that is to live under a government ought first by his own consent to put himself under that government'. Every he? Every man? What about the other 50% of the population? I suppose in one sense I must have noticed the absence of woman from these statements; but I somehow assumed that that had to be taken for granted in 17th century England.

But if we ask '*why* it was taken for granted – not only by men but even by Leveller women who canvassed, agitated, petitioned, leafleted and lobbied for the vote of their menfolk and apparently never even thought of asking for it themselves' – then certain questions 'about the overwhelming influence of the Bible' are opened up that would mandate 'a bigger rethink of the past' than most academic historians have contemplated. The same is true of certain literary historians: e.g. so far as their support for sexism and their resistance to change are concerned, compared to the reactionary forces of the Islamic, Judaeo-Christian and Far Eastern religious traditions, the 'liberal humanism' that is the *bête noir* of post-structuralism seems a paper tiger. To take the ultimate stand against sexism you would have to launch a direct attack on virtually every fundamentalist (i.e. *unsullied* with liberalism or secular humanism) religion on earth, as well as other articles of faith such as certain fundamental tenets of Freudian psychoanalysis which, in their historical,

NOTES189

clinical, impact on women have caused far too much suffering to be described or rationalised as anything but quasi-religious, pseudo-scientific instruments of repression (Miles, pp. 216-17).

2. After directing *The Red Shoes* Michael Powell returned to the identical '*Faust*-like conflict' in the film version of Offenbach's opera *The Tales of Hoffman* (1951). In its final episode 'The Story of Antonia', the heroine, who is a singer suffering from consumption, is warned by her father to beware of the burning ambition that had previously destroyed her mother, who was a celebrated *diva*. The sinister Dr Miracle (whose death's-head make-up is reminiscent of Lon Chaney's in the first film version of *The Phantom of the Opera*) summons up the voice of Antonia's dead mother who, through her statue as a prima donna, calls to her daughter in a sublimely eerie aria commanding Antonia from beyond the grave to sing, divinely, just once more. Horrified, Antonia's father and her suitor, Hoffman, implore Antonia not to risk her life and soul by singing. Surrealistic images of hellish flames emerge from and blend with the image of innumerable hands applauding Antonia's fatal song which is conducted, as in an immense theatre, by the demonic Dr Miracle. Antonia, of course, dies immediately after having sung (compare George du Maurier's portrayal of the death of Trilby). What seems particularly interesting about Antonia's case is that the spirit of the girl's mother urges her on to artistic achievement. The father and the suitor, as usual, embody the forces of normality, morality, fertility, domesticity, safety and so on, that are (here as elsewhere) dramatically and dialectically opposed to the heroine's artistic ambitions.

3. So far as I know, the following arguments made, millenia ago, by Plato, have never been refuted. There is, Plato concludes, no profession which is peculiar to woman as woman or man as man: 'natural capacities are similarly distributed in each sex, and it is natural for women to take part in all occupations as well as men'. For instance, 'one woman may have a natural ability for medicine or music, another not . . . and one may be good at athletics, another have no taste for them; one be good at soldiering, another not'. Like individual men, individual women 'may be philosophic or unphilosophic, spirited or spiritless'. Therefore, the idea that 'men and women need the same education, and that education will operate on the same nature in both sexes is no impossible day dream but in accordance with nature; it is the contrary practice that seems unnatural'. Although Plato observes that women generally will be 'the weaker partners', in any given occupation, he also acknowledges that 'a good many women are better than a good many men at a good many things'. And if the 'only difference apparent between them is that the female bears and the male begets', that is not a difference relevant to the argument that males and females with comparable capacities 'ought to follow the same occupations'. See *The Republic*, trans. Desmond Lee (Part VI, Book 6), pp. 233-5.

4. It's interesting that Auerbach compares the heroine of George du Maurier's bestseller to characters created by George Eliot, one of the very few novelists allowed entry, along with Henry James, into F. R. Leavis's 'great tradition'. Leavis himself would not have allowed the lesser George to be compared in any way except dismissively to the greater. In freely discussing them together, Auerbach is closer to the artistic tradition, which has always been demonstrably less snobbish and exclusive than the critical tradition. For

instance, George du Maurier, who immensely admired Henry James, told
him his idea for the story of Trilby and urged James to write it. James
thought the idea was very interesting – he himself had displayed an interest
in mesmerism in *The Bostonians* as well as in various other works and was
subsequently delighted with the tremendous success of du Maurier's most
popular novel. See Henry James's *Notebooks*, ed. Leon Edel and Lyle H.
Powers (1987), pp. 51–2 (entry for Monday, 25 March, 1889 and the note
to this entry on p. 571). By the way, as an example of the continuing
interactions between works in differing as well as comparable literary and
theatrical traditions, it is interesting to note that, in *The Bostonians*, Olive and
Verena read the works of George Eliot, and so James pays homage to her
artistry. It is also interesting to note, to say nothing of adding to the store of
completely useless information, that Andrew Lloyd Webber's hit musical
version of *The Phantom of the Opera* opened in London at Her Majesty's
Theatre, which was built by Beerbohm Tree on the proceeds of *his* hit stage-
version of *Trilby*.

5. For instance: whether or not the individual women interviewed personally
    believed this to be a good thing or a bad thing, all of them agreed that, today
    as yesterday, girls are constantly being psychologically conditioned to
    believe that women are not, and/or ought not to be, as ambitious as men.
    This identical message emerged from the results of a debate at Cheltenham
    Ladies' College (reported in *Out of the Doll's House* – see Holdsworth
    (1988), pp. 39–40), where the majority of students concluded that if girls
    who study medicine, law and so on, do not, finally, become top surgeons,
    judges and professors, 'it will only be because they genuinely do not want
    to' and because 'the professional side of life means less to a woman than it
    does to a man'.

    > In other words, they feel it will be their own choice, not male ego [or gender
    > conditioning] that holds them back and keeps them content to play second fiddle.
    > The Cheltenham girls did not question why this should be. They simply
    > accepted it as feminine and natural.

    But *mutatis mutandis* and by the same token, girls academically outshine the
    boys in other schools, where males are conditioned to believe that to make
    good grades is to be a sissy. In either case, so conditioned are gender roles in
    schools and professions of different kinds, that there is no way to generalise
    about male or female nature on the basis of the way men and women perform
    in any of them.
        So far as individually single-minded and ambitious girls are concerned, as
    one woman observed (she herself was struggling to combine a successful
    career as an actress with being a devoted wife and mother), things today are,
    comparatively at least, somewhat easier for gifted young Alcharisis.
    Although comparably ambitious women still may be deemed 'unnatural' and
    'unfeminine' in certain quarters, they are, at least professionally, free to fight
    for their right to success without apology and without agonising over
    internal conflicts between the competing demands for time, emotional
    energy, etc., made by family life, and/or by their own equally genuine
    desires and needs to be loving and devoted wives and mothers. Things are,
    now as ever, hardest of all for the women who want it all and journalistic
    effusions about celebrities who have managed to combine brilliant careers
    with happy marriages, etc., tend to evade the most obvious point about

them: it is much, much, easier to 'have it all' *after* you already have it made professionally.

6. For instance, Dr Miriam Stoppard recently singled out this taboo as the central topic in her popular and influential advice column (see *TV Times*, 28 January–3 February 1989, p. 82):

> In the past, women have rarely confessed to having no maternal instincts, or surprisingly few, but now more women feel free to admit to what they feel is a biological inadequacy. It is no such thing, of course. Maternal instincts are under hormone control — if you don't have the hormones, you don't have the instincts. Many women revel in the joy children bring, but there is a downside — loss of freedom, career and identity, and feelings of isolation. [She thus advises the woman ('not a high-powered career woman') who couldn't face the thought of having children, not to risk having a child in the hope that she 'might want it when it arrives'] . . . I don't think you are abnormal [and] I certainly don't think you should gamble with the life of a child. So accept yourself as normal and contact others (in the British Organisation of Non-Parents) who feel as you do.

And a lot of women do. In a poll of single women commissioned for *New Woman* Magazine (see the New Year Issue, 1989, pp. 12–13), 'more than half (54 per cent) the women who didn't have children said they didn't want them'. This result appeared 'contrary to fashionable thinking — that a woman's urge to bear children is so strong that she is compelled to indulge it however adverse her circumstances' – but it is 'probably a pretty accurate reflection' of what many women today actually feel.

And so, on the one hand, it is obviously true that, like the Biblical Rachel who cried out 'Give me children or else I die', some women, today as yesterday, will go to virtually any lengths to have children of their own – see, for instance, Susan Hill's harrowing account of her own efforts to have another baby in her forties (in *Family*, 1989). On the other hand, it is just as obviously true that many other women will go to any lengths not to. As Rosalind Miles observes in her discussion of the struggle for birth-control (*The Women's History of the World*, p. 204),

> The staggering range of devices and potions from pre-history to the present day, with women worldwide straining every nerve for non-motherhood, also casts an ironic sidelight on the myth of the 'maternal instinct'. Anything and everything, it seems, that could possibly have conferred the blessing of infertility was pressed into service.

For that matter, social attitudes towards female fertility remain as achingly ambivalent and contradictory in life as they do in art. As Julie Burchill observes in her essay on the screen goddesses, Garbo, Monroe and Bardot – none of whom 'had visible children' –

> society can blather on all it likes about the sanctity of motherhood, but the girls on film it has always worshipped — not just this trinity but all the fictions — are ritually removed from humdrum women by their sexy sterility
>
> (*Girls on Film*, p. 156).

By very much the same token, at the chic Park Avenue party in Tom Wolfe's *Bonfire of the Vanities* (pp. 333–4) the women came in two varieties. First, there were women in their late thirties and in their forties and older, all of them skin and bones, 'starved to near perfection'. Second, there were women in their twenties or early thirties, 'the so-called Lemon Tarts, mostly blondes, the sort of women men refer to, quite without thinking, as *girls*', the

third or fourth wives of the rich male guests. What was entirely missing from
the party was

> that manner of woman who is neither very young nor very old, who has laid in a
> lining of subcutaneous fat, who glows with plumpness and has a rosy face that
> speaks, without a word, of home and hearth and hot food ready at six and stories
> read aloud at night and conversations while seated on the edge of the bed just
> before the Sandman comes. In short, no one ever invited . . . Mother.

7. See, for instance, the interview between the journalist and the artist in
Margaret Atwood's *Cat's Eye*, (p. 90).

> '. . . My husband's been terrific [says the artist], he gives me a lot of support,
> some of which has been financial.' I didn't say which husband.
> 'So you don't feel it's sort of demeaning to be propped up by a man?'
> 'Women prop up men all the time,' I say, 'What's wrong with a little reverse
> propping?'

Fair enough. But in marked contrast to this eminently sane and sensible
point, here are the two most inane of all the sexist theories about talented
women that I encountered in the process of writing this book.

According to both Michael Powell and Norman Mailer, a beautiful young
woman's artistic performance will, somehow, be miraculously enhanced if
she has sexual intercourse with some older, Svengali-type male. And thus
these male supremacists provide us (themselves?) with a kind of tutorial (as
opposed to a crassly commercial or crudely exploitative) justification for the
old casting-couch routine. 'I never let love interfere with business, or I
would have made love to Moira Shearer.' 'It would have improved her
performance,' boasts Michael Powell (*A Life in Movies*, p. 656). Powell
does not, however, go on to say whether having sexual intercourse with the
young ballerina would have improved his own professional performance as
director of *The Red Shoes*. Nor does he say whether making love to anybody
else, or to a whole lot of other men, would have effected a comparable or
even greater improvement in Moira Shearer's performance in the film. Still
one does wonder, if not, why not? By very much the same sexist token, in
his so-called biography of Marilyn Monroe, Norman Mailer posits the
theory that the old Hollywood mogul, Joseph Schenck, must have seen
'something' in the young starlet that made her seem 'truly his protégée . . .
annointed by him to receive an old man's gold – those secrets he is at last
obliged to communicate to another.' After all – or so Mailer informs us – an
'old sultan' is 'capable of smuggling anything into the mind and the body of
a young women'. Mailer does not tell us precisely what, if anything, in the
way of knowledge, etc., a young women is capable of communicating into
the mind and body of an old sultan for the obvious reason that 'less is known
about the true transactions of fucking than any science on earth' (*Marilyn: A
Biography* (1973), pp. 69–70). If there is a more inane observation, in ancient
or modern literature (high or low), it would be fun to know what it is.

8. As Archer and Simmonds go on to observe, 'Without a child to justify
herself, Marilyn Monroe would embark on spasmodic efforts to create
houses beautiful'. Likewise, when Judy Garland's 'contempt for her own
inability to keep husband, family and career in equilibrium grew too strong,
her recourse was to take to the scouring pads or frantically cook herself into a
state of grace'. Moreover, as Rupert Christiansen reminds us, it was some

ultimate kind of fulfilment as 'a normal woman' that Maria Callas tragically sought from the awful Aristotle Onassis 'whose interest in her singing extended only as far as the glamour and status she had incurred'. 'Now at last I am a happy normal woman of my age, even though I have to say that life for me really began at forty' Callas brightly proclaimed to *Life* magazine in 1964. 'The truth was that she was about to plummet into a period of barren misery, without marriage to Onassis or a resuscitated career.' (Christiansen, *Prima Donna*, pp. 310–11).

Archer and Simmonds argue that misplaced social and personal premiums on fame, commercial success, diva-status, etc., also contribute to the destruction of talented women. Yet there's no way for a beloved star of either sex to avoid the kind of public adoration that has followed ikons such as Marilyn Monroe, Maria Callas, Elvis Presley and James Dean beyond the grave. Moreover, the novelist David Lodge (*Working With Structuralism*, p. 163) has described, as a hopelessly 'vain endeavour', the New York Fiction Collective's 'consciousness-raising sessions' which were 'designed to eliminate the counterproductive addiction to "success" '. Very like performing artists,

> Novelists are driven by the dream of personal success (why else would they persist in such a difficult, laborious, psychologically taxing activity?) and their relationships with their peers usually include strong feelings of rivalry. They compare jealously advances, sales, terms of contract. They deeply resent – even socialist novelists deeply resent – paying income tax on their writing earnings, and often get into serious difficulties on this account. I do not mean to imply that novelists are a peculiarly mercenary group of writers. It is simply that they recognise . . . that their fortune in the market – the readiness of strangers to risk or expend money on their creative work – is a significant criterion of achievement. Not the only one, of course – we also want to be loved, respected, praised by the discerning (we are insatiable) – but an essential one, because an objective one. Indeed I believe most novelists, even 'literary' ones, would, forced to choose, prefer to be judged by the market (assuming it is free from censorship) than by any other institution. . . . The literary market, then, has functioned historically not merely as a means of material production and distribution of prose fiction, but as a kind of sounding board for the novelist's own sense of his literary identity and achievement. But the literary market can fulfil that function only as long as it is accessible to all works of merit. It may produce a good deal of rubbish, but it must not exclude the good. There must be a general faith that, sooner or later, any novel of real value will find a publisher. I personally believe that this is still true of the British publishing world. But it may not be true of America, and, if present trends continue, it may one day no longer be the case here. *That* will be the real crisis for publishing and for the novel.

9. Compare the highly romantic sense of obligation as well as inspiration manifested by Dame Janet Baker at her final performance in 1982 (Christiansen, *Prima Donna*, pp. 332–3):

> Acknowledging the final applause, she held up above her head the lyre she had been using as Orfeo, as if to direct the audience's tribute back to the spirit of music itself. It was a gesture that signified the depths of her idealism and her somehow Victorian conception of the nobility of the singer's calling, with its exalted mission to communicate the essence of music – but it amused a certain section of the public. Her diary of her last year as an opera singer was published to patronizing sneers at her reflections on art and life; and a glossy magazine nicknamed her 'Dame Granite'. Peter Hall, who knew her well and produced

that last *Orfeo*, saw it from another angle in his diary: 'My goodness, she seems
to be together, that woman. She knows what she wants, and she knows the
sacrifices she has to make in order to get it. She also treats her talent not as a meal
ticket, but as a serious responsibility that's got to be used to the full. She's a very
remarkable person.'
A very remarkable singer too, if in her case the two can be separated.

CHAPTER THREE

1. For further discussion see Terence Hawkes (1986), *That Shakespeherian Rag:
   Essays on a Critical Process*, Methuen, pp. 80–1: 'It will come as no surprise to
   those with a taste for Eliotic humour to learn that there really was such a
   song, as B. L. McElderry has pointed out. The work of the almost
   eponymous team of Gene Buck and Herman Ruby (words) and David
   Stamper (music), "That Shakespearian Rag", with its chorus,

   > That Shakespearian rag
   > Most intelligent, very elegant,
   > That old classical drag,
   > Has the proper stuff, the line, "Lay on Macduff"

   was one of the hit numbers of 1912.' Eliot, of course, interpolated the extra
   syllable in 'Shakespeherian', as well as adding the four 'O's.

2. Critics in the middle of the twentieth century, such as L. C. Knights and F.
   R. Leavis, derided the kind of old-fashioned, extra-textual questions – e.g.
   'How Many Children Had Lady Macbeth' – that post-Victorian critics,
   notably A. C. Bradley, had raised about the extra-dramatic life of Shakespeare's critics. Critics of a future age may find equally dated the late
   twentieth-century preoccupation with Othello's sexuality on the part of
   white male critics who raise the following extra-textual questions and well
   nigh invariably answer them in a way to assure that the sex act between the
   black man and the white woman was (a) not physically or (b) not
   emotionally or (c) in either event not mutually satisfactory. Here are some
   representative questions raised by such distinguished and influential critics as
   Stanley Cavell and Stephen Greenblatt. Precisely when, if ever, did Othello
   and Desdemona achieve congress? Did he penetrate her sufficiently to cause
   the wedding sheets to be stained with her virginal blood? If not, was he
   therefore in doubt about her virginity as well as his success as a lover? If he
   did bring her to orgasm, did her passionately erotic response itself unsettle
   Othello? After all, both Catholic and Protestant writings had condemned
   'excess' in married love as akin to adultery and this may have resulted in
   Othello's 'buried perception of his own sexual relations with Desdemona as
   adulterous'.
   Contrast the remarkably straightforward portrayal of the relationship in
   Verdi's *Otello* as described by Catherine Clement (in *Opera, or the Undoing of
   Women*, trans. Betsy Wing (1989), Virago Press, pp. 122–3):

   > In a twinkling of an eye [Otello] and Desdemona overstepped all distances: skin
   > color, the differences of class and age. How, knowing the end of the story, can
   > one not be moved? Look at these beautiful lovers who give themselves in a
   > sublime duet in which nothing concerning desire or its sources are hidden. . . .
   > He told her about his wars, his deserts, his slavery; she wept and sighed while she

listened to him. Then they return to the exchange made at the beginning of their lovemaking, they sing together the 'I' and 'you' of gift and countergift that they call 'their love.' And we see them pass from war to tears, from pity to atonement, and attain utmost desire.

CHAPTER FOUR

1. Blacks and women have justifiably complained about the either/or victim/ threat stereotypes that in effect deny them equality while casting them as the Other. The recent emergence of the career-bitch as a stereotype usually opposed to the bimbo-stereotype is a kind of modern variant on the old binary opposition between the prima-donna and the *ingénue* stereotypes, likewise implying that if a woman refuses to play the passive *ingénue*-victim-bimbo role then she *must* therefore be a threat/career-bitch/prima-donna. So powerful is the tendency to see everything in terms of these stereotypes that people in real life are victims (even as blacks are often victimised by the police) because they are erroneously seen as threats, or defined as threats (even as women are defined as career-bitches) because they won't put up with being patronised or victimised.

2. In seemingly contradictory arguments about dramatic identifications in the *Poetics*, Aristotle observed that the greatest tragic heroes are neither better nor worse than we are but 'like ourselves', although they should simultaneously seem superior to us in some way. It has also been argued that literature provides us with ideal characters whose virtues inspire us to emulate them. But Aristotle's apparently mixed up qualifications seem more descriptive of the actual processes of identification than the notion that art inspires us to emulate its personifications of virtue. It could be that we most powerfully sympathise with and identify with characters who are like ourselves in having certain flaws and (like Rick or Hamlet) are comparably vulnerable to the 'heart ache and the thousand natural shocks/That flesh is heir to' while also being somehow our superiors (braver or more glamorous) and so inspire our desire to be like them. The blindingly obvious fact that these forms of identification, empathy and admiration may attach us to glamorous villains and villainesses as readily as to virtuous characters has caused difficulties for critics ever since Plato called attention to it in *The Republic* – for further discussion see Hawkins (1985), pp. 14–60.

3. A good test of which characters women find most attractive are the parts which actresses most covet, and they are traditionally the wild, 'wicked', parts: Cathy, Scarlett, Cleopatra. It is interesting that the film versions of so many works discussed in this chapter are directly or indirectly associated with Vivien Leigh, the actress who got the most coveted film part of them all. Laurence Olivier, who was going to Hollywood to star as Heathcliff, wanted Leigh to play Cathy in *Wuthering Heights*, but the part had already been assigned to the beautiful but perhaps too ladylike Merle Oberon. Then David O. Selznick cast Leigh as the definitive Scarlett in *Gone With the Wind*. Subsequently she begged Selznick to let her play opposite Olivier as the second Mrs de Winter in *Rebecca*, but he gave the part to Joan Fontaine for the obvious reason that even in the drab sweater and skirt Leigh wore in her

screen-test for the part, she looked far more like the beautiful Rebecca than the comparatively plain *ingénue* required by the script. Most people would agree that Fontaine is ideally cast in the Hitchcock film: she's prettier than the narrator as described in the book, but perfectly communicates her youthful sincerity, sense of inadequacy and eagerness to please. Most women can identify with her. On the other hand, there are probably more women of all ages living today who have wished they looked like, or were like, Vivien Leigh as Scarlett O'Hara than any other actress playing any other role in any other film ever made. For further discussion, see *Scarlett's Women: Gone With the Wind and its Female Fans*, by Helen Taylor (1989), Virago.

4. A whole book could be written on structural affinities between certain works of 'high' literature and popular hits. For instance, the soap-opera *Dynasty*, like *Rebecca*, owes its basic structure to *Jane Eyre*. Indeed the *Jane Eyre* outline governs the structure of innumerable Romantic plots wherein the nice, but not fabulously wealthy or aristocratic, young heroine is beloved by the master of a great estate who is in some way haunted by the spectre of his first wife or some dark shadow of the past.

Compare, also, the 'Disaster Plot' formula that governs Albert Camus's *The Plague* and Peter Benchley's *Jaws* (and its various sequels) wherein an honourable person, or a group of good people, discover that something of great danger is threatening a whole community that responds by pretending the danger does not exist and otherwise evades responsibility before finally uniting to resist the terror. The Cover-up Disaster Plot, wherein the person who tries to warn the public about the catastrophe is thwarted by vested interests and/or ultimately reviled if not finally killed for telling the truth, governs many post-Watergate films and TV shows, including the impressive film of Ibsen's *An Enemy of the People* starring Steve McQueen, that stressed its modern relevance.

It is, structurally speaking, also interesting to compare 'Open Endings' in popular genres and 'high literature'. For instance, in one ending to Dickens's *Great Expectations*, Pip and Estella are reconciled and in the other they go their separate ways. Much the same thing happens in the last two chapters of *Gone With the Wind*. If, as a friend of mine did, you thought Mitchell's novel ended with Scarlett running home to Rhett's arms (see the last lines of the penultimate chapter quoted on p. 33 above) and so put it down without having read the final chapter, you would describe the novel as having a happy ending implying a sure and lasting reconciliation between Scarlett and Rhett. The last chapter, of course, ends with Rhett's exit ('I don't give a damn') and the prospect of reconciliation is left in doubt. Therefore, 'Did Scarlett ever get Rhett back again?' is the most famous open question in popular American lore. One could argue that Mitchell's experiment in suggesting alternative futures for her characters is more effective because it is less self-consciously precious than John Fowles's experiment with three alternative endings to *The French Lieutenant's Woman*, wherein (a) the protagonist does not get off the train to meet Sarah in Exeter, but marries Ernestina; (b) he finally is united with Sarah and their child; and (c) he and Sarah are estranged forever in the end. For full discussion of Fowles's endings - it would be interesting to know what he would say about Mitchell's - see David Lodge, 'Ambiguously ever after: problematical endings in English fiction' in *Working With Structuralism* (1981), pp. 143-

55. And compare also Harold Pinter's screenplay for *The French Lieutenant's Woman* where the movie within the movie ends happily while the affair between the stars of the movie ends unhappily.

5. As Madame de Merteuil observes, the dice in the game of love have always been loaded in favour of men, for whom 'defeat means only one victory the less'. For a woman, the social and biological stakes are far higher (or were until the emergence of AIDS) and a pregnancy or socially frowned on love affair could mean ruin. In 'this unequal contest', women are lucky not to lose, while men are only unlucky 'when they do not win'. Moreover, she observes, promises 'reciprocally given and received can be made and broken at will' by men alone (see p. 180). It was bad form (and still is – see *Fatal Attraction*) for a woman not to accept the end of an affair with good grace, but a man could threaten the woman with loss of reputation or worse if she wanted to end the relationship before he did: thus a 'woman's prudence' had to be most 'skilfully employed in undoing the same bonds' that a man would 'simply have broken'.

6. Throughout this novel, Scarlett's alternative identifications with her parents reflect her internal affinities with both of them as well as oppositions between the conflicting traits she inherited from and shared with her father and mother (pp. 86–7):

> For all the Tarleton girls were as unruly as colts and wild as March hares, there was an unworried single-mindedness about them that was part of their inheritance. . . . They were sure of themselves and of their environment. They knew instinctively what they were about, as did the Wilkeses, though in widely divergent ways, and in them there was no such conflict as frequently raged in Scarlett's bosom where the blood of a soft-voiced, overbred Coast aristocrat mingled with the shrewd, earthy blood of an Irish peasant. Scarlett wanted to respect and adore her mother like an idol and to rumple her hair and tease her too. And she knew she should be altogether one way or the other. It was the same conflicting emotion that made her desire to appear a delicate and high-bred lady with boys and to be, as well, a hoyden who was not above a few kisses. (pp. 86–7)

Compare the single-minded (though in widely divergent ways) women in *Daniel Deronda* – on the one hand Mirah Cohen and on the other hand the Alcharisi – with Gwendolen Harleth, who is subject to conflicting impulses, emotions and ambitions.

7. Gwendolen compares becoming a governess to entering a penitentiary; and only someone enamoured of the idea of being subject to constant scrutiny while in continual servitude should cast the first stone at her for that. The life of a governess really was rather like being in some pentitential order (see the painting of 'The Governess' (1844) by Richard Redgrave, 'a study in loneliness', reproduced by Flora Fraser in *The English Gentlewoman* (1987), p. 149). But, then, that was an unmarried woman's lot. Indeed, job-satisfaction outside marriage was a prospect yet undreamed of by gentlewomen (save for fantasies of triumph on the wicked stage) and so it is with palpable irony that George Eliot compares Gwendolen's predicament to the truly tragic fate of a gentle*man* forced to do work he deems beneath *his* abilities:

> Naturally her grievances did not seem to her smaller than some of her male contemporaries held theirs to be when they felt a profession too narrow for their

powers, and had an *a priori* conviction that it was not worth while to put forth their latent abilities. Because her education had been less expensive than theirs, it did not follow that she should have wider emotions or a keener intellectual vision. Her griefs were feminine; but to her as a woman they were not the less hard to bear, and she felt an equal right to the Promethean tone. (*Daniel Deronda*, pp. 320 1)

All women (regardless of their 'latent abilities') are traditionally supposed to recognise the nobility in doing servile, monotonous, thankless, low-paid or non-paid work deemed unworthy of the superior powers of their brothers.

8. What's traditionally 'unwomanly' is not hard work *per se*, but professional success in competition with men. See, for instance, Frank Kennedy's historically representative perspective on how well-born working women ought to behave in *Gone With the Wind* (pp. 637, 640):

> Frank had never heard of a woman in business anywhere. If women were so unfortunate as to be compelled to make a little money to assist their families in these hard times, they made it in quiet womanly ways - baking as Mrs. Merriwether was doing, or painting china and sewing and keeping boarders, like Mrs. Elsing and Fanny, or teaching school like Mrs. Meade or Mrs. Bonnell. These ladies made money but they kept themselves at home while they did it [and they also turned it over to their husbands] as a woman should. But for a woman to leave the protection of her home and venture out into the rough world of men, competing with them in business . . . . Frank wished he could hide in the dark back room of his store and see no one. His wife selling lumber! (p. 637)

And then (same song, second verse) compare the ideally feminine component of the American work-force extolled by *Look* magazine in 1956 (quoted in Friedan (1963), pp. 52–3):

> The American woman now works, rather casually, as a third of the U.S. labour force, less towards a 'big career' than as a way of filling a hope chest or buying a new home freezer. She gracefully concedes the top jobs to men. This wondrous creature also marries younger than ever, bears more babies and looks and acts far more feminine than the 'emancipated' girl of the '20s or even '30s.

See also Frank's view of how women can remain feminine and still get what they want in *Gone With the Wind* (p. 640).

> It was not that Frank had never seen commanding women before this. Atlanta, like all Southern towns, had its share of dowagers whom no one cared to cross. No one could be more dominating than stout Mrs. Merriwether, more imperious than frail Mrs. Elsing, more artful in securing her own ends than the silver-haired sweet-voiced Mrs. Whiting. But no matter what devices these ladies employed in order to get their own way, they were always feminine devices. They made a point of being deferential to a man's opinions, whether they were guided by them or not. They had the politeness to appear to be guided by what men said, and that was what mattered.

And still does. Note the emergence of the career-bitch stereotype as opposed to the sweet thing who gets her way by being or seeming charmingly deferential to men. Male critics who condemn feminist critics for not making the requisite historical and cultural distinctions between works produced in different periods by differing cultures seem to think that differing periods and differing cultures have offered more to women, in the way of differing options, than they actually have.

9. In contrast to their delicately nurtured counterparts in Victorian England

(but compare Cathy's childhood adventures with Heathcliff), many girls in the Old South acted with the same freedom from restraint as boys. Thomas Page of Virginia recalled that girls ran about the plantation yard wishing they were boys, and getting half-scoldings from mammy for being tomboys and tearing their aprons and dresses: 'Half-scoldings were also half-approvals.' Their introduction to the proprieties of ladyhood came much later. On these points, see Wyatt-Brown, pp. 138, 153, 231-2: 'From birth to the boys' "clothing" stage', girls and boys alike were allowed the same wild outdoor activity that often led to common accidents; getting lost in the woods, being thrown from ponies, falling from great heights, hurting themselves with firearms left casually about. One Virginia parent delightedly told her husband that the children were 'employed all day making bonfires'. Southerners were averse to strict regulation of young girls, and a little girl from England who visited the Blair plantation on the Eastern shore was described by her hostess as much 'to be pitied': 'The poor thing is stuck up in a chair all day long with a Coller on, nor dare she even to taste Tea fruit Cake or any little Triffle offer'd her by ye company'. Although stricter controls became increasingly fashionable during the ante-bellum era, one J. G. Clinkscales vividly remembered that in his pre-Civil War childhood 'many of the young girls could ride as well as their brothers, and not a few of them could handle firearms with great accuracy and skill'. Fathers took their girls fishing. Sometimes they went on hunting trips, too. Like Scarlett, Daphne du Maurier's Rebecca is also described as having behaved like a boy when she was a little girl: 'She should have been a boy', says Mrs Danvers. And before she dies, Brontë's Cathy wishes she were 'out of doors', half-savage and hardy, and free . . . and laughing at injuries, not maddening under them! (*Wuthering Heights*, p. 126). The ubiquity of this sort of gender-bending suggests that's what's bent are the gender stereotypes. See also Emelye's plea to Diana in Chaucer's *Knight's Tale*. 'Ne never wol I be no love ne wyf':

> I am, thou woost, yet of thy companye,
> A mayde, and love hunting and venerye,
> And for to walken in the wodes wilde,
> And noght to been a wife, and be with childe.

10. An amusing illustration of the unending interaction between 'high' literature and popular genres occurs in Truman Capote's *Breakfast at Tiffany's*, wherein the narrator asks Holly Golightly to give him an example of something that, in her opinion 'means something':

> '*Wuthering Heights*', she said, without hesitation. . . .
> 'But that's unreasonable. You're talking about a work of genius.'
> 'It was, wasn't it? *My wild sweet Cathy*. God, I cried buckets. I saw it ten times.'
> I said, 'Oh' with recognizable relief, 'oh', with a shameful, rising inflection, 'the *movie*'.
>
> (*Breakfast at Tiffany's*, p. 59)

The line 'My wild sweet Cathy', is a line comparable to 'The stuff that dreams are made of'. It ends the movie starring Laurence Olivier and Merle Oberon, but I can't find it in the book, although it clearly echoes Nelly's description of Cathy as a 'wild, wick slip' who had 'the bonniest eye, and sweetest smile, the lightest foot in the parish'. By the way, the name of the

American cartoon cat was also inspired by this film: the cartoonist thought the incessant calling of the name 'Heathcliff! Heathcliff!' was the funniest thing he had ever heard in his life.

11. The term 'gypsy', of course, derives from 'Egyptian', and Cleopatra is dramatically described as a tawny 'gypsy' in the opening lines of Shakespeare's play. And (as stressed in the notes to the World's Classics edition of *Wuthering Heights*, p. 344) the key word in various descriptions of Heathcliff is 'gypsy': the adult Heathcliff is introduced as 'a dark-skinned gypsy in aspect' (p. 3) and the child Heathcliff is derided as a 'gypsy brat' (p. 35). The point here is not to argue for direct influence but that the term is obviously ideal for establishing, in one word, that a given character of either sex is exotic, alien, heathen, anti-social, free-spirited, wild, magical, etc.

12. The call of the wild in works of this kind is so powerful that it has by now become a cliché that, should there be a conflict between them, any truly romantic love affair *must* override the respectable attractions of a 'good match', so that the fair heroine finally rides off into the desert with her Sheik of Araby. As corny and generally unrealistic as all this is, it points to the best things that can be said in favour of romantic and sexual love in life or art: they are just about the only things powerful enough to break down tribal barriers. 'And thou, what need'st thou with thy tribe's black tents/Who hast the red pavilion of my heart?' For real-life examples, see Lesley Blanch's accounts of Western women, Isabel Burton, Jane Digby, Aimée Dubucq de Rivery and Isabelle Eberhardt, who sought and sometimes found true happiness on *The Wilder Shores of Love* (reprinted 1984, first published 1954).

13. Alice Walker here treats a woman defined by her husband as 'nothing' and by society as an 'Inessential Other' (if ever there was one) as a heroine worthy of admiration and respect. Obviously, the emergence of newly dignified character types often encourages, even as it results from, a heightened social consciousness or from social change. For instance, as the population ages more interest in the artistic depiction of older characters may emerge, as the success of Angela Lansbury in the popular series *Murder, She Wrote* could attest. But today as yesterday, older women are rarely if ever portrayed in starring roles except in detective novels about Miss Marple or spin-offs from novels by Agatha Christie such as *Murder, She Wrote*. Thus Alison Lurie pointedly describes the literary traditions and taboos she violates throughout *Foreign Affairs* by featuring a heroine portrayed as no man's, indeed, 'no one's mother, daughter or sister'. For, of course, traditionally speaking:

> The few older people – especially women – who are allowed into a story are usually cast as relatives. . . . People over fifty who aren't relatives are pushed into minor parts, character parts, and are usually portrayed as comic, pathetic, or disagreeable. Occasionally one will appear in the role of tutor or guide to some young protagonist, but more often than not their advice and example are bad; their histories a warning rather than a model. [Yet the real world is] full of people over fifty who will be around and in fairly good shape for the next quarter-century; plenty of time for adventure and change, even for heroism and transformation.
>
> (Lurie (1984), pp. 206–7)

Nowadays, although mothers appear on lots of commercials, Tom Wolfe's line, 'nobody invited Mother' is pretty accurate with reference to modern popular genres except the occasional soap-opera whose audience requires one, or cute situation comedies that require stereotypically cute mothers: the grand *Roseanne* is a laudable exception. The monster-type in the great tradition, such as Grendel's mother (the first noteworthy female in English literature) or the mothers in plays by Tennessee Williams, now seems extinct but their memory should be preserved, since they had far more dramatic clout than most mothers in films and on TV nowadays do. About the only thing that can be said about the ones on screen today is that since they are safely attached to a man and confined to the home, they are far less likely to get killed or raped in front of millions of impressionable viewers than single women who work outside the home and are thus portrayed as fair game. For other current stereotypes, see Steinem (1983), p. 328 ff:

> Television . . . proves Margaret Mead's conclusion that in a patriarchy, widows are the only women honored in authority. If you're born female, what you have to do is marry the newspaper publisher, senator, corporate stockholder, or whatever man has the position you want. . . . When he dies, you may be allowed to carry on in his place. . . . A powerful woman on television is allowed to be an older woman and a widow like Mrs. Pynchon on the Lou Grant show.

Steinem also notes that although 'a really poor person or family is rarely a major part of a TV series at any time (it's too depressing)', a Ph.D. thesis could be done on why comedies focus on working-class or middle-class families while melodramas focus on the rich and powerful. 'Personally I think it's a semiconscious plot to preserve the social order. The idea is to convince us that it's *fun* to be poor, but being rich is a terrible burden we shouldn't want to try'. On portrayals of women, the good news is that the best parts in 1988 films were virtually all women's parts, some very unconventional, such as Madame de Merteuil and Dian Fossey, and most played by superb actresses in their forties.

14. By now it is rare for a criminal, a monster or a villain *not* to be portrayed sympathetically in popular genres. See the old actor's account of this phenomenon in Gail Godwin's *The Odd Woman*, pp. 285–6.

> 'But there are villains today, too, aren't there?'
> 'Well-l-l,' drawled the old actor. 'Yes and no. . . . Today, a villain always has a *side*. He's no longer all bad, all wicked. He affects no waxed mustache, no stealthy step nor evil eye, nor hollow voice. He no longer consorts with other vile degenerates in foul and frowzy dens of iniquity. Your today's villain is often a sympathetic character who has a perfectly good psychological excuse for wrecking the lives of others.'

The fact that he has no redeeming features, and therefore affords audiences with a respite from having to feel sorry for the monster/villain, may help to explain the popularity of the awful Freddy in the *Nightmare on Elm Street* series. To say nothing of J.R. in *Dallas*, whose depravity has nothing to do with deprivation.

15. These same processes of imaginative identification with a given character or with a given situation are recorded as occurring on and off the stage in very different historical and literary contexts. For instance, describing the days back in Corinth when he himself was in love and suffered from the pangs of jealousy, St Augustine remembered how he 'used to share the joys of stage

lovers and their sinful pleasure in each other', and when they were parted pity led him to 'share their grief', since the 'more a man is subject to such suffering himself, the more easily he is moved by it in the theatre' (see St Augustine's *Confessions*, pp. 55–7). The same process occurs on stage: 'By the image of my cause I see/The portraiture of his', said Hamlet of Laertes. 'My tears begin to take his part', says Edgar of King Lear, 'he childed as I father'd'. There is a kind of consolation in this. When we see such characters bearing our woes we feel less alone in misery: 'How light and portable my pain seems now,/When that which makes me bend makes the King bow' (see *King Lear*, III, vi, 108–9).

16. Prospero here realises Isabella Linton's dream of having her penitent enemy beg for mercy and only then granting him a measure of forgiveness. Perhaps the ultimate revenge-fantasy involves having power so great that the renunciation of vindictiveness itself is a manifestation of absolute power, as it is in the cases of Prospero and of Edmond Dantes. It seems to me that, like Shakespeare in *The Tempest*, Alexandre Dumas created a paradigmatic wish-fulfilment fantasy in *The Count of Monte Cristo*, wherein the victim of a cruel conspiracy – very like Prospero – achieves unlimited wealth and knowledge on a treasure island, and having brought his old enemies to utter destruction, finally renounces vindictiveness and sails off into the sunset with his beautiful child/mistress/wife. But the Count of Monte Cristo, very like the right Duke of Milan, decides the rarer action is in virtue than in vengeance only after he has brought the villains who betrayed him to their knees. With no conceivable hope of avenging herself, Isabella cannot pity Heathcliff.

References

Allott, Miriam (ed.) (1970) *Wuthering Heights: A Casebook*, Macmillan, London.

Andersen, Hans (1924) *Fairy Tales*, illustrated by Kay Nielsen, George H. Doran, New York.

Archer, Robyn and Diana Simmonds (1986) *A Star is Torn*, Virago Press, London.

Armstrong, Karen (1986) *The Gospel According to Woman*, Elm Tree Books, London.

Atwood, Margaret (1982) *Lady Oracle*, Virago Press, London.

Atwood, Margaret (1989) *Cat's Eye*, Bloomsbury Press, London.

Auerbach, Nina (1982) *Woman and the Demon: The Life of a Victorian Myth*, Harvard University Press, Cambridge, Mass., and London.

Augustine, St (1964) *Confessions*, trans. R. S. Pine-Coffin, Penguin Books, Harmondsworth, pp. 55 7.

Avedon, Richard and Truman Capote (1959) *Observations*, Simon and Schuster, New York.

Bacall, Lauren (1979) *By Myself*, Jonathan Cape, London.

Baldick, Chris (1987) *In Frankenstein's Shadow: Myth, Monstrosity, and Nineteenth-century Writing*, Clarendon Press, Oxford.

Bate, Jonathan (1986) *Shakespeare and the English Romantic Imagination*, Oxford.

Belsey, Catherine (1985) *The Subject of Tragedy: Identity and difference in Renaissance Drama*, Methuen, London and New York.

Blanch, Lesley (1984) *The Wilder Shores of Love*, Abacus Press, Tunbridge Wells (first published 1954).

Blixen, Karen (1934) *Seven Gothic Tales*, Putnam, London.

Blixen, Karen (1958) 'Babette's Feast' and 'Tempests' in *Anecdotes of Destiny*, The University of Chicago Press, Chicago.

Blixen, Karen (Isak Dinesen) (1964) *Out of Africa*, Jonathan Cape, London (first published 1937).

Bloom, Allan, with Harry V. Jaffa (1981) *Shakespeare's Politics*, University of Chicago Press, Chicago (first published 1964).

Bloom, Allan (1987) *The Closing of the American Mind: How Higher Education Has Failed Democracy and Impoverished the Souls of Today's Students*, Simon and Schuster, New York (see also Hovey, 1988).

Bowen, Peter with Martin Hayden and Frank Riess (1972) *Screen Test*, Penguin Books, Harmondsworth.

Bromley, Roger (1989) 'Rewriting the masculine script: the novels of Joseph Hansen', in Longhurst, pp. 102–17.

Brontë, Charlotte (1980) *Jane Eyre*, ed. Margaret Smith, Oxford University Press, Oxford.

Brontë, Emily (1981) *Wuthering Heights*, ed. Ian Jack, Oxford University Press, Oxford (see also Allott).

203

Burchill, Julie (1986) *Girls on Film*, Virgin Books, London.

Burke, Kenneth (1964) 'Literature as an equipment for living', in *Perspectives by Incongruity*, ed. Stanley Edgar Hyman, Indiana University Press, Bloomington, Indiana.

Butler, Marilyn (1987) *Literature as a Heritage, or Reading in Other Ways*, inaugural lecture, 10 November, Cambridge University Press, Cambridge.

Campbell, Joseph (1988) *The Hero With a Thousand Faces*, Paladin, London (first published 1949).

Capote, Truman (1958) *Breakfast at Tiffany's*, Hamish Hamilton, London.

Cather, Willa (1982) *The Song of the Lark*, intro. A. S. Byatt, Virago Press, London (first published 1915).

Cavell, Stanley (1979) 'On *Othello*', in *The Claims of Reason: Wittgenstein, Skepticism, Morality and Tragedy*, Oxford University Press, New York.

Charney, Maurice (ed.) (1988) *'Bad' Shakespeare: Revaluations of the Shakespeare Canon*, Associated University Presses, London and Toronto.

Chaucer, Geoffrey (1974) *The Complete Works of Geoffrey Chaucer*, ed. F. N. Robinson, second edition, Oxford University Press, Oxford.

Christiansen, Rupert (1986) *Prima Donna: A History*, Penguin Books, Harmondsworth.

Clement, Catherine (1989) *Opera, or the Undoing of Women*, Virago Press, London.

Cohen, D. M. (1980) 'The Jew and Shylock', *Shakespeare Quarterly*, **31**, 53–63.

Cooke, Alistair (1976) 'Shakespeare in America', in *Pattern of Excelling Nature*, ed. David Bevington and J. L. Halio, Associated University Presses, London and Toronto, pp. 17–25.

Culler, Jonathan (1983) *On Deconstruction: Theory and Criticism after Structuralism*, Routledge & Kegan Paul, London.

Davis, Lennard J. (1987) *Resisting Novels: Ideology and Fiction*, Methuen, London.

de Beauvoir, Simone (1988) *The Second Sex*, trans. H. M. Parshley, Picador, London.

Dean, Leonard F. (ed.) (1961) *A Casebook on* Othello, Thomas Y. Crowell, New York.

Defoe, Daniel (1981) *Roxana*, ed. Jane Jack, Oxford University Press, Oxford (first published 1724).

Drabble, Margaret (ed.) (1985) *The Oxford Companion to English Literature*, Oxford University Press, Oxford.

du Maurier, Daphne (1940) *Rebecca*, Garden City, New York.

du Maurier, George (1947) *Trilby*, in *Novels of George du Maurier*, with Introductions by John Masefield and Daphne du Maurier, Pilot Press, London (first published 1894).

du Maurier, George (1931) *Trilby*, with preface by Gerald du Maurier, J. M. Dent & Sons (reprinted 1978).

Dworkin, Andrea (1988) *Letters from a War Zone*, Secker & Warburg, London.

Eiseley, Loren (1971) 'Instruments of darkness', in *The Night Country*, Scribner, New York.

Eliot, George (1967) *Daniel Deronda*, ed. Barbara Hardy, Penguin Books, Harmondsworth.

Eliot, T. S. (1939) *Old Possum's Book of Practical Cats*, Faber & Faber, London.

Evans, K. W. (1970) 'The racial factor in *Othello*', *Shakespeare Studies*, **5**, pp. 124–40.

Fetterly, Judith (1978) *The Resisting Reader: A Feminist Approach to American Fiction*, Indiana University Press, Bloomington.

Fiedler, Leslie (1960) *Love and Death in the American Novel*, Criterion Press, New York.

Fitz, L. T. (see also Linda Woodbridge) (1977) 'Egyptian queens and male reviewers', *Shakespeare Survey*, **28**, 313–14.

Fitzgerald, F. Scott (1950) *The Great Gatsby*, Penguin Books, Harmondsworth.

Flamini, Roland (1978) *Scarlett, Rhett, and a Cast of Thousands*, Collier Macmillan, New York.

Fowles, John (1966) *The Magus*, Jonathan Cape, London.

Fowles, John (1969) *The French Lieutenant's Woman*, Jonathan Cape, London.

Fowles, John (1974) *The Ebony Tower*, Little, Brown, Boston and Toronto.

Fraser, Flora (1987) *The English Gentlewoman*, Barrie & Jenkins, London.

Friedan, Betty (1963) *The Feminine Mystique*, Dell Books, New York.

Gardner, Helen (1955) 'The Noble Moor', *Proceedings of the British Academy*, London.

Gardner, Helen (1982) *In Defence of the Imagination*, Clarendon Press, Oxford.

Glover, D. (1989) 'The stuff that dreams are made of: masculinity, femininity and the thriller' (see Longhurst, pp. 67–83).

Godwin, Gail (1974) *The Odd Woman*, Berkley Medallion Books, New York (see also George Gissing (1893) *The Odd Women*).

Gombrich, E. H. (1972) *Symbolic Images: Studies in the Art of the Renaissance*, Phaidon Press, Oxford.

Graves, Robert and Raphael Patai (1983) *The Hebrew Myths; The Book of Genesis*, Greenwich House, New York.

Greenblatt, Stephen (1980) *Renaissance Self-Fashioning*, The University of Chicago Press, Chicago.

Griffen, Jasper (1982) *The Small Oxford Book of Snobs*, Oxford University Press, Oxford.

Habicht, Werner (1989) 'Shakespeare and theater politics in the Third Reich,' in *The Play out of Context*, ed. Hannah Scolnicov and Peter Holland, Cambridge University Press, Cambridge.

Halliwell, Leslie (1978) *Halliwell's Filmgoer's Book of Quotes*, Granada Press, London.

Hawkes, Terence (1986) *That Shakespeherian Rag: Essays on a Critical Process*, Methuen, London.

Hawkins, Harriett (1985) *The Devil's Party*, Clarendon Press, Oxford.

Hill, Christopher (1989) 'History and the present', 65th Conway Memorial Lecture, South Place Ethical Society, London.

Hill, Susan (1989) *Family*, Michael Joseph, London.

Hirsch, E. D. Jr (1987) *Cultural Literacy: What Every American Needs to Know*, Houghton Mifflin, Boston.

Hitchens, Christopher (1989) *Prepared for the Worst: Selected Essays and Minority Reports*, Chatto & Windus, London.

Holdsworth, Angela (1988) *Out of the Doll's House: The Story of Women in the Twentieth Century*, BBC Books, London.

Hovey, Kenneth Alan (1988) 'The Great Books versus America: reassessing *The Closing of the American Mind*', *Profession 88*, The Modern Language Association of America, New York, pp. 40–5.

Ibsen, Henrik (1980) *Ibsen: Plays Two (A Doll's House, An Enemy of the People, Hedda Gabler)*, trans. Michael Meyer, Methuen, London.

James, Henry (1967) *The Bostonians*, ed. Leon Edel, Bodley Head, London (first published by Macmillan 1886).

James, Henry (1987) *Henry James's Notebooks*, ed. Leon Edel and Lyall H. Powers, Oxford University Press, Oxford.

Jones, Ernest (1953) *The Life and Work of Sigmund Freud*, Penguin Books, London.

Joyce, James (1977) *Ulysses*, with 'Ulysses: a short history' by Richard Ellmann, Penguin Books, Harmondsworth.

Kermode, Frank (1986) *Romantic Image*, Routledge & Kegan Paul, London (first published 1957).

Kesey, Ken (1962) *One Flew Over the Cuckoo's Nest*, Marion Boyars, London.

Kimball, Robert (ed.) (1984) *The Complete Lyrics of Cole Porter*, Vintage Books, New York.

Kirkland, Gelsey with Greg Lawrence (1987) *Dancing on my Grave: an autobiography*. Hamish Hamilton, London.

Lacan, Jacques (1972) 'The seminar on "The Purloined Letter" ' ('Le seminaire sur "La lettre volee" '), trans. J. Mehlman, *Yale French Studies* **48**, 38–72 (see also Muller and Richardson (1988)).

Laclos, Choderlos de (1961) *Les Liaisons Dangereuses*, trans. W. K. Stone, Penguin Books, Harmondsworth (first published 1781).

Leroux, Gaston (1986) *The Phantom of the Opera*, ed. Peter Haining, W. H. Allen, London (first published 1911).

Lessing, Doris (1973) *The Golden Notebook*, Granada Press, London.

Lodge, David (1981) *Working With Structuralism*, Routledge & Kegan Paul, London.

Longhurst, Derek (ed.) (1989) *Gender, Genre and Narrative Pleasure*, Unwin Hyman, London.

Lurie, Alison (1984) *Foreign Affairs*, Random House, New York.

MacCabe, Colin (1986) *High Theory/Low Culture*, Manchester University Press, Manchester.

MacCabe, Colin (1988) *Futures for English*, Manchester University Press, Manchester.

Mailer, Norman (1973) *Marilyn – A Biography*, Hodder & Stoughton, London.

Maltin, Leonard (1988) *TV Movies and Video Guide*, Signet Books, New York.

Mann, Thomas (1947) *Doctor Faustus*, Penguin Books, Harmondsworth.

Markham, Beryl (1988) *West With the Night*, Penguin Books, Harmondsworth (first published 1942).

Marlowe, Christopher (1971) *The Plays of Christopher Marlowe*, ed. Roma Gill, Oxford University Press, Oxford.

Marx, Karl (1977) *Karl Marx: Selected Writings*, ed. David McLellan, Oxford University Press, Oxford.

Maslow, A. H. (1962) *Towards a Psychology of Being*, Van Nostrand Press, Princeton, New Jersey.

Medved, Harry and Michael (1986) *Son of Golden Turkey: The Best of the Worst from Hollywood*, Angus & Robertson, London.

Melly, George (1989) 'Cole's Errant Nymph', *The Independent Magazine*, 13 May.

Miles, Rosalind (1988) *The Women's History of the World*, Michael Joseph, London.

Mitchell, Margaret (1936) *Gone With the Wind*, Macmillan, London.

Montrose, Louis Adrian (1983) ' "Shaping fantasies": figurations of gender and power in Elizabethan culture', *Representations* **1**, 61–94.

Muller, John P. and William J. Richardson (1988) *The Purloined Poe: Lacan, Derrida, and Psychoanalytic Reading*, Johns Hopkins University Press, Baltimore.

Nabokov, Vladimir (1974) *Lolita*, Corgi Books, London (first published 1959).

Newman, Karen (1987) ' "And wash the Ethiop white": femininity and the monstrous in *Othello'*, in *Shakespeare Reproduced: The text in history and ideology*, eds. Jean E. Howard and Marion F. O'Connor, Methuen, London and New York.

Olivier, Laurence (1986) *On Acting*, Weidenfeld & Nicolson, London.

Orkin, Martin (1987) *Shakespeare Against Apartheid*, Ad. Donker, Craighill, South Africa.

Perry, George (1987) *The Complete Phantom of the Opera*, Pavilion Books, London.

Pinter, Harold (1976) *The Birthday Party* in *Plays: One*, Methuen, London

Plato (1974) *The Republic*, trans. Desmond Lee, Penguin Books, Harmondsworth.

Poe, Edgar Allan (1902) 'The Masque of the Red Death' in *Tales of Mystery and Imagination*, Oxford University Press, London.

Porter, Cole (1984) *The Complete Lyrics of Cole Porter*, ed. Robert Kimball with foreword by John Updike, Vintage Books, New York.

Portis, Charles (1968) *True Grit*, Simon and Schuster, New York.

Powell, Michael (1986) *A Life in Movies*, Heinemann, London.

Praz, Mario (1933) (reissued 1970) *The Romantic Agony*, 2nd edn, transl. from Italian by Angus Davidson, Oxford University Press, Oxford.

Quinlan, David (1987) *Wicked Women of the Screen*, B. H. Batsford, London.

Richards, Janet Radcliffe (1982) *The Sceptical Feminist*, Pelican Books, London.

Ridley, M. R. (ed.) *see* Shakespeare (1958) *Othello*.

Riese, Randall and Neal Hitchens (1988) *The Unabridged Marilyn*, Corgi Books, London.

Rogan, Johnny (1988) *Starmakers and Svengalis*, Macdonald Queen Anne Press, London.

Rosenberg, Marvin (1980) 'Shakespeare's tragic world of "If", *Deutsche Shakespeare-Gesellschaft West*, Jahrbuch, 109–17.

Scherman, David (ed.) (1979) *Life Goes to the Movies*, Time/Life Books, Amsterdam.

Scheuer, Steven H. (1988) *Movies on TV and Videocasette: 1988–1989*, Bantam Books, New York.

Shakespeare, William (1958) *Othello*, ed. M. R. Ridley, Methuen, London.

Shakespeare, William (1981) *The Complete Works of William Shakespeare*, ed. Peter Alexander, Collins, London (first published 1951).

Shaw, George Bernard (1937) *Pygmalion*, in *The Complete Plays of Bernard Shaw*, Odhams, London.

Sheehan, Neil (1989) *A Bright Shining Lie: John Paul Vann and America in Vietnam*, Jonathan Cape, London.

Shipman, David (1970) *The Great Movie Stars: The Golden Years*, Bonanza Books, New York.

Smith, D. Nichol (1916) *Shakespeare Criticism*, World's Classics edn, Oxford University Press, Oxford.

Sparrow, John (1981) *Grave Epigrams and Other Verses*, Cygnet Press, Burford, Oxfordshire.

Sprinchorn, Evert (1968) 'The handkerchief trick in *Othello*', in *The Columbia University Forum Anthology*, ed. Peter Spackman and Lee Ambrose, Columbia University Press, New York, pp. 201–10.

Steinem, Gloria (1984) *Outrageous Acts and Everyday Rebellions*, Flamingo Paperbacks, London.

Stoppard, Tom (1982) 'Is it true what they say about Shakespeare?' *International Shakespeare Association Occasional Paper No. 2*, Oxford University Press, Oxford.

Taylor, Helen (1989) *Scarlett's Women: Gone With the Wind and its female fans*, Virago Press, London.

Thurman, Judith (1982) *Isak Dinesen: The Life of Karen Blixen*, Weidenfeld & Nicholson, London.

Tomkins, Jane (1989) 'West of everything' (see Longhurst (1989), pp. 10–30.

Tuchman, Gaye, Arlene Kaplan Daniels and James Benét (1978) *Hearth & Home: Images of Women in the Mass Media*, Oxford University Press, New York.

Twain, Mark (Samuel Langhorne Clemens) (1955) *The Adventures of Huckleberry Finn*, J. M. Dent & Sons, London (first published 1884).

Twain, Mark (1986) *The Adventures of Tom Sawyer*, ed. John Seelye, Penguin Books, Harmondsworth.

Vidal, Gore (1977) *Matters of Fact and of Fiction*, Random House, New York.

Vidal, Gore (1983) *Pink Triangle and Yellow Star*, Granada, London.

Vidal, Gore (1987) 'Dawn Powell, the American writer', *New York Review of Books*, 17 November.

Walker, Alice (1985) *The Color Purple*, The Woman's Press, London.

Widdowson, Peter (ed.) (1982) *Re-Reading English*, Methuen, London.

Wolfe, Tom (1981) 'Loverboy of the bourgeoisie' (Cary Grant), in *The Kandy-Kolored Tangerine-Flake Streamline Baby*, Pan Books, London (first published 1966).

Wolfe, Tom (1988) *The Bonfire of the Vanities*, Jonathan Cape, London.

Woodbridge, Linda (see also L. T. Fitz) (1984) *Women and the English Renaissance*, University of Illinois Press, Urbana and Chicago.

Wyatt-Brown, Bertram (1982) *Southern Honor: Ethics and Behaviour in the Old South*, Oxford University Press, New York.

FILMS

Dates for films are mainly from Steven Scheuer's guide to *Movies on TV and Videocassette*, Bantam Books, New York, 1988. Virtually all of the best films cited in this book are available on video, and the worst ones occasionally turn up on late shows on both sides of the Atlantic.

A Chorus Line (film, 1985); *A Little Night Music* (film, 1978); *A Midsummer Night's Sex Comedy* (1982); *A Star is Born* (1937, 1954, 1976); *A Streetcar Named Desire* (film, 1951); *Adventures of Robin Hood* (1938); *All About Eve* (1950 – this film was the basis for the Broadway musical, *Applause*); *The African Queen* (1951); *Alien Nation* (1989); *Amadeus* (1984); *An American Werewolf in London* (1981); *Angel Heart* (1987); *Baby Boom* (1987); *Bedazzled* (1967); *The Best Man* (film, 1964); *The Big Sleep* (1946, 1978); *The Bostonians* (1984); *Breakfast at Tiffany's (1961); Butch Cassidy and the Sundance Kid* (1969); *Cabin in the Sky* (1943); *Casablanca* (1942); *Coal Miner's Daughter* (1980); *The Color Purple* (1985); *Damn Yankees* (1958); *Dangerous Liaisons* (1988); *Death of a Centerfold: The Dorothy Stratten Story* (1981); *Desperate Journey* (1942); *Dr Faustus* (1967); *Farewell, My Lovely* (1975); *Fatal Attraction* (1987); *Five Graves to Cairo* (1943); *The Forbidden Planet* (1956); *The French Lieutenant's Woman* (1981); *Gone With the Wind* (1939); *Gorillas in the Mist* (1988); *Gypsy* (1962); *Henry V* (film, 1945); *High Noon* (1952); *King Kong* (1933, 1976); *Kiss Me Kate* (1953); *Laura* (1944); *The Maltese Falcon* (1941); *Man Hunt* (1941); *The Man With Bogart's Face* (1980); *The Man Who Would Be King* (1975); *The Masque of the Red Death* (1964); *Mephisto* (1981); *Mr Smith Goes to Washington* (1939); *North by Northwest* (1959); *Notorious* (1946); *One Flew Over the Cuckoo's Nest* (1975); *The Phantom of Hollywood* (1974); *The Phantom of the Opera* (1925, 1943, 1962, 1983); *The Phantom of the Paradise* (1974); *The Plainsman* (1936); *Rambo: First Blood Part II* (1985); *Ran* (1985); *Rebecca* (1940); *The Red Shoes* (1948); *Richard III* (1956); *Slave Girls of the White Rhinoceros* (also titled *Prehistoric Women*) (1967); *She Done Him Wrong* (1933); *Smiles of a Summer Night* (source for the Broadway musical and film, *A Little Night Music*) (1955); *Snow White and the Seven Dwarfs* (1937); *Spartacus* (1960); *Star 80* (1983); *Star Wars* (1977); *The Stepford Wives* (1975); *Sunset Boulevard* (1950); *Superman II* (1981); *Svengali* (1931, 1955, 1983); *The Tales of Hoffman* (1951); *Tarzan, The Ape Man* (1932); *Tempest* (John Cassavetes) (1982); *That's Dancing* (1985); *The Tempest* (Derek Jarman) (1979); *The Thief of Bagdad* (1940); *Theatre of Blood* (1973); *Throne of Blood* (1957); *The Trail of the Lonesome Pine* (1936); *The Treasure of the Sierra Madre* (1948); *True Grit* (1969); *The Turning Point* (1977); *Werewolves on Wheels* (1971); *West Side Story* (1961); *The Wild One* (1954); *The Wizard of Oz* (1939); *The Wolf Man* (1941); *Wuthering Heights* (1939).

Index